And Then I Peed My Pants...

My Misadventures in New Motherhood

By Meagan Phillipson

First Edition, 2014
First published in paperback 2014 by
Mevach Press

National Library of Australia
Cataloguing-in-Publication Entry

ISBN 978-0-9923810-0-4

Copyright © Meagan Phillipson 2014

All rights reserved. Except under the conditions described in the Copyright Act 1968 of Australia and subsequent amendments, no part of this publication may be reproduced, stored in a retrieval system or transmitted in any form or by any means, electronic, mechanical, photocopying, recording or otherwise, without the prior permission of the copyright owner.

Mevach Press (ABN 79 342 161 681)

www.mevach.com

Cover art copyright © of Alice Carroll 2014

In memory of Beouf,

thanks for the humour gene.

Friday

My waters broke at 3 AM on a Friday morning. I awoke thinking great, now I have to add incontinence to the list of pregnancy indignities. Then I realised it wasn't pee and nudged The Hubby, telling him that I had wet my pants but not really if he knew what I meant. Of course, he did not. When he was awake enough to realise what I was trying to say, he began to panic and this sent me off in a panic. We both understood this was it. The time had finally arrived.

He rang the hospital to tell them what had happened, only to be advised to go back to bed and wait until daylight before driving in. Since I was in no pain, we took the advice and eventually fell back into a fitful sleep. I awoke twisted up in a sea of precautionary beach towels The Hubby had laid out. Seems he had expected a woman's waters breaking to be an event of biblical proportions.

We later wandered into the hospital and were greeted by slightly panicked midwives questioning where we had been and where our overnight bag was. It was in the car, along with five other bags that we left behind until we were assigned a room. For overly organised people, we gave the impression of the exact opposite. Turned out they had meant to come in quite literally at daybreak so they could set me up an antibiotic drip to ward off any infection.

Once I was admitted and set up on a drip, the waiting continued. In the afternoon our obstetrician came along to tell me that I would be induced if active labour had not started by the next morning. He also added casually that, oh by the way, he wouldn't be available for the birth because he was chairing an obstetrician convention in town.

My heart sank through the floor.

"But…but that is why we booked you, to know who will be there at the birth."

He wasn't fazed by my outburst. I felt my anger rise towards his positive can-do attitude, the same one that ironically attracted me to him in the first place. A birth was an everyday event for him whereas the conference had been months in the planning. Yet for me, a first timer, the order of importance was the exact opposite.

"Not to worry, there are lovely obstetricians who regularly fill in for me."

"So who will be filling in?"

"Uhh not sure yet, we are still ringing around."

"You're 'ringing around'?"

"It's a bit tricky since everybody is attending my conference. We've got a great turnout, over 300 obstetricians! Not to worry, we'll work it out."

I give The Hubby a look. He seems just as unnerved. The obstetrician leaves the room and I start to cry. This is a highly unusual event for me, as I am not an overly emotional person - at least not overtly so.

"So let me get this straight, there are 300 fucking goddamn obstetricians in town this weekend and I can't even get one of them to attend the birth of our child?!?"

"Honey calm down, we are in a good hospital and any doctor who works here is more than capable of delivering our child."

"That's not the point, you know I hate fucking doctors, you know I wanted to choose my own and now he is gone. Fucking gone! Now I get some random fucking pot luck doctor. That's not what we're paying through the fucking nose for!"

If all other cues are not obvious enough, The Hubby can always tell when I am angry by the rise in swearing. The more I sound like a sailor on shore leave, the more intense my anger. He seemed to get the message pretty quickly that I was pissed off no end.

With little alternative though, we settle in and have dinner. Nothing happens until midnight, when some labour pains begin and disappear. By 3:30 AM they have become painful but not significant enough to be called active labour. They are enough, however, to prevent sleep and cement my desire for an epidural when the time comes.

The dawn arrives without me progressing any further. Minus anything happening fast, it looks like I will be induced. I am scared of the option but, really, I'm scared of any options because they all lead to the great unknown of childbirth. I resign myself to fate. The hospital cannot leave me too long with my waters broken, it is too dangerous to the baby and myself.

The midwives tell me to eat a full breakfast in preparation for the day ahead. It seems strange to do something so normal on a day that is anything but. We eat and then wait the time down.

Saturday

I have skipped over this part of the story and keep avoiding the writing of it, as though I am trying to neatly airbrush a blemish from a photo. It would be far easier to lie and say I was induced and we celebrated a routine entrance of our baby into the world. But that is not the truth and does not reflect the story of how we became a family.

I was induced at 9:30 AM, after eating that full breakfast which then threatened the whole day to explode from my mouth with each contraction.

The process of induction wasn't as scary as I had imagined. The contractions were controlled by the amount of oxytocin hormone dosed through the drip. The pain started off slow and similar to what I had experienced overnight.

The plan was to have the contractions build in regularity and then call in the anaesthetist for my epidural once active labour was established. I was assured by the midwives that I could back out from the epidural at any stage, despite me increasingly asking if it was time yet. I sensed they were testing to see if I really wanted one or was just speaking from fear.

By the time the anaesthetist arrived, I was glad I had been so insistent. The pain had grown in intensity and was inescapable. I was taken quickly through all the potential side effects and asked to sign a waiver in case any of them came to fruition. I probably would have signed a death warrant for my own mother at that stage – I just wanted that damn epidural in me, pronto.

Like induction, the epidural insertion also wasn't scary but mostly because it wasn't a foreign concept to me. I've had two injections into the spine for an old back injury so had a rough idea of what was to come. The insertion was made and the drug began to work down the spine, through the groin and down to my feet like hot fire. I was prepared for this sensation and didn't flinch. Instead, I stared intently at a small graze on the linoleum floor below and bit my lip, hard.

From there on, the contractions were still noticeable but they no longer carried a sharp edge of pain. They were more like blunt pressures and I felt random pain elsewhere. It was as though my body was trying to find an alternative way to tell my brain what was going on. At some point it felt like ants were crawling across my ribs and I started to scratch madly. I experienced waves of hot and cold flushes. My blood pressure dropped a few times and I feared fainting or throwing-up, or both at the same time.

And then something took over. I stopped being the self-conscious usual me and flipped into some alternate reality. I was there but very much apart from everyone else in the room. The Hubby had been putting a cool towel over my face and I grabbed it, planting it firmly over my eyes where it remained. I retreated further into my own zone.

I remember arching my back, breathing in ways I never knew I could and making strange cooing sounds to relax. The tiny part of my logical brain that was still functioning wondered whether I was possessed.

Apparently I said lots of things that day, most of which I can't remember. I do remember one particular midwife in the team of midwives and calling her 'Lovely Linda' whenever she appeared by my side. She was an island of calm and confidence in this weird sea I found myself floating in belly-up.

I don't recall but I also apparently promised to bake everyone in the room cupcakes, especially the people with the nice drugs. I also apparently vowed to marry the anaesthetist once same sex marriages were legal in our state.

There were moments of clarity though. At 3 PM a shift change took place for the midwives and a rather gruff one came in to ask Lovely Linda for an update. The gruff midwife then let out a sigh and joked, "Well, we've been going this long and no pushing. I think Mum's lying back too much and is being a bit lazy!"

I ripped the towel from my eyes and shot her daggers. Clearly Mum was not impressed. Mum had been going since 3 AM the previous day with not much sleep and way too much adrenaline. Mum was looking around for the first available object to ram up this midwife's nearest orifice.

"I haven't pushed because nobody told me it was time to."

The midwife didn't back down.

"Well you should be able to feel with your body when to push."

"I can't because everything is numb."

She grabbed one of my legs and moved it back on the bed, where it then promptly flopped to the side. She turned to talk to Lovely Linda, as though I was suddenly not there again. It was a move that grated me deeply, as it made me feel like I was nothing more than a vessel holding back the arrival of a baby.

"You can't do anything with this one. Her legs are like dead tree stumps."

I have never been one for confrontation but her lack of sensitivity hit a very raw nerve. I pointed my finger at the midwife and was about to scream "FUCK YOU!" at the top of my lungs when Lovely Linda appeared at the side of my bed.

"It won't be much longer, how about I stay around until the birth?"

I could have made a thousand cupcakes for Lovely Linda on the spot. Much to my relief, the other midwife disappeared from the room and I went back into my zone.

From that point on, time became fluid. It didn't seem to travel the same way as it normally does. An hour passed by in what felt like five minutes. While another minute felt like ten hours. With the guidance of the attending midwives, I had apparently been pushing like a trooper for 90 minutes. Yet still, no baby.

And then in swanned my obstetrician, fresh from his blessed conference. Another moment of clarity hit me. I remembered all my fear the previous day about who would be attending the birth and realised I never did find out which obstetrician was going to be there.

I must give him some kudos for doing the decent thing in the end yet, with hindsight, his entrance seemed like just turning up for the show stopper while the midwives had performed the grunt work. I could have thrown him out but didn't have the energy to focus outwards.

The midwives and the obstetrician huddled in the corner and discussed tactics. He then explained to me what they were about to do and what I would have to do on their signal.

"We're going to use a suction cap. You have been pushing for well over an hour and the baby hasn't moved a centimetre. Its head is stuck at the last station."

I yelled out in frustration. Couldn't they have worked this out beforehand? All those pushes and energy, wasted. And now they were asking me to muster even more energy.

The suction cap was placed and I was told when to push. I felt an almighty pressure but only dull pain. I beared down on cue.

Nothing.

"Ok, we're going to do that again. When we say go, you push as hard and for as long as you can."

"Go."

I looked within me and found anger. I looked again and, just in time for the next contraction, found the reserve of strength they were asking of me. I pushed with my whole body. I pushed and pushed until every last fibre of my being is a spent force. The clock showed 5:51 PM.

"Open your eyes!"

I pulled the towel from my eyes and looked down to see two arms flailing out from the sides of a small body and a black hole mouth. It looked like a sea creature from the deep. This purple, wet, shivering body was planted on my chest and let out an enormous wail.

"It's a boy!"

I looked over to The Hubby, who was crying. I was crying too but more from exhaustion and relief that the ordeal was finally over. The celebration could come in a few minutes, when I was fully back on planet Earth and we were back in our room.

But then things went downhill.

"I'm not happy with the blood loss."

"The placenta is stuck."

"We have to stem the bleeding."

The obstetrician stopped talking about me like an object and turned back towards me.

"I'm sorry but you have to go to surgery. Now."

I was annoyed. Outraged in fact. Why should I go anywhere? Haven't I been through enough already? Just leave me alone to calm down and welcome my son.

Yet it wasn't up to me to decide. Before I could form the words, more people appeared with a board and used it to slide me across into another bed. The anaesthetist reappeared like magic to provide me with a top-up to the epidural. The obstetrician went to scrub up.

For a brief moment there was silence in the room. The midwives took their chance and worked with me to push the placenta out, which we managed between us. I was relieved, hoping this would save me from being wheeled away. It was not to be. The obstetrician re-emerged.

"She's still bleeding; we need to get her into theatre."

The enormity of what was happening hit me and I started to panic. I looked around for The Hubby as they started to wheel me away. Our eyes locked and suspended us together amid all the action. He appeared just as lost as me at the suddenness of what was happening.

"Look after the baby, please."

I felt like adding that I meant look after him now, in five minutes, for life if need be. But there was no time for clarification.

"I will. I love you."

"Love you too."

Girlfriend Needs to Get her Roots Done

It is very hard to describe what happened next. In fact, I can't. And I don't think I should. I don't want to be one of those women who wear their childbearing stories like proud battle scars, which are paraded out with some kind of demented pleasure to scare first-time pregnant women. I didn't find that fair when I was pregnant and I don't find it fair now postpartum. Besides, I'm not proud of what happened or that I managed to get through it. I am traumatised, deeply.

The only thing I will say about what happened during the surgery is the strange effect shock has on the mind, particularly memory. I remember bits and pieces, as I was awake with only the epidural and meditation techniques on my side. The obstetrician swears he told me what happened but I can't recall a word he said other than barking at me to "relax your legs".

Yet I recall vividly being wheeled out afterwards and seeing the back of a woman's head as she was wheeled past me into the theatre where I had just been. I remember looking at that head and thinking "girlfriend needs to get her roots done". It's somewhat reassuring to know, even in deep shock, I can still be a superficial bitch.

I also remember realising on the way to my room that I had a son. This may sound strange but it was a very strange headspace I was in that day. I cried out in reflex "my baby, my baby!" only to be assured he was ok and with my husband.

It was there on the hospital trolley that I bonded with him. I needed to be with my sea creature from the deep and I knew he needed me too.

After that I remember being back in my room. The Hubby was rocking the baby in his arms. He said he was just calming down and I was unsure who he was referring to. They both looked exhausted. The delivery would have been an extremely arduous day for the both of them too.

While I was in surgery, he had called his parents and some close friends to tell them the good news. The baby was weighed, measured, a belly button made and first photos taken. I felt a pang of disappointment for missing it all. I asked The Hubby to call my parents and tell them the good news. He had waited because he knew how much I had wanted to make the call, but I didn't have the energy. It was another moment I lost.

At my insistence The Hubby went home to get some much-needed rest. The feeling in my legs was slowly coming back and a midwife gave me some pre-emptive pills for the pain.

The bassinet was placed next to my bed and I was instructed to buzz if the baby woke during the night. I looked over to see him sleeping and realised I hadn't even seen his face properly.

"Hey, hello…"

We settled in for the night and I floated off on whatever drugs they had given me.

Code Red

I awake to the baby screaming. Out of reflex, I move to get up but am stopped by the catheter and other tubes tying me down. I reach over towards the bassinet, forgetting I have a cannula in the back of my hand that is attached to a drip. I knock it accidentally on the bed rails and the pain jolts me fully awake.

Suddenly, an alarm goes off in the machine attached to the drip. I must have knocked something out of place. A red light blinks the room alight with its urgency as the baby's screams grow louder.

I press the buzzer and wait for help.

And wait.

I press it again. Still nothing.

The baby is within reach and I extend my hand again, this time more carefully. I rub his belly in an effort to calm him. It's no use. I then try to pick him up but can't get on an angle to use both hands. Besides, I had only ever been handed babies by their mothers. I realise I have never picked up a baby and don't know how.

I lay back and cry. And then I do the only thing I am able to – I buzz again for help.

A midwife finally arrives and attends to the machine.

"No worries, these machines are a bit temperamental sometimes."

She continues to fiddle with the machine, seemingly oblivious to the screaming bassinet between us.

"Could you please pass him to me?"

"Oh, yeah sure."

It was the first time I held my son if you don't count him being planted on my chest in the delivery suite, which I don't. His body is stiff with tension. I don't know how to go about calming him so I try what feels right.

"Shhh shhh, it's ok, Mummy is here…"

The screaming continues to grow in intensity, as though my intervention has made the matter worse. His body arches back further with each scream. I feel like a failure at the starting gun.

"Hmm, someone sounds a bit hungry."

The midwife lifts up my surgical gown and yanks out my breast. I am too tired and drugged up to protest but flinch at this unannounced intrusion. After what happened in the delivery suite though, I am somewhat resigned to being treated like an object.

I watch as the midwife brings the baby to my breast and rubs the nipple under his nose before tracing it down to his mouth, which gapes open in response. She pushes his face deep into the soft pillow of skin and he suctions on. I let out a small yelp at the sensation.

"Relax, let your shoulders drop. The more anxious you are, the longer it will hurt."

I call on my meditation techniques again and try to space out. The process reminds me of the surgery the night before. I remember staring at a corner of the theatre while rhythmically breathing through it all. My mind fixates on the memory of that image.

Suddenly my right leg begins to twitch around and I can't still it. The midwife again appears oblivious to what is outside her point of focus.

"Well done, Mum! He's attached beautifully."

I look down and my baby is quietly feeding. He has found the comfort he was seeking and, in return, gives me comfort through a rush of hormones the action releases. We swap sides with minimal fuss and it all seems so innate, so wonderfully natural. I tentatively stroke his hair and look down to see my leg has stilled.

The midwife settles him back down and hands me some more tablets to swallow. We both drift off to sleep, with me hoping for the new day to hurry up so The Hubby can return.

Take Two

I awake again later that night, this time disorientated and gasping for air. My heart races out of my chest as my lungs search out the air they are craving. I am disorientated and don't know where I am and why this bed isn't the bed I normally sleep in.

I realise I am in hospital, then remember what has occurred and fall into further panic. I repeatedly press the buzzer. It has become a lifeline, an umbilical cord to meet all the needs I cannot satisfy myself.

I keep pressing away. I desperately need someone, anyone, to come in and tell me it will all be ok.

A midwife bursts into the room.

"Calm down, it's ok, shhh, shhh, shhh…"

Somewhat embarrassingly she is talking to me, not the baby who is fast asleep. It is a good call, one she probably makes several times a night in rooms across the ward. She strokes my hair and continues to whisper calming words. It works and my lungs find oxygen.

I turn my head towards the drawn curtains on the window. My eyes are out of focus and I can't quite straighten them. They slowly blink shut as the midwife's hand retreats from my hair.

It is still dark.

Little Old Man

Sunrise. It is the first full day of a new life for us as parents and for him; our son. The Hubby arrives and I have never been so glad to see him.

What a strange experience to finally be able to study my baby's face for the first time. I am surprised at how much he looks like me. The nose is unmistakable – it is the same distinct button nose that I and many people in my family have. I hold up one of his hands, which looks like a miniature version of my father's.

I was shocked at these points that were intrinsically from me. In my mind he was to look exactly like The Hubby, who looks strongly like his mother and she in turn exactly like her mother. I didn't even think for a moment that my genes would be in the running.

Indeed, I had already grown attached to the alternate child in my mind. That baby's blue-eyed, blonde Germanic features sat in stark contrast to my dark Irish features. I was prepared for people to ask whether I was the nanny and laughing it off as a loss in the genetic lottery. And yet here he was, a dark-haired boy sporting my family's trademark nose and stumpy fingers.

The baby starts crying and snaps my attention back into the room. The Hubby looks at me for direction. What do we do? Perhaps he is hungry? Or did his first poo? Oh dear, we haven't changed a nappy ever. Do we call a nurse? Are we allowed to pick him up without their permission?

Yes, we figure, he is our son. I shuffle up in bed and The Hubby cautiously lifts him from the bassinet and to my breast. Like the night before, breastfeeding seems effortless and any prenatal worries disappear from view.

After he is done, he begins to wail. This puzzles me because I thought he'd be full and fall back asleep. A passing midwife hears the racket and comes in. She places him upright on The Hubby's lap and shows him how to burp a baby. He looks so tiny in The Hubby's man hands, which are busy rubbing folds of wrinkly skin from the base of the spine to his oversized wobbly head. The two of them seem engaged in a private struggle to see who can be more physically awkward.

"He looks like a little old man being burped."

"Yeah, he kind of does."

The baby concurs by letting out a giant burp. And with that, Little Old Man gets his nickname.

Boab Trees

A midwife walks in and takes a look at me in bed.

"Ok, it's time to get the catheter and those tubes out so you can go have a shower."

I have been itching to get out of bed all morning. My back is killing me now that the sensation has returned to the lower half of my body. The Hubby leaves the room to give me some privacy, which seems a farcical gesture after what he witnessed the day before.

The tubes are removed and I am free to move about. The midwife helps me to the edge of the bed and points out a chair halfway to the bathroom. I stand then move my foot forward. It slips about five centimetres. I glare down at the errant foot. My brain knows how it should move, what it looks like when it moves, but the physical parts are not cooperating.

I take another step and then another one. My legs are wide apart and I am hunched over in anticipation of pain. I walk like a crab but at least I'm walking.

I'm well on the way to the bathroom and look defiantly past the chair in the hallway and towards the door. But then my ankles start to wobble around. I look down again and notice they are rounded balls. I lean over on the chair for support and to get a better look.

"What the fuck is wrong with my feet?"

The midwife looks down.

"Oh, that can happen after birth."

"Why didn't anyone tell me?"

There was no reply but I had already learnt there were a number of things I wasn't told about birth. It was starting to feel like a mass conspiracy to encourage childbearing among sane women. Having ankles that looked like boab trees was just another thing. At least they only look weird and don't hurt, I think cheerily to myself.

I make it to the bathroom and open the door. Like Pavlov's dog, my bladder springs into action at the sight of the toilet bowl. There is greater urgency than normal and I pull down my pants as I shuffle towards the seat. But it's too late. Unlike when my waters broke, I have really done it this time. I have peed my pants.

I freeze mid-stride and consider my options. First things first, I bury any evidence under some papers in the bin.

"Did you say for me to have a shower too?"

"Yes, if you feel up to it."

In truth I don't but it's too humiliating to let the midwife know what just occurred. I run the shower and get in, shivering from the effort of standing up.

I look down again, too frightened to touch anything down there. I gingerly run the hose over the area and feel a stinging pain that has me grabbing at the wall.

I start to worry about what exactly happened during the surgery. If I can't get to the toilet, perhaps my pelvic floor muscles are gone. I try to put the thought out of my mind. The doctor should be around later to explain it all.

When the pain has subsided enough for me to move, I turn off the shower and dry off. A midwife had kindly given me the tip to use a hairdryer for downstairs because a towel would be too rough. It's the most literal and best blow job of my life.

I crab-walk back to bed and slide in, careful not to place pressure on anywhere between my hips and feet. The pain is unbearable but I feel more human for having had a shower. The midwife offers some more tablets and I fall back asleep.

It was the 80s

2:30 AM. Two days have passed by. A midwife comes in and Little Old Man is screaming. He is hungry and I have nothing left in me to feed him. The initial ease and excitement of breastfeeding has gone. He is waking too often to feed and we are both exhausted.

Two midwives stand in the hallway outside my door. I was on the way to the toilet and hear them talking about my case in whispered conversation.

My milk supply is low, they agree, before concluding that the root cause is massive blood loss and shock. Oh and I look terribly pale and drawn, apparently.

They enter my room, one holding Little Old Man while the other holds a clipboard. Will I consent to him being bottle fed formula?

One midwife advises me that the baby is crying because he is hungry and I don't have enough milk just yet. The other thrusts a clipboard in my direction and asks me to sign. I read the form in the half light – it is for parental consent to formula feeding.

"I don't want him on formula."

Little Old Man cries out louder as though he is begging me to sign. His desperate cries make me feel the pain of his hungry belly myself. The midwives shoot each other an impatient look as I continue to waver. The bad cop midwife with the clipboard turns the screws a bit harder.

"We know, but do you want a baby who is breastfed exclusively or one that is able to spell his name in kindergarten?"

I look at Little Old Man and sign. They take him back up to the nursery for a feed and I am left behind. The silence in the room after his all-consuming screams is maddening. I fold over on myself and sob uncontrollably against the wall. I feel so powerless, so utterly useless in my new role as a mother.

Another midwife later comes in to try to discern what the problem is with my breastfeeding, as though losing nearly two litres of blood is not a problem enough.

"Was your mother able to breastfeed?" she asks.

"I don't know."

I try to remember any conversation with my mother on the topic but it's not something that comes up casually.

"I think she once said I was bottle fed."

The midwife looks exasperated.

"Yes but why?"

"I don't know, because it was the 80s?"

She laughs and confirms with me it was nothing to do with her physical ability.

"If she had an issue, like chronic mastitis, then the odds are you may trip over the same issue."

The next morning, I ring my mother to get confirmation of why she did not breastfeed. She dismisses the midwife's theory as akin to reading tea leaves. She then continues on to say in her day midwives were just a bunch of hairy arm-pitted hippies obsessed with breastfeeding and to take no notice of them.

My mother is probably right, except for the hairy arm pit hippy bit, yet the idea of having someone else to blame than myself is alluring. Particularly when that person is my mother.

So why didn't she breastfeed?

"Well, it was the 80s darling. Plus, I waited and my milk never seemed to come in."

To understand this comment, you need to firstly understand my mother. During the 1980s, she was a very happy exponent of the minimal-effort-instant-packet-mix-women-can-do-it-all generation of women. She would give anything a go regardless of the price tag if it promised to fix her problems and save time.

The add-on about her milk not coming in makes me giggle into the phone. I imagine her looking at a screaming hungry baby and then at her breasts, wondering why they didn't do whatever it is they are meant to do before reaching for the bottle in frustration.

After I hang up, the scene strikes me as sad. Perhaps nobody told her about colostrum and that not much milk is produced in the first 72 hours. Perhaps a midwife didn't grab her breast uninvited to illustrate how to attach a baby. Perhaps she gave up before her body was ready to give it a real go.

I feel like calling back to apologise for any insensitivity but resist. It is enough to have changed to a gentler perspective of her based on my own experiences.

Tidal Wave

Before The Hubby leaves the hospital for the day, I let him in on where my headspace is at. All afternoon I have noticed my mood getting worse. The weight of depression is one I unfortunately know all too well. Luckily, I also remember that the 'baby blues' kick in around day three when the pregnancy hormones drop and the breastfeeding ones arrive.

"Honey, my hormones are coming in…"

"Oh. What do these ones do?"

"If I get upset over the next couple of days, then please don't think this is how I really am. It's just the hormones readjusting. Remember, how they told us about baby blues in the antenatal class?"

He looks at me warily before smiling.

"Thanks for the heads-up. It's good that you have such an understanding of yourself."

And it's true. I feel ready for whatever waves of sadness are about to wash over me because I am able to see them gathering on the horizon and know how to ready myself mentally. The Hubby squeezes my hand and pats Little Old Man on his way out the door.

The night passes much like the ones before it. I wake up in panic a few times, although not as bad as the first night. The baby screams out in hunger. I try to feed him and then helplessly call the buzzer when my attempts don't satisfy his hunger. Each time they take him to the nursery, I try to block out the mental image of him being fed formula. I just don't want to know.

Although harmless to the observer, the image of a formula feed is a highly confronting one to me. My body has failed to meet something very instinctive and, in doing so, has created a compulsion so strong that it has consumed me.

I love my son. I love him with every last breath in my body. True to the cliché, I would gladly get run over by a bus if this meant I could save him. When he cries or rests his head on me, my body literally aches for him. When he makes sweet facial expressions or puckers his big fish lips during feeding, tears of joy flood my vision.

I cannot control these physical reactions. Oxytocin is a strange and, at times, marvellous hormone. As I am coming to realise, it is also powerful enough to hijack my entire mood.

During the night I start to cry without end. I fall asleep crying, I wake crying and I feed Little Old Man crying. Compounding the tears is a crushing wall of anxiety. The adrenaline from the first couple of days has worn off and the fear from the birth and surgery have caught up with me. The sense of being braced for whatever comes is evaporating quickly. I am drowning under the relentless waves.

By the 5 AM feed, the midwife asks if there is anything she can do. I think for a moment and recall a work colleague, Ros, telling me to call if I ever needed a mum. At the time I found the comment strange. I have a mum, she lives in Sydney. In the hospital room though, I was beginning to understand what she had meant.

"I know this is probably unusual but could you please call this number at 7 AM and ask Ros to come in to see me? She is a friend of mine."

"Sure, no worries at all."

The last add on to my request was a bit of a stretch of the truth to justify my randomness. Ros wasn't really a friend, or at least not the kind of friend I would make a call to at 7 AM in the morning in such a demanding manner. We had only met a couple of months prior to me going on maternity leave. Yet something clicked between us and I knew we could be good friends in time. Perhaps this was the speedy entrance to that time.

I hand over a piece of paper with her number on it and feel instantly calmer for having followed my gut feeling. There doesn't seem to be much else to anchor myself on to at this point.

I climb back into bed and try to fall back asleep. Like the nights before, I look out the window into the blackness and pray for the morning to come.

Hot Mess

"Hey, morning."

Ros is standing over my bed, looking down on what must look like quite the sight. I sit up and push aside a night-table full of nipple shields, tissues and spare pads the size of surfboards. I then pat my normally perfectly coiffed hair somewhere near back into place.

"I'm sorry, I must look like a hot mess."

"Oh don't worry about that, how are you more importantly?"

It is the first time since the birth that someone has asked me that. How am I? I start to formulate an answer but quickly tear up.

"Oh love, it's ok…"

Ros sits on the bed and I blurt out everything from the waters breaking on without censorship. Her eyes grow wider as I continue. It is the first time I have told anyone the story of Little Old Man's birth. Somewhere in my head I had concluded the birth experience was normal and I was just being oversensitive. Judging from the look on her face, though, this was not the case.

I finish the emotional vomit onto Ros with a crescendo of personal humiliation.

"…and then, and then I peed my pants"

Shame registers somewhere in me – not only at the last admission but also at the crying itself. This really, truly is not my style. I am the pillar of strength for all my friends. I have listened for many hours as some have cried on my shoulder but never did the same myself. And now here I am – returning the favour to someone with whom I have zero credit.

I apologise and wait for Ros to call me crazy and walk out of the room. Instead, she reaches out her hand and strokes my arm.

"Oh love, you've been babied that's all. Your body has been through so much and is full of hormones. It is perfectly normal to be upset so don't apologise. And for the record, pissing your pants is perfectly permissible when you're either drunk or postnatal."

To my surprise, I laugh.

"But what if my pelvic floor is really gone?"

"Haven't you been told what happened in the surgery?"

"No. I keep waiting for the obstetrician but he never comes…"

"You don't have to wait for him. The midwives can read your notes to you too. Do you want me to go up to the nurses' station and get one to come down?"

I nod and she leaves the room. A ball of nervous energy rises up in me. What if something went terribly wrong? Maybe this is why they haven't told me. Maybe they are trying to protect me until I am stronger.

Whatever the case, I conclude I have the right to know and would rather deal with the definite than whatever scenarios my mind conjures up.

I sit up and wait for Ros and the truth to return.

Bent-Up Grill

The nurse enters the room with a blue folder and sits on the end of my bed. She opens it up and asks me what I wanted to know.

"Everything."

"Everything?"

"Everything."

And so she began to read out from admission on what had occurred. Some of it I knew but other bits I was hearing for the first time. It turned out I had second degree tearing but my pelvic floor was thankfully intact. The peeing in the bathroom episode was normal and happens to most women after delivery because muscles are stretched out of shape. I was relieved, pardon the pun, to know I wouldn't have to spend the rest of my life wearing adult nappies.

The nurse continues to read out my notes. My leg flinches back to life again when she reaches the blood loss and the surgery. I pretend to be bouncing my leg on purpose. I look over to Ros to see concern on her face.

"...and that is about it until this morning."

"And those drugs they keep giving me, what are those?"

"Morphine."

"Holy crap!"

"You need to keep taking them otherwise you will be in a lot of pain."

The idea of taking such a strong drug didn't really sit well with me but I feel more at ease consenting to them now. The notes didn't make for pretty listening but they were mine.

"Thank you for telling me what happened to me." I offer somewhat pathetically.

"You're welcome, it is your right to know."

Indeed.

Part of the Furniture

The baby blues were thankfully subsiding as quickly as they arrived. The absolute desperation was slowly being replaced with the routine of motherhood. It was a predictable pattern centred purely on the wants and whims of the baby: eat, feed, settle, sleep, eat, feed, settle, sleep and so on.

The only choice I had in the matter was what I did with those small windows of opportunity when he was asleep. The midwives told me to sleep when he slept, which I mostly did. But I also took the opportunity to call friends and connect with the outside world out of fear of completely losing the plot.

The longer I was there, the more I noticed the rhythm of the hospital day. There was the trolley troll who would come around mid-morning and bark at me for not finishing my breakfast yet so she could take the tray. There was also the bin lady, who took out the garbage which was filled with all sorts of unspeakable things. And then there were the other mothers and babies.

Having been there for a few days, I now considered myself a veteran. I knew the sounds of the ward and could accordingly guess where other women were at in the birthing process. One night I heard a foetal heart monitor thumping away in the room next door. The next morning a baby's wails filtered through the walls. I then later saw a very dazed-looking woman emerge from the room and walk gingerly to the nursery.

Every evening the incidental sounds of the ward lessened, with visitors leaving and the ward settling down into its skeleton night staff. It was then that I could hear all the babies up and down the ward let out their cries. It was like cicadas gearing up on a summer eve, only louder.

Before I gave birth, every baby sounded the same. Yet listening to these babies day after day, I learnt that their cries were as unique and individual as their fingerprints. Some sounded like sheep, others like ravens, hawks or angle grinders. My favourite sounded like one of those dalek robots from *Dr Who*.

For my baby, I was able to pick his cry from the first night on. I could hear it approaching whenever the midwives were wheeling him back from the nursery after a break. My top was open and I was ready to go by the time his bassinet barrelled through the door with him in a fit of hungry rage.

The Hubby looked on in amazement at this growing awareness and asked how I knew. The bookish nerd in me wanted to give a logical answer but I didn't have one. I just knew.

Escape

I have been in hospital for four nights and this is the fifth, which was an extension by my request because I hadn't felt quite ready the morning before when we had to make the decision. By the evening though, we had all reached a point where we felt ready to go.

I reached this point first, when a midwife came in and chastised me for having Little Old Man attached to the breast for too long. She said he was burning calories and shouldn't be awake for more than an hour. This came after another midwife had chastised me for only attaching him for 10 minutes a side, suggesting I let him attach for as long as he wants in order to stimulate milk production. She, in turn, was preceded by a midwife who had sworn ten minutes a side was all that was necessary. I snapped at the last in this parade of well-intended midwives and told her it was my business. She sighed and said it was up to me if I wanted an overworked baby.

The more shift changes I see, the more conflicting information I receive. At the beginning I lapped up every piece of advice, turning my behaviour to the perspective of the latest midwife. I trusted each implicitly, as I had always respected the opinion of medical professionals as superior to my own uneducated hunches.

Yet the conflicting advice was disheartening and increasingly annoying. I have been burned too many times by the Shouldn't Brigade. I don't mind following suggestions of what I should do, even if it is conflicting with other advice. I will give anything a go to get my milk flowing and have a well-rested baby.

No, what gets me is the advice telling me what I shouldn't do, as it is limiting and makes whatever it is that I'm doing my fault even though I am following the advice of another midwife.

The Shouldn't Brigade is also messing with my growing confidence and understanding as a mother of what is best for my child. When I think I have worked out something for myself, in comes a midwife to tell me I shouldn't do that. I take their advice within reason but am increasingly questioning where the harm is in whatever it is that I'm doing.

Another midwife later enters my room and frowns at me for letting Little Old Man settle on my arm. I try to explain he is only calming down after a rather testing feeding session.

"Ohhh, but you shouldn't let him settle on you! He'll be sleeping in your bed until he is four years old! You'll regret this later..."

Perhaps this is true if I let him settle on me every single time but I am only allowing it when he has been really upset. I figure the last few days have been hard on both of us and he needs some slack while trying to learn the ropes of being alive.

As what will be our last full day in hospital wears on, my annoyance turns to anger as I battle with what feels like constant running interference. The door to my room opens and closes regularly without anybody knocking or checking if any of the inhabitants are asleep. It is a private room yet feels like anything but with nurses, cleaners and the meal trolley troll all treading their way through. By the time The Hubby returns with dinner, I let him know my thoughts.

"I want to go home tomorrow."

"Are you sure you're ready? I don't want you to push yourself."

"No, I'm ready. The midwives have been great but their help is starting to turn into a negative."

The Hubby looks surprised at this comment but he doesn't spend 24 hours in the ward. It is only later that night that he sees my point. The Hubby has taken over doing the formula feeds and goes up to the nursery to get a bottle. A midwife refuses to issue him with more than 30ml at a time even though Little Old Man has been easily going through more than that in one go. We know this because another midwife had earlier given us a whole bottle of formula.

The Hubby stomps around the room in frustration, knowing that he will only have to go back up again soon to get another 30ml while a screaming baby baulks at his empty mother and half formula feed.

The next morning both myself and Little Old Man are discharged. We exit the front doors and I wait with the baby capsule for The Hubby to drive up. I can't quite believe that we're going home as a family, it seems so strange, as though we're breaking some kind of law by taking him into our exclusive care.

We pack our little bundle of sleeping joy into the car and The Hubby carefully exits the car park. It is a nervous drive, with every bump and careless driver noted with caution. I watch the streets pass by out the window. Everything looks foreign after nearly a week spent holed up in a hospital room. Life has been intensely in my face with a newborn but in other ways it is also distant from me now.

I watch someone ride to work and another wait at the lights with their morning coffee. The scenes are about as foreign as watching someone land on the moon.

Back home, we burst through the doors with The Hubby tending to the baby capsule, overnight bags, a camping mattress, and a pile of other things. I wish I could help but I don't have the energy. I head for my chair and sit down, exhausted by the twenty steps it took to get there.

The living room looks exactly as I left it, complete with the half-opened mail I went through on the morning we drove in. I realise The Hubby probably hasn't been in there either since the birth – commuting in a daze between our bedroom and the hospital.

I am in pain but couldn't be happier. Nobody can walk in on me anymore without knocking. No more nosey midwives grabbing at my breasts, no more trolley troll and nobody else coming in just as I've fallen asleep. It is me, The Hubby, Little Old Man and our fish tank.

For better or worse, I am home.

Home Sweet Home

I had another panic attack on our first night at home. The pressure of breastfeeding compounded with the anxiety around the birth and the sense of panic grew and grew until the point of no return. The lack of sleep, physical pain and random screaming fits from Little Old Man didn't help much either. Nobody can prepare you for how relentless life with a newborn really is. They can tell you in words but the meaning is hollow until you go through it yourself.

The night began as it did in the hospital. The Hubby or I would feed him depending on whether it was breast or formula time, then we would rock him gently to sleep and sneak off to bed. By the time we just snuggled back down, he was either awake again for a cluster feed or a bout of wind.

There was barely a minute where both of us were in bed at the same time.

We had continued the rooming-in arrangement from the hospital to increase the chances of my milk coming in. Yet a newborn baby is not the best sleeping partner. I have no idea where the saying 'sleep like a baby' comes from because it does not match what I have seen so far. Babies sleep more like drunk homeless men – they make loud random noises, startle easily, cry themselves to sleep, fart with abandon and end the night by pissing themselves. Hardly what I would deem paragons of good sleeping habits.

With both of us on high alert, every noise Little Old Man made woke us from what little sleep we were getting. By the middle of the night, things had reached desperation point. We had already resolved to move his cot into the hallway in the morning and, if that failed, further off into the living room.

I took the baby downstairs and tried to breastfeed him. He got some milk but it wasn't enough. I was still struggling with the idea of feeding him with formula. The midwives had always taken him away to the nursery to do it or The Hubby did while I walked off. It was easier to let others feed him with formula than face my own demons.

And now those demons were right there, sitting alongside me while I considered what to do with the screaming babe in my arms. There was nobody to do the dirty work but me. I knew I had to swallow whatever emotion was stopping me from feeding him. It wasn't fair or sustainable to go wake The Hubby and make Little Old Man wait in the process. But I couldn't make the first move. I froze in my indecision.

I picked up the phone and rang a breastfeeding advice line. I gave them the context as if I was talking about someone else: emergency surgery, milk didn't come in cause of the shock and blood loss, baby not getting enough food, comp feeding, unsure what to do next. The woman chipped at my façade as I went.

"Oh you poor thing, oh how awful, I'm so sorry…"

Eventually she chipped enough that I broke down and couldn't stop. It was 2 AM and I was blubbering on the phone to an absolute stranger. She offered the same practical advice that I received at the hospital. Try the baby on the breast, then provide expressed milk, then formula feed and then express for the next feed when baby is settled. Repeat ad infinitum.

I hung up and felt anxiety rise in me. I had done the steps right up until formula feed and there was no way round it. I went to the kitchen and headed towards the formula but stopped short. I turned and marched up the stairs to the sleeping hubby.

"I can't, I can't, I'm so sorry…"

"What? What is it?"

I handed Little Old Man to The Hubby and bent over the bed, gasping for air. As my breathing slowed I was overcome with a sense of defeat. It seemed so stupid. Why can't I bloody feed him the bottle?

"What's the matter?"

"I just couldn't feed him the formula. I couldn't do it."

"Let's go do it together then."

And so we did. The Hubby patiently explained how to measure out the formula and I watched as he fed Little Old Man. I focussed on my breathing, trying to calm myself into the role and thanking The Hubby for his patience.

I knew the next time it would be me doing this alone. There would be no way around this, only through.

Drawing Lines

Little Old Man had taken a break from crying and I took my opportunity. It was 4 AM and I sent a text to Sans, a dear friend in Perth, to see if she was still awake. She was. Thank God for the time difference and a little insomnia on both sides.

I retold the night and my panic at the bottle. As a Mum of two boys herself, she got where I was coming from and knew I wanted only the best for my son. It was a relief to be understood by someone I trusted as a solid sounding board. Sans listened and listened until I had no words left to say. And then she spoke.

"No matter how hard the night, remember that the sun will rise in a couple of hours. And when it does, draw a line under everything that has gone before and start afresh into the new day."

"Ok."

"And promise me that you will feed him tomorrow with the bottle yourself."

"Ok, I will."

I hung up and looked out the window with Little Old Man nestled in my arms. The darkness didn't seem as formidable as it did at the hospital.

Sans was right, the sun would soon rise. A new day was on the cusp of breaking and, with it, a line would be drawn.

Tits out Friday

The midwives at the hospital had said one way to make my milk happen was to have skin-to-skin contact. I decided for the day I would carry round Little Old Man on my chest with only a jacket to keep us warm.

During the morning it went well. He snuggled in close and slept in longer blocks than he previously had. The jacket was more than sufficient to keep us warm in addition to the body heat we generated. It was amazing how much heat a little snoring bundle could generate.

I looked down at him often in a sleep-deprived daze and smiled at his curled-up lips. He was so tiny and I couldn't believe my luck that he was finally here with us. I could feel my body reacting to his proximity and hoped this was the hormones ramping up.

By mid-afternoon he was awake. With a newborn it seems there are only two states: asleep and awake. And by awake I don't mean sitting up happily and giving smiles. No, awake means screaming with hunger until sufficiently fed, burped and cradled. At that point, with any luck, they promptly fall back to sleep in order to gather energy for the next round.

Little Old Man fed at the breast a couple of times but it wasn't enough. I pleaded for his patience and he screamed out his impatience. We circled each other a few times in this way at each feed. The gaps between sleep and awake got smaller as his underlying hunger continued to build. We were locked in battle and I was too caught in the moment to see what was happening.

At the next feed, The Hubby intervened by gently suggesting he take over with a bottle of formula. Close to tears, I remembered my promise to Sans on the phone the night before. I snapped out of one battle and turned to the other.

"No, let me do it."

"Are you sure?"

"Yes, I have to learn. I have to start offering it to him."

The Hubby handed me the bottle and I popped it in the gaping hole of a mouth. He continued to scream, oblivious to the solution right there. I tried to tickle the roof of his mouth with the teat to get him to latch on.

"Come on baby, don't make this any harder on me…"

Pleading. The last resort of a desperate parent. I took the teat out of his mouth and The Hubby walked him round the room to settle him down a few notches. It seemed to do the trick, at least long enough to give the bottle another go. I placed the teat under his nose and traced it down into his mouth. Bingo! He latched on and started to gulp as soon as he realised there was something worth sucking for.

Little Old Man polished off the entire bottle and burped loudly. He looked contented and at peace with his belly for once. I felt so guilty for having so far denied him that sensation while in my arms.

As if The Hubby had read my mind, he added,

"You're giving this your best shot, honey."

"I know."

I zipped up my jacket and studied Little Old Man's face, trying to lock this contented look into my brain as a reminder to never get back to where I had been in the past few days.

Dinner, Take Three

The Hubby looked in the fridge and sighed. There was some chicken that was about to go off but neither of us had the energy or inclination to cook it up. Our diet since coming home from the hospital consisted of cereal, toast, the occasional takeaway and whatever leftovers we could find at the back of the freezer.

When The Hubby went shopping, he picked up some fresh vegetables and meat in the hope of inspiring himself into cooking. For my own part, my energy levels were so low that I could barely make toast. The end result was me operating in ever diminishing circles of energy. I had even struggled that morning opening a new bottle of milk. I had never felt so tired or weak in my life but figured this was par for the course.

The Hubby started to chop up the chicken and some vegetables. He looked through the pantry for some inspiration of what to do with it before holding aloft a packet sauce he found.

"You know what, we're going to have a proper dinner tonight."

"Huh?"

"Yes, we're going to sit down at the table and eat dinner like we used to."

"Oh honey, I don't think we'll be able to."

"Well, we've got to give it a go. I'm sick of eating separate meals on the couch. I want to spend some time with you."

Time with me? Was he delirious? I haven't exactly been the most sparkling company of late. Besides, where was I going to find the time to sit down and have a proper meal?

"We're going to eat together, even if takes all night."

I sighed and agreed to try before grumbling at the unnecessary pressure this placed on us. What was the big deal with eating a proper meal all of a sudden?

As is his forte, The Hubby cooked a lovely looking meal. He served it up and we both sat down at the dining table. It felt like such a lifetime ago when we had last sat together that the act was almost silly.

We picked up our cutlery and, as if on cue, Little Old Man started to scream.

"Sorry, I'll have to get him."

I returned to the table and picked up my fork while nursing him on the other arm. The Hubby looked deflated.

"This isn't what I had in mind."

"Well, what do you suggest I do? Let him starve?"

"You're starving yourself!"

"What do you want me to do? This is what having a baby is like, I'm sorry that doesn't fit in with your ideal of having dinner together."

"We're going to have dinner together, it's important."

"Fine! Just let me feed him and we can reheat dinner in the microwave."

A tense truce was held in the room. I fed Little Old Man in silence and then rocked him back to sleep in his pram. We warmed the dinner and began again.

There were two more interruptions, which we both took turns in dealing with. The end result was a lukewarm meal for each of us and a kind of contented baby. But we persisted and ate a proper meal together.

"Thank you for making the effort of cooking."

"No, thank you for agreeing to eat it with me."

It seemed like a strange thing to thank someone for but he was being sincere. When I had calmed down and went along with his great experiment, I saw the point he was trying to get at. Yes, it was only dinner but it was also so much more. It was about looking after ourselves both physically and as a couple.

If we allowed everything to slide for the sake of the baby then we ran the risk of not working as a team at the very time in our lives that we needed to the most. And that would help no one, least of all the baby.

Reality Check

After sitting at the breakfast table for five minutes, I stood up out of pain. It had been two weeks since the birth and the pain from the stitches was not going away. In fact, it seemed to be getting worse. I went to see my usual doctor, unsure of what to expect.

Until that point, I had only very gently touched anything below the belt when washing in the shower as per instruction from the hospital. I was petrified of knowing what a wreck it all looked like. It certainly still felt like a bent-up grill, complete with stitches and odd bumps where they shouldn't be.

I nervously entered the doctor's office and explained what had happened during the delivery and the current situation. It was the very last place on the planet I wanted to be because I knew where it would be leading.

"Hmm, sounds like we should have a look."

I nodded reluctantly and assumed the position on the examination table.

"Oh dear…"

The way she said it made my heart sink. It was part pity, part shock. Not really a tone I want to hear from a medical professional, particularly not when referring to myself.

"The stitches have only half dissolved and are infected. We'll need to pull them out. You should feel better afterwards."

I feel my leg starting to twitch and stare firmly at the holes in the ceiling tiles.

"Ok let's do it, anything is better than this pain."

She starts to take the stiches out. I curl my fingernails into the palm of my hands to stop myself from edging off the table.

"You know, if you lived a hundred years ago or in a developing country, you would be dead."

"Uh huh…"

"You've really been through the wars, haven't you? I've had six kids and nothing like this."

Stop talking. Stop talking.

"There we go. All done."

I sit up and get dressed. The vainer part of me wants to ask her if it looks as bad as I imagine but she seems to have already answered that. I feel like a physical wreck, an irretrievable mess.

The doctor checks her computer to see my results from the hospital blood tests.

"Did they put you on iron supplements?"

"No."

"So you're not taking any?"

"No, why?"

"You should be. You're very anaemic. It wouldn't be helping your breastfeeding efforts."

She writes a few scripts and I limp back over the car park like a prized fighter. It is the first time I've been outside for about a week. I go to the chemist and find out the wait for scripts will be twenty minutes. I feel like whining that I just want to go home to bed but remember I'm in civilisation and not in my baby bubble.

I look at the waiting chairs in the chemist and shudder at the thought of having to sit in the car to drive home. I remember the supermarket is next door and, for whatever mad reason, decide this would be a great way to fill in those twenty minutes even though I'm already puffed out.

I walk two aisles, pick up a bag of tortillas and cheese to justify my excursion, and line up to pay. All around me are people going about their everyday business. They have no idea what a feat it was for me to stand among them. The pain is unbearable so I stare at the full trolley ahead of me to distract myself.

I imagine the energy involved in collecting all those items, bagging them, carrying them to the car, out of the car, into a kitchen, and then preparing them into meals. Microwaving a tortilla with some cheese on it seems like a much more do-able option.

The woman with the full trolley interrupts my thoughts.

"Excuse me, would you like to go ahead of me? You only have two items."

I nod and shuffle forward. It is small gesture of kindness, one I have made myself many times. Yet the woman has no idea how much she has saved me. In my mind, she is not just polite but a supermarket fairy.

I return to the chemist as discreetly as one can when crab-walking in public and pick up my scripts. I then face the challenge awaiting me at the car. I slowly lower myself into the driver's seat and brace myself for the surge in pain. But it doesn't come.

Perhaps the good doctor was right about feeling better afterwards.

The Midnight Runners

It has been a few days since I got my stitches out. Despite the promising early signs, the pain was not getting any better. It was actually getting worse. A lot worse.

"Honey, I can't sit."

"What do you mean?"

I'm kneeling on the couch with my arms dangling over the back. It was a position I discovered in the last few weeks of my pregnancy when I needed relief from the weight of the baby pressing down. Now it was helping me avoid another pressure, this one more acutely painful.

I ask for the phone and pause momentarily over who to call. I start by ringing the maternity ward to ask for advice on whether I should come in. It's late on a Friday night and they are the only ones I can think of who might answer the phone. They are concerned the infection has spread and suggest I call an after-hours service at the hospital.

I ring and the receptionist asks for a detail of the problem to gauge the emergency. I feel anxious about retelling the story of the birth yet again but the pain gives me little choice.

"Oh dear, you poor love. I'll book you in for an appointment tonight. There is one free on the other side of town in an hour."

"I'll take it."

I didn't care if it was on the other side of the continent at that point. The pain was so intense.

The Hubby looks on concerned.

"So who is going to drive you there?"

"What do you mean? I can drive myself."

"Not like that."

I grit my teeth and smile. I know he means well but I have come to resent the feeling of being helpless. The Hubby has kindly looked after me since the hospital and I freely concede he has been a lifesaver. Still, knowing this doesn't make me feel better about having to be looked after. In those moments where I have tried stubbornly to do things for myself, I have ended up doubled over in pain or needing to lie down to recover.

Before I begin to argue the point of not being that helpless, another shot of pain sears through me. I know it is time to cede my pride.

"Ok, so who is going to drive?"

Little Old Man is fast asleep in his pram. It seems pointless to put him in the car capsule and potentially wake him.

"We could get Em and Sue?"

"Isn't it too late?"

"They said to call them any time of the day or night if we needed anything…"

"I feel bad though."

"Don't. You would do the same for them if the situation was reversed."

As it turns out, they were on their way home from a concert and were happy to drive me. How odd that people could be out enjoying themselves at a concert, I think to myself. They arrive twenty minutes later and we are on our way.

I lay across their back seat and look up at my friends, thanking them for making the trip out so late. It's moments like these that are a reminder of how important friendships are – particularly the ones where you know a call for help will be answered regardless of what the clock says.

At the clinic the doctor calls me in and I explain the situation. He takes my temperature and writes a new prescription for antibiotics and stronger painkillers. He seems quite willing to give me whatever strength painkillers I want – right up to morphine. In his enthusiasm, he comes across more like a drug dealer than a doctor. I opt for pain relief that is strong but not knock-me-out strong. Given how careful I was about medication during pregnancy, I feel like my postnatal self has morphed into a walking pharmacopeia.

"Don't worry, it's very normal to get reoccurring infections in surgery stitches. You should be fine with some more rest. Just keep up the pain medication and see your regular doctor if you are not better in a week."

On the way home, we stop at the chemist. Em and Sue buy chocolate as a midnight snack and we set about devouring the evidence before reaching home. We drive down the deserted streets and tell each other stories of our medical emergencies over the years and the crazy doctors we've seen.

The rush of sugar and pain medication makes me feel silly and I start laughing without end. It's the first real laugh I've had since the birth. Maybe it was the stress of the night and pain leaving me. I knew I would be ok. All I needed was time and some rest.

White Rage

I am jealous of a formula tin that sits on my kitchen bench. It comes from a supermarket, where rows and rows of tins sit waiting to provide babies with easy nourishment. The Hubby bought little tetra paks of formula when we came home from the hospital to tide us over until my milk was at full supply.

I have learnt to live with formula but feel cheated by its continued existence in our lives. All the midwives at the hospital were so positive and adamant that breastfeeding would work out. I believed them wholeheartedly because they said what I desperately wanted to hear. Only one, a lactation consultant, dared to raise the prospect that perhaps my milk would never fully come in. I shut down and told her we were done talking.

Back home, without a word between us, The Hubby and I both began to realise that formula would be more than just a temporary fix. Then he bought the tin – better value for money than the tetras, he said. I couldn't argue the logic and said nothing. Even so, I hated that tin on sight and was angry at its existence.

And I still hate it. I hate the sense of failure I feel when I see it, even though I know I have done everything in my power to make my milk happen. Above all, I am jealous – a feeling I never thought I would possess towards an inanimate object. But that object provides the one precious bond I would dearly love to give my son but can't quite seem to. Not just yet, at least.

There are no words to explain my strength of conviction on breastfeeding. It is an innate desire and extension of the physical bonds of pregnancy. It is a conviction borne on that illogical sea of postpartum hormones that still wash over me. And, if I were to be truthful, it is also partly fuelled by the perfectionist in me who strives to do everything right and best.

If I had been asked while pregnant, I would have shrugged philosophically and said I'd like to breastfeed but if it doesn't work out then *c'est la vie*. I saw the benefits and was sold on the antenatal classes espousing the simplicity of it all. The ease with which it began and the can-do attitudes of the midwives further entrenched these messages. Yet the initial enthusiasm has since been worn away by the daily reality of a screaming baby after another failed attempt at feeding.

I should add here that I don't have a problem with women choosing formula. To breastfeed or not is a highly personal and individual choice that I respect absolutely, even more so now I realise how hard it can be if something goes wrong. No, my problem is that my choice of breastfeeding has been taken away from me.

This lack of choice is forcing me to live with formula. As the midwife so kindly pointed out at the hospital, yes I would like my child to be able to spell his name at kindergarten. That doesn't mean it has been easy to swallow the sense of anger and disappointment in me.

I have called formula every insult my mind could muster – 'that white powder', 'kiddy cocaine', 'pig swill', 'industrial sewage', 'factory milk', 'white poison'. This is all despite me knowing it keeps my son alive and enables him to thrive. The pull of hormones cannot be explained, only experienced.

And in the background a harder truth looms ever larger, despite me struggling wildly against it; perhaps I should just give up on breastfeeding altogether. The fact is, I am sick and my body needs to recover big time. I am dealing with infections, pain, anaemia, trauma; plus all the normal sleep deprivation and recovery issues that other women go through. Perhaps having one less pressure would help me back to health.

But I can't let go, my hormones have a vice-like grip. They are as unrelenting in intensity as my feelings towards that tin, the one that sits on my kitchen bench.

Circles

In the week following my trip to the after-hours doctor, I did everything he advised. I rested and let The Hubby look after me without constant protest. I also took my painkillers and antibiotics as prescribed rather than only when I felt they were absolutely necessary.

The pain subsided to the point that I finally felt like I was heading in the right direction. I was desperate to get out of the house and into the fresh air but I knew not to push it. The recovery time needed after the supermarket expedition was enough of a reminder to take it easy. I waited another week before I felt strong enough to leave the front door. And then I did.

Recovery from surgery and blood loss isn't quick and I am learning to respect my physical limits. I am also mindful that I was housebound for the month before the birth. Even if the surgery hadn't happened, I still would have been starting from a pretty unfit point.

I began my return to normal life by walking to the letter box to get the mail, which sent me diving back onto the couch to rest. After a few days of this though, I felt I had mastered the walk. I then moved beyond the letter box and in ever increasing circles around our house. I first walked around a small park in our complex. When I got used to this, I expanded to walking to front drive. I am now set to walk across the street.

My ultimate goal is to do the walk I used to do daily before getting pregnant. At the moment though, I like the security of being close to home in case the pain gets too much and I need to pull the pin.

We'll see how it goes. Recovery is no race – as long as I remember this and don't get diverted by stubbornness then I should be fine.

Welcome to the Barnyard

Little Old Man makes weird noises, lots of them. It is like a secret language that The Hubby and I are slowly deciphering. The first we learnt was The Goat – a cry of hunger that builds in crescendo until he begins to bleat like a goat. The sound initially crushed me until I realised a trick to bypass my hormones. I imagined the cry sounded like a goat and I felt less affected and able to get on with providing him with what he needed.

Based on this discovery, and that the association makes the cries easier to memorise, we have sought to find a barnyard animal or object for all his cries. To date, Little Old Man makes the following noises:

The Donkey – A sound made during feeding, usually when he is midway and trying to keep the sucking action up.

The Rusty Gate – Similar to The Donkey but with just the high pitch repeated. Also tends to be made during eating time.

The Seagull – A sound produced randomly during sleep. There seems to be no purpose for this sound other than to startle us from our sleep, as though he's just checking if we're paying attention at all times to his every want and desire.

The Tugboat – Another sleep sound of debatable purpose. I maintain it is him dreaming.

The Steam Train – Similar to the tugboat's horn but repetitive in nature. Also a sound made during sleep and often accompanied with facial movements that infer he is dreaming of a feed.

The Yappy Dog – Another random sleep sound designed to ensure we are paying attention. Like The Seagull, The Yappy Dog will depart as soon as it arrives.

The Hungry Piggy – When I was pregnant, Little Old Man's nickname was Ferkel (German for piglet). While we didn't know it when we gave the nickname, it has proven to be very apt given the noises he makes before, during and after feeding time. He doesn't sound like just one piglet, he sounds like about a dozen piglets in feverous search of food. After feeding, the grunting is less desperate and more contented.

The Strangled Cat – This is not a cry I wish to hear at any time of the day but especially during the graveyard shifts. The cry is of an overtired baby at the end of their tether. And it signals hours of settling work ahead. The scream is desperate and ends with the last millilitre of lung capacity being shunted past the vocal chords. Not that I have heard a cat being strangled but I imagine the sound is quite similar.

The Duck – This is when he is slowly waking up and his mouth is aware before he is that there is a hungry belly to be fed. The resulting sound of the sucking is something like a desperate Daffy Duck.

Cute Cat – A cute meow sound that is a much more favourable feline sound than Strangled Cat. Cute Cat comes out after a long crying session or when Little Old Man is really tired and not quite sure what his next move is.

Desperation Stations

"This is crazy. Neither of us have slept right in weeks!"

"I'm dead on my feet. I was up four times last night."

"Yeah, I was up four too."

"What are we going to do? We can't go on like this. Nobody can survive this."

The Hubby and I are eating breakfast together. It is a rare occurrence that we are both awake at the same time. Except for around midday, we mostly operate in different time zones. The rare meeting allows us to console each other after another bad run.

The only person in the house who seems to sleep enough is the one person interrupting everybody else's sleep. Little Old Man gets up once every two hours. That doesn't mean we have two hours of rest between feeds. No, each feed and settle cycle takes forty five minutes – leaving us with a grand total of one hour and fifteen minutes of peace if we're lucky.

The one trick we've found is tag-teaming the feeds so each of us gets a break in between getting up. But even then our sleep is interrupted by the baby monitor going off in the bedroom and the other one getting up to respond and return later.

On some nights, one of us will sleep downstairs on the lounge to allow the other to have at least a four-hour block of sleep. This favour is then returned during the day when the well-rested one looks after Little Old Man while the other parent has a siesta.

"Maybe we should bring your mother out from Germany?"

"Oh no, she'd panic that we're not coping."

"But we're not coping!"

"Is there someone else, someone closer?"

"My Mum?"

We both laugh. My mother is in Sydney but not at all what you would consider hands-on.

"Aunty Judy?"

"Do you think she would be useful?"

"Well, she did have three kids and helped raise her grandchildren."

"Maybe…"

The idea is bizarre and hints at our absolute desperation. My family is anything but close. Aunty Judy is lovely but I'm about as close as having a cup of tea and polite conversation with her every six months or so when I visit home. It is not the kind of relationship where I could ask her to drop her life and move interstate for a couple of weeks to help out with an unwieldy newborn.

Yet here I was running through her childrearing credentials to The Hubby as though she was on the short-list for a job she didn't even apply for and possibly didn't want.

"So what do we do?"

"I don't know, I just don't know…"

We sat there in silence, both trying to solve the same puzzle before us. How do we handle this son of ours? This two-legged chaos? I began to think out loud.

"Maybe….maybe the solution isn't to get someone in to help with him but rather to help with all the other stuff in running a household while we get through the early days?"

"What do you mean? Like a cleaner?"

The Hubby sounded suspicious but was willing to hear me through.

"Yes and a red card that we can each use once a week to order takeaway if the day has been too much. We can also restock our frozen leftover supplies so we stop living on toast."

"Surely we can do this ourselves. It's not that much…"

"It is that much when you've got a newborn and a wife who is still recovering and can't do her share of the housework. I feel awful not being able to help more than I do. You're not Super Dad and nobody is expecting you to be."

"Hmm, I'm not sold on the takeaway bit."

"Well at least the cleaning. It would save us a couple of hours of non-baby time."

"True. Let's look into it."

And so we did. It seemed lazy, almost decadent, to get a cleaner. Rich people had cleaners, not people like us. But it was a measure to get us through and it wasn't like we were spending the money on anything else. Our old spending habits had disappeared thanks to our new hermit lifestyle. Gone were the dinners out, shopping expeditions and morning coffees. Our budget went only to grocery shopping and the occasional buy for Little Old Man.

A couple of weeks after finding someone, our house sparkled and we felt slightly less pushed for time. And something unexpected happened – a clean house made life seem less desperate. There was a sense of order once again in at least one aspect of our insular lives. Preparing a few frozen dinners for storage also helped us claw back a bit from the edge. A sleep-through was not yet in sight but at least we had a little more pep to push ourselves towards it.

Rooted

I keep recalling the back of the woman's head and her bad roots. Every time I do, I become quite anxious and my leg starts to jump about. I didn't expect this part of the baby experience.

I remember the last time I saw them – the bad roots were sitting in a postnatal physio class at the hospital a couple of days after the surgery. I kept catching myself looking over at this head of hair and then shifting my attention back to the physio. I hoped this would go unnoticed.

Then the woman attached to the roots raced over to me after the class. I braced myself for a tirade beginning with, "What the fuck are you looking at?" Instead, I got a pleasant greeting.

"Hi, I'm Alison. Your husband was speaking with my husband this morning in the lounge area. Our waters broke at the same time and I was waiting on you to finish in surgery before being wheeled in for an emergency C-section. We had our boys on the same day!"

I froze on the spot and momentarily didn't know what to say. In panic I said the first thing that popped into my mind, which was the story about why I thought she needed to get her roots done. It was the most random and insensitive introduction I have ever given myself. She seemed to take it well or was perhaps being ultra-polite before she could safely back away.

"I actually had a hairdresser's appointment booked for the day my water broke."

"Well, I'd really love to go to the hairdresser with you when we're out of here."

This wasn't a flippant add-on. I really, desperately, did want to go to the hairdresser with this stranger. As though fixing Alison's hair would magically fix the cyclone of emotions and memories swirling inside me.

We chatted a bit further, mostly because I wanted to prove I wasn't some postpartum loon. From what she said of her own story, it sounded like she had been through the wars too. The Hubby passed on our contact details to her hubby.

Given all the similarities, I had hoped she would contact me rather than write me off. I sensed we needed each other because only we could understand what the other was going through.

The few people who know I had a rough time have reassured me that I have a healthy baby boy and this is all that matters. Yes, his safe arrival is a blessing beyond words yet it does not negate the anxiety, insomnia and nightmares that arrived with him. I wish it were that simple but it isn't. I know recovery for me will involve more than just the physical side.

Weeks have now passed since the birth and I think about Alison every day. How is she doing? Is she struggling like me? I look in my inbox to see if there's an email from her, apologising for taking so long to get in contact. Newborns and all, you know. But there is nothing.

With each day of silence that passes, I am coming to realise that getting Alison's roots done or waiting for time to heal all is not going to make things go away. No, I need something more to achieve that. I need help.

Junk in the Trunk

There's a moment during feed time when Little Old Man opens his eyes. He looks up and directly into my eyes. It is as though his gaze is shooting right through into my heart. And, like the hormonal fool that I am, I fall for this look every single time without fail. Perhaps, I think excitedly, this is the moment that he recognises me as more than just the random figure that provides food. I start cooing at him

"Awww, I love you too my little prince…look how beautiful you are…look at…"

And then it happens. Well, more to the point, shit happens.

There is something deeply unnerving about someone looking you straight in the eye while they shit in your lap. Naturally, Little Old Man has a nappy on but the 3mm protective shield of plastic doesn't really feel like it counts when he lets rip.

The natural reaction is to jump up and change the offending nappy. Yet I have learnt the hard way that there is no point changing the nappy mid-feed. He may not be finished with his business, as breastfeeding and nappy changes seem to relax his bowels. So there I sit with a warm, slightly humid, feeling enveloping my lap.

The Hubby has his own strategy to deal with this phenomenon by placing a precautionary towel between the offending zone and his lap. I find this does little but offer psychological comfort. Someone is still shitting on your lap. That said, The Hubby's desire for comfort is understandable given he has had to change his own pants twice after falling victim to a Number 3 evacuation*.

Once Little Old Man's misdeed is done, it is as though he wishes to prolong the torture by insisting on being burped as per usual feeding routine. I try rolling him on his tummy but no, he wants a specific burping position. I place him on my shoulder with the nappy only centimetres from my nose. The smell is ripe to say the least.

In that moment, I have thought of what the smell reminds me of. If you wish to not exclude a certain dish from your diet, then skip the next paragraph.

The closest analogy I have come to is if you took a rotisserie chicken, stuck it in a plastic bag on the back seat of a car, wound up all the windows and left it baking for five days in the summer sun. That is what baby poo smells like. And don't pull that face – I did warn you.

* A Number 3 is a Number 2 that has escaped the parameters of the nappy boundaries and freely seeps over clothing, skin etc. of person holding the baby. Sorry, I should have warned you of this definition too.

Snomit

The arrival of a baby has exponentially increased my knowledge of bodily functions. During the hospital stay and directly after, the learning curve centred on my own bodily functions and weird postpartum side effects like boab tree legs and lock jaw. With those now mostly gone, the focus is on learning the bodily functions of babies.

Since day one, Little Old Man has been giving us a crash course in all things poo. He was born with a PhD in Pooology. As such, I endearingly call him by his alternate nickname – 'Mummy's Little Shit Machine' – as I wipe off the third Number Two for the morning. They are impressive displays of bowel movements and much of the conversation I share with The Hubby sadly revolves around the latest find in a nappy.

Not to be outdone, the other end of Little Old Man is equally capable of surprise and discovery. He can produce burps loud enough to be heard from another room. He can also make a noise that sounds like it should be accompanied by vomit but isn't. And he can do sneaky vomits, where a puddle of white liquid silently falls out the side of his mouth. The first warning - a warm sensation on my pants or shoes - always come too late.

The latest bodily function to emerge is the Snomit. Little Old Man could be mid-meal and suddenly turn his head and sneeze vomit in my direction. He never sneezes in the opposite direction, no, no. He prefers to spray milky bile all over my clothing so I end up looking like I've been attacked by one of those cans of fake snow. He doesn't limit his efforts to me. The Hubby's black T-shirts are also a particularly beloved target. They seem to be the baby equivalent of a red rag to a bull.

There is nothing we can do to fix his lack of control. He is, after all, only a baby. All we can do is laugh and take it with good grace until he is old enough to be taught otherwise. Here's hoping that the general public are just as understanding when we are out and he unleashes the latest snomit or, worse still, poo-nami.

Whatever Works

There is a new way to end sentences in our house: 'whatever works'. The full sentence should be 'whatever works to stop him from crying'.

And we have tried almost everything in this endeavour.

When Little Old Man cries after a feed, the main way to calm him down is to go for a walk. But riding the pram along a footpath does very little. No, in order to soothe him, the pram must ride over every available rough surface. To the casual observer, I must look like a psycho mother. Instead of using the perfectly maintained footpaths of my neighbourhood, I walk him along whichever green, gravel or dirt track I can find.

The Hubby and I are now on the constant lookout for uneven surfaces. We talk triumphantly of our latest discoveries of a metal grating, construction site or cracked concrete drive. I have even considered buying a piece of rock-climbing wall and laying it across the dining room for added convenience.

When we catch ourselves in the absurdity of our new hobby, one of us will utter the oft-repeated words that make our madness somehow sane: 'whatever works'.

In this vein, we have also driven around at all hours with a screaming baby in the back. We keenly search out speed bumps to run over and dodgy roads in urgent need of repair. The bumpier the better in terms of settling. Don't question the logic, it's like magic.

My husband swears by turning Little Old Man 360 degrees clockwise (but not anti-clockwise) when he is unsettled during feeding. I run over my feet with the pram. He parks the pram next to the fish tank. I play music that I listened to often while pregnant. He believes 5ml of formula make all the difference between scream and sleep. I whisper the weather forecast in his ear.

And all this is done under the same banner, the same slogan of hope that all sleep deprived parents undoubtedly find themselves saying at some point: 'whatever works!'.

Whatever works indeed.

Out of Time

I drove past some office workers today that were milling outside a coffee shop and fought the urge to scream at them. They probably went to bed at a respectable hour, slept for a decent amount in one block and then went to work in the morning at the same time as they always do. They even have the audacity to feel so 'tired' by these luxuries that they spontaneously make more time to buy coffee. Those bastards. They have a pattern to their lives while I, on the other hand, am beholden to the anarchic world of newborn sleep.

The moment of madness did make me think about how not enough sleep messes with both my head and life in general. Sleep deprivation is officially considered a form of torture and some governments use it against prisoners of war. So instead of waterboarding, the US Government could have issued each inmate at Guantanamo Bay with a newborn baby to care for. It probably would have been enough to turn the most hardened terrorist into an informer.

For as much love and joy as they bring into our lives, any half-honest parent will admit that having a newborn is indeed a slow form of self-inflicted torture. They offer no escape or mercy in the face of parental begging for just one hour of sleep.

The only way to outsmart them is to try to reconstruct your sleeping pattern around theirs. Yet if you follow the advice of resting when your baby rests, the result is a sense of jetlag that just doesn't quite correct itself. You steal an hour or two here and maybe get a four-hour block if you share the feed/settle shifts with your partner. And while your sleep may add up to eight hours over a 24 hour period, you don't feel nearly as refreshed as if you had slept those eight hours all in one go. It is enough to survive, sometimes barely, but not enough to prevent looking and feeling like a parent zombie.

The other alternative is sticking roughly to our sleep pattern and bridging the gaps with coffee. As I have discovered though, the result is a quick slide into mayhem. The more tired you are, the less able you are to deal with someone screaming in your face for two hours at a time. You will come to realise the hard way that coffee is not your friend – it is an energy chimera.

The psychological aspect of sleep deprivation is what I experienced when driving past the office workers. It is the sense that you are out of time and out of sync with society. You sleep randomly, wake even more randomly and do things at odd hours. Even when you do manage to do things at regular hours, like go grocery shopping at 3 PM, all the randomness of your day beforehand makes you feel like an imposter in a world you don't belong to anymore.

After a few weeks like this, you realise that time is a relative construct and humans have instituted communal routines. Most people go to bed before midnight, get up around sunrise and go to work or otherwise fill the daylight hours constructively. Shops, offices, cafés and other shared spaces are all open during the daylight hours and early evening, which reinforces the unconscious commitment of people to this rhythm.

For those falling outside this norm, like new parents, life can be lonely and isolating. When you are awake, the world is asleep and vice versa. You don't belong to the majority anymore. You are beholden to the sleeping patterns of someone who is oblivious to day and night because their brains are yet to develop a circadian rhythm.

For the record, I did end up resisting the urge to yell out the window at random strangers. Luckily I had racked up enough sleep the night before to enable me to drive on with my last shred of human dignity intact.

Work Horses

My breasts, or Girls as I prefer to call them, led a pretty charmed life up until Little Old Man arrived on the scene. Before him, all they had to do was look pretty and demure in the occasional cleavage enhancing top. They never worked a day in their lives.

Now, they work round the clock. When Little Old Man isn't at them, they are busy producing milk or being hooked up to an expressing machine to encourage more production. The expectation I have placed on them to perform is enormous. They must catch up to Little Old Man's hunger levels and enable me to minus out the formula from his diet. There is no space for another alternative in my mind.

To aid this, I went to the doctor and was prescribed a galactagogue. At first the term reminded me of an undergrad university subject I did on ancient Greek mythology to fill up my timetable. I imagined a goddess bearing a full chest of udders, standing triumphantly on a rock and gazing out into the distance while her hair tousled out behind her. But no, a galactagogue is merely a drug or herbal remedy that is given to women hoping to increase their milk production.

I have been taking my galactagogue tablets all week. Every morning I wake up and look at my Girls, hopeful that today will be the day that milk happens. And every evening I go to bed deflated in more ways than one and praying that tomorrow will be the day. But the day never seems to come. The goddess of milk seemingly doesn't wish to pay me a visit.

The prescription was only short and I have just taken my last tablet. I'm unsure whether I could have taken it for much longer, as they have intensified the rise in hope and fall into a sense of personal failure. I can't even get to where I want to be with some performance enhancing drugs.

I attach Little Old Man and we have our little moment of bonding before the bottle gives his belly the sense of fullness he desires. It was a big step to be ok feeding him the bottle and I still wish I could take that step back. I accept though that I can only do so if my body complies. It is a temporary ceasefire of sorts in my war with the tin on the kitchen bench.

Welcome to the Insane Asylum

The Hubby and I arrive at the first community Mother's Group on time and with a sleeping baby. We can't quite believe our luck on both fronts. I scan the room for Alison and her bad roots but she is not there. I have given up on hearing from her but still look around if I see some mums.

The group is officially called a Parent's Group to be inclusive but there are fifteen mothers and only two dads. The babies range from two weeks to four months. Looking round the room, it is reassuring to see the dark circles and haggard look tends to fade as the baby's age increases. I watch on as the older babies gurgle and laugh on the floor mats. It is nice to see there is hope that Little Old Man may soon give something back to us other than screams and sleepless nights.

At first people sit there politely waiting for instruction from the facilitating midwife on what the point of the group is. She asks if there are any questions and someone raises their hand. From there, the questions fly around the room while other parents call out the answers. The session devolves quickly into anarchy, with no agenda and all sorts of bodily functions on display. The midwife seems strangely pleased with proceedings.

The Hubby and I turn to each other, relieved that we are clearly not the only ones struggling with wind, multi-coloured poo and mysterious leaks out the side of the nappy. The parents with older babies reassure the parents of younger ones and everyone shares random tips. I gain an audience when showing the glass nail file I use on Little Old Man because it doesn't grate the skin around his fingernails.

Reminiscent of the hospital physio session, I get out of my chair after the formal proceedings are done and introduce myself in ways that I wouldn't dream of in normal social settings. But this is not normal. Or perhaps, more to the point, this is the new normal where it is ok to start a conversation based on shared challenges that you never imagined existed pre-baby.

I look at The Hubby, who seems equally puzzled by the loss of my old self-conscious self. But I realise the need to step forward into the baby fray to build a broader network of allies.

Everyone in the room is struggling in similar ways with their tiny bundles of love and chaos. It is sink or swim and we're all reaching out for the same lifeboat. So why not admit what you're doing and reach out together?

Destination: Nowhere

Little Old Man made random noises all night. He gave a slight reprieve in the morning but then ramped up to full-pitch crying after lunch. The situation is made trickier by the fact that I am flying solo for the first time since the birth since The Hubby has returned to work. It is almost as though Little Old Man senses this new scenario and is testing out my mummy mettle.

The stress caused by the screaming builds in the house like a localised pressure system. I try to settle him in every way I know how but nothing works, not even begging. The urgent scream continues unabated.

At least I know the source of his discontent and can sympathise accordingly. The day before he had his six-week immunisation shots, which has caused a slight fever. I give him pain relief as directed and wet his brow with a cool cloth but his protests are unrelenting.

I feel panicked and want to get out of the house. But I can't just walk out on him, it doesn't work that way. So I strap him into his car capsule and load us both into the car. This evokes even more screaming but who cares at this point?

"Come on, we're going to pick up your father."

We technically don't have to leave for over an hour but I don't care. It is time for a drive in the hope that this action will do its usual magic. I turn up the car radio to drown out his crying, choosing music that I listened to when pregnant in the hope this might soothe him as a vague memory.

We travel to the opposite end of the city, along expressways and lightly congested roads to avoid having to stop the rolling motion. All the while I sing along loudly to the music, hoping the sound of my voice would further aid soothing.

When we opted for disposable nappies, I said I would offset this ecological vandalism by planting a tree. Now here I was driving my diesel car around for no other reason than trying to gain a moment of sanity. At this rate, I will have to plant an entire forest to make up for the ecological footprint caused by our son's arrival on earth.

I sing and drive until my voice starts to fade. And then, amid the noise I have created, I hear in the back what I have been craving for hours. It is the one and only answer to every desperate mother's pleas with a screaming baby: silence.

I look at the clock on the dash and take the next left to head back towards The Hubby's work. I will be there to pick him up on time as though the day had progressed like normal, even if it had been anything but.

Not on his Wall

We went back to the obstetrician for my routine postnatal check-up. I really didn't want to go and asked The Hubby if we could skip it altogether. I'm not a fan of confrontation, especially with doctors who up until the birth I had perceived as always knowing better.

No, we had to give some honest feedback, The Hubby argued. Not just for our sake but also for the sake of future patients that this doctor would look after. I knew he was right – it was an argument I was too polite and shattered to have at the time but needed to. This still didn't make the prospect any easier to criticise someone who saved my life, even if it is their job to do so.

The obstetrician ran through the usual questions and had a look downstairs, noting that everything was healing up just fine. I had to agree with him. The infection was long gone and the physical pain had subsided to the point that I almost felt back to normal. Indeed, the only thing slowing me down was the anaemia.

"Is there anything else you wish to discuss?"

"Well actually…"

My husband launched in first, choosing the shit-sandwich method of feedback; compliment, a dollop of constructive criticism in the middle, then compliment again. The doctor nodded as The Hubby spoke and then looked at me.

"Um, I tend to agree. Prenatally you were there even though I know you had a lot on that weekend. But you disappeared when it came to the postnatal care and this made me unnecessarily upset. I felt left in the dark. I mean, even the receptionist on your front desk knew what kind of stitches I had when she quizzed me over an appointment request a few weeks ago."

Blank stare.

"So I just, um, I just thought perhaps you would appreciate some feedback from the perspective of a first-timer…"

"I see. Well, we don't have to connect up for the next pregnancy."

"Err, I guess not."

"I wish you both well."

And with that, he stood and shook my husband's hand. I felt the same sense of being an errant child that I did at the hospital and like I was being scolded for the audacity to query my treatment. My cheeks flushed red in anger but I kept my cool.

We walked out of his office and past a wall filled with photos of smiling babies he had delivered over the years. They served as beaming advertisements for the good doctor's work. I wondered where the pictures of the equally beaming mothers were. Or the midwives who had done the hard yards.

"Our son is not going up there."

The Hubby nodded.

And, with that, my treatment and absolute trust in doctors ended.

Help!

Shortly after my run-in with the obstetrician, I did get the help that I knew I needed. When I returned from the hospital, a community nurse came to see how we were settling in. After she asked how the birth went, she fished around in her purse and handed me a brochure entitled something like 'So you had a difficult birth?'

The brochure was for a postnatal counselling service. I chucked it at the bottom of a pile of other brochures I got at the time. I thought counselling was too naff and not for me. But then I kept thinking about the brochure and came back to call the hotline. It was one of the more prudent decisions I have made since becoming a parent. I could have trooped on valiantly for a while longer but decided it was wiser to preserve the emotional energy required to do so for better use.

In the end, it didn't take much to help me get beyond what had happened. What I needed the most was to talk about it and learn a few relaxation techniques to stop my leg jumping about when I reflected on the hospital exprience. It also really helped to have someone objective listen to my story and tell me that what I went through was not normal but my reactions were. Anyone, no matter how emotionally strong they are, would have freaked out to some degree in circumstances similar to mine.

Combined with talking about it, what has really helped has been the passing of time away from the birth and first few weeks. Time, as the saying goes, is the greatest healer. I don't think I'll ever get to the point where I will forget what happened but I hope, in time, to be ok with it.

Multi-Talented

With a baby screaming out his demands at will, it is hard to get much else done. Often the only option left is to hold him over one shoulder while using the other free hand in any way possible. In some sad way, this challenge has become part-game, part-second nature for me. I have become the queen of one-handed multi-tasking and am learning to be more dexterous with my feet than I ever imagined possible.

My crowning moment came at a time of the morning that I don't wish to think about. It was still dark but I had been awake long enough for my confused stomach to churn into action. It was then that I remembered the loaf of bread in the fridge. Mmmh, carbs sweet carbs. Nothing else has had the ability to turn me into a carb-eating machine quite like pregnancy followed by breastfeeding.

Little Old Man was fed and settled so I tried to put him in his pram to sleep. As I let go, his body curled into a ball and his face soon followed. He was ramping up from peaceful to screaming in seconds. I picked him up quickly in the hope that he wouldn't notice the slight interruption and fall back asleep. Success, it worked.

But that still didn't solve my stomach's rumbling. I gently placed him over my shoulder and used my one free hand to open the fridge, take the bread out, pull the tag thing off, get two slices out, pop them in the toaster, unscrew the lid on a jar of peanut butter, get out a bread knife and plate, take toast out and (the trickiest part of all) smear peanut butter on the toast. Breakfast is served, Mummy style!

I started to munch triumphantly on the toast but then knocked the knife off the bench. Not to worry, I thought to myself, and used my toes to pick it up by the handle. I lifted it to knee-height and bent the rest of the way to pick it up. Some people, possibly The Hubby, might find this sad but I was proud.

With a bit of flexibility I managed to keep a baby asleep and meet my own needs. What's not to love about that?

Foie Gras Baby

One of the selling points of exclusive breastfeeding is that the breast apparently only produces as much as the baby needs. I say apparently because I have met a number of concerned breastfeeding mothers with babies that never seem satisfied.

With Little Old Man, the challenge with the bottle part of his feed is different. Given there is an endless supply of formula, the trick is being able to pick up on the cues of when he wants to stop or take a break. It's a challenge because I don't think even he really knows the answer. He is still learning when he feels full and judging the lag between eating and feeling satiated. And let's face it, on that front a lot of adults – myself included – sometimes have issues with learning the difference too. The eyes can be bigger than the belly, as the saying goes.

I watch his facial expressions and listen out for unhappy grunts. When I'm unsure, I take the bottle away and see what happens. If he starts to cry and won't let up, even with some gentle patting, then I pop the bottle back in his mouth. When I do this and continue on past the point that I think he should be full, then it results in one of two things. Either he happily falls off to sleep or throws up the entire contents of his stomach all over my lap.

Mother Nature is pretty clever. I have a greater amount of respect for her ingenuity after going through pregnancy although she kind of screwed me around on the birthing front. Despite being quite vomit laden, I imagine this phase of learning to feed will result in both of us knowing where his boundaries are.

My only hope in the meantime is that I am not over-feeding him into some plumped up goose. For this, along with many other reasons, I wish I had the certainty and supposed simplicity of exclusive breastfeeding.

Rejection

It is hard to be rejected in life, even harder when the one doing the rejection is your child. But that is exactly what has happened. Little Old Man has had enough of breastfeeding and is on strike. I can hardly blame him, I almost feel like doing the same. It is, after all, maximum effort for minimal gain. In contrast, he enjoys the easy flow of formula from a bottle when we have both given up on another boob session.

While I can understand his rejection of the breast, it is hard to accept on an emotional level. There is some part of me that continues to be compelled to believe I must be able to provide for him. This body gave him life and for whatever reason, it continues to want to give him that life through the milk it produces. It is instinctive, a deeply engrained physical reflex that is proving so very hard to fight.

Yet fight it I must. I can't do anything else when he won't attach. It is now to the point that even the mere suggestion of a breastfeed sends him into flailing fits of protest. I can't even get the bra unstrapped before he starts. His little baby brain has made the connection between breast and frustration. The Girls are no longer a source of comfort or food.

While it is hard to accept, I need to respect that his revulsion to the concept is as uncontrollable as my compulsion. He is programmed to seek out food and warmth with minimal effort. When these two things are lacking in supply, his body is quick to spring into screaming action. His body wants swift resolution to these deficits so it can continue using its calories to build up the brain and body.

Using all his energy to suck at a low supply was never a long-term strategy.

The problem is that my instincts are gridlocked with his instincts. I have to cede to his, I just have to. There is literally no choice when he has made his so clear. The problem is, I don't know how.

Express Delivery

It had to happen. Although, as it turns out, not quite in the way I had feared. For the next 24 hours I am not breastfeeding Little Old Man. That is not to say though that I'm giving up altogether. Instead, I have come up with an ingenious third way. I am giving us both a break by expressing.

Yes, the midwives all said baby on breast is the best and most efficient way to stimulate milk production blah blah blah. But I am also realistic about the prospects of stimulating any further than the level I am currently at. Perhaps this was a salient point directly after the birth but I have been struggling for eight weeks now with little improvement. The only thing this method seems to be increasing is frustration levels on both sides.

While it is hard to admit defeat on never getting full production, it is the only viable option I have. Giving up altogether is not going to happen. And I don't think it should. Expressed milk is milk all the same, just delivered in another manner.

I am prepared for the next day or so to be hard but nobody said being a mother was easy.

Sweet Relief

It has now been 48 hours since I stopped trying to put baby to breast at every feed. I have put him on once mid-feed, when he wasn't desperately hungry and I wasn't desperately in need of the pump. He attached beautifully, like he used to at the beginning before we wound ourselves into a stress ball. Although he couldn't talk, I sensed Little Old Man felt the same sense of relief. His back no longer arched his body away from me and there were no screams or endless relatching.

It is as though a great weight has been lifted. If breast time works, then it works. If not, well he can finish off the bottle and then I pump. I am trying to adjust my view.

The Hubby has been a surprising source of lactation advice. He used the analogy of me coming home starving and he saying dinner would be ready in three hours. If this happened, I would be pretty agitated and start rummaging through the pantry. It is the same with Little Old Man. When he is hungry, he doesn't want to wait or have to sip drops through a half-functioning straw. No, when he wants food then he wants it now! Or five minutes ago, to be exact.

I am extending this analogy as a way of coming to terms with the situation. In this way, I see expressed milk as an entrée, formula as the meat and veg, and any breast time as a bonus dessert. The Girls still have value but not as the mains.

Do the Math

Since it went so well, I continued to exclusively express after the initial trial run until it officially became the new norm. It was a liberating step to make, one based on my gut feeling rather than the conflicting advice from a steady stream of midwives, lactation consultants and lactivists.

Expressing has also had benefits other than stress-relief. It has also allowed me more flexibility in the feeding routine. Now I can express when my breasts need it rather than sit there in pain while the baby half attaches and screams about the lack of flow.

The ability to consistently measure my milk supply through expressing has also helped me accept reality. On a good day I manage to produce between 200-250ml a day of milk. Yesterday Little Old Man chomped his way through one litre of formula. While this was unusually high, 250ml still doesn't come close to his average intake.

The maths still don't add up even if you double my supply amount on the grounds that babies are far more efficient at drawing milk from a breast than a pump.

The situation is still upsetting but at least I can start to accept it now there is an objective number attached. The lactation consultant's prediction at the hospital has proven right. It's true. I never got my full milk supply. Period. I can't change this reality but I can change the way I deal with it to a more positive viewpoint.

The ability to measure has led me to question whether expressing is useful at all. Naturally, the experts would say any amount is better than nothing but is the amount I produce enough to deliver the much-touted benefits of breast milk?

I donned the other hat from my pre-Mummy life as a researcher and went in search of an answer beyond the vague response of "every drop counts". Although I couldn't find a definitive scientific study to really nail the number, I did find dozens of websites and forums touting 3 ounces (or 118 ml) as the magic number.

It was an answer that both relieved and confirmed my actions. 118 ml is an achievable goal with the amount of pumping I do.

Maths, as I have learnt, can work for and against me in the battle with the bottle.

Heaven and Hell

I never know how the day is going to be until about mid-morning. Some days Little Old Man is an absolute dream to parent. He sleeps lots, eats with minimal fuss and even gives a gummy smile during play time. On such days I feel ten-foot tall and like I have finally got the hang of this motherhood thing. I smile contentedly to myself and smoothly pre-empt his every need. We work together as a team, connected by that invisible bond that will always stretch out between us.

Other days, however, he is a wee bit more on the high-maintenance side of things. It will start early, usually around 5 AM, where he wakes screaming at full bolt. He may display glimpse of hope that he will resettle after a quick feed yet, a few hours later, it is clear the miracle of sleep is not going to happen. Indeed, he probably won't sleep again until nightfall – preferring to drive me completely spare by staying awake until he is overtired and screaming non-stop.

As much as my mother and mother-in-law would like to advise otherwise, there is no suggestion I haven't tried to stop this cycle. I sing, dance, rock, hum, settle, feed, burp, feed again, burp again, hold him, distract with squeaky toys, rub his belly, massage his feet and the list goes on.

The last resort in my toolbox is to leave him to cry, which I find so hard to do. I refer to my go-to advice book, which I call *The Baby Bible*, for some guidance on how and whether to do this. The good book states that sometimes babies can have all their needs met and just want to cry out their frustrations. And, it adds, there is nothing you as the parent can do other than provide a safe environment and reassuring voice every so often so they don't completely lose the plot.

The advice makes sense on a logical level. I have seen how Little Old Man can seemingly have every potential need met yet still scream on regardless. Yet I find it so hard to respond to this situation by placing Little Old Man in his bassinet and then walking out, closing the door behind me.

When I manage to do so, I go to the furthest end of the house and make noise to drown out his strangled cat cries. I watch television or have a shower while praying he will learn quickly the invaluable lesson of self-soothing through these experiences, just as the *Baby Bible* promises.

All the while my heart remains in that room. I berate myself for not being able to settle him through loving gestures. I feel guilty for the anger that has settled in my chest after having him scream at my face for hours on end. And then I tell myself to toughen up and fear a future where Little Old Man turns into a spoilt brat toddler because Mummy was too soft and never allowed him the space to learn to self-settle.

When I've been through this cycle and my anger turns into sympathy, then I know I am ready to go back into the room and pick him up. It is usually less than 15 minutes but by this stage his face has almost turned purple from all the crying. I look at his tears and my confidence from the heaven days crumbles. I conclude that I am the worst mother to have ever walked the planet for letting this happen, then hold him close and whisper apologies into his ear.

After he has performed this form of torture on me, he usually settles for about 30 minutes. After that, he might wake and the whole cycle begins again from feed on. Or he may sleep on but this is a rare reprieve. Once a hell day has begun, it rarely ends mid-way.

The oscillation between heaven and hell days reminds me of how much my mood and outlook is dependent upon him. If he has a good or bad day, then so do I. The days are no longer planned around how I am feeling or what I would like to get done. I know it will shift in time as he phases out of newborn but at the moment the connection is intense. He is the sun and we are the universe that revolves around him.

The Cult of Breastfeeding

I broke the code in Mother's Group and I don't think the facilitating midwife was very happy about it. She probably had a concealed code red button somewhere that she pressed to alert Midwife Central of this breach. I'm joking clearly yet to some extent breastfeeding really does feel like one major conspiracy theory run with almost cult-like fervour.

It began when a mother in the group questioned whether it was worth continuing to breastfeed with low supply. Yes, yes of course and straight from the breast is preferable to promote stimulation came the reply. Every drop counts.

Something flinched inside me and I found myself mid-sentence before I realised.

"Actually, milk is milk. At this stage postnatal it doesn't matter if the baby gets it direct from your breast or via expressing into a bottle. It's not like you're going to stimulate much more supply than what you currently produce unless you take a galactagogue. Also, from the research I've done, it seems that the benefits of breast milk kick in at around 118 ml per day. If you can manage at least this, then the effort is worth it for your baby. If not, then don't sweat it for a few drops."

Silence.

All the midwife's previous reaffirming of other comments was notably absent with me. The mothers looked at me, some nodding and others just staring blankly in sleep-deprived comas.

"It's such a relief to hear that, thank you."

"Yeah it's so good to know the effort is worth it. I produce triple that and breastfeed as well!"

And therein lies the paradox of breastfeeding advice as I have experienced it. The focus is on the absolute ideal of baby on breast rather than what is possible or – God forbid – best for both baby *and* mother. It is very baby-centric, which is a valid point, but some balance is required also. This may even encourage women in some cases, such as low supply, to continue on where they may have given up altogether.

I first realised the need for balance when reading a popular breastfeeding book that advised to feed with a cracked nipple, even an infected one with pus oozing from it because that won't harm the baby to digest. Well goody for the baby but what about the harm caused to the mother? I haven't had the pleasure but I imagine there might be a bit of pain involved in having a seeping wound sucked on by a ferociously hungry newborn.

Back in the room, the conversation moved on and a few interested women circled me, craving to speak more about something that hadn't been raised before. We had all fallen for different reasons into using express pumps and were going along fine except for the nagging doubt over whether there was any benefit. Nobody had received any advice other than the glib line that every drop counts. I found the situation wrong. Where were the midwives to back us up or at least inform us fully in our choices?

While this may have been important for others there, for me it was largely an academic point. The morning reconfirmed my decision to make up a breastfeeding schedule with zero interference. I've been burnt too many times by conflicting and biased information – first at the hospital and then later by community nurses and hotlines.

I can't bring myself to trust midwives anymore so I avoid them altogether. I don't even trust them to weigh my son, as crazy as that may sound. My guides have become the internet for all things breastfeeding and the family doctor for all of Little Old Man's check-ups and immunisations. And this is sad.

There is so much pressure placed upon women unnecessarily not so much by the advice given but by the way it is continually couched in the benefits. The advice seems to carry the underlying message that "yes this can be difficult as all hell but think about your baby first! Don't slack off and deprive them!"

I would guess nearly all mothers want provide their newborns with the much-touted benefits of breast milk. I have yet to meet a mother who hasn't tried everything before letting go of breastfeeding as an option, especially first-timers in those early days. This group are particularly vulnerable since it is all new and they have to work out in a sleep-deprived haze what is best for their baby while being bombarded with advice.

It is less than ideal for health care professionals to step into this vulnerable space, run an agenda and then move on if milk doesn't happen. If a baby can't exclusively breastfeed then there are other ways that may involve some milk or simply just leave open bonding and comforting opportunities.

A more realistic approach could help struggling mothers like me avoid completely melting down. Focussing on the problem-free exemplar or quoting the *World Health Organisation* guideline of six months exclusive breastfeeding helps nobody.

All it does is set a high bar not many women are able to attain for a multitude of reasons. To be exact, only 14% of Australian women are still exclusively breastfeeding by six months[1]

Good on those who defy the statistics and reach the ideal but that doesn't mean the other 86% of us can't be cut some slack.

Mamma Jugs Fudges the Truth

The old adage in marketing is that if something sounds too good to be true then it probably is. In hindsight, all the antenatal classes that covered breastfeeding were just that. Maybe it is an attempt by midwives to bump up the exclusive breastfeeding rates a few percentage points. Or maybe they just really believe their own spin.

The following are benefits touted by the advocates and the reality as I have found it:

A) *Breastfeeding is free* – this is true for those who don't have any issues getting the right amount of milk when it is needed. For the rest of us, breastfeeding can be quite expensive. There are costs in renting or buying a pump (which can run into the hundreds of dollars), buying the bottles for the hire pump (ours were two for $60),

---

[1] Australian Government Department of Health and Ageing, Australian National Breastfeeding Strategy 2010-2015, published 2009, page 7.

seeing a doctor for complications, buying prescribed medications to increase milk production or treat mastitis, buying herbal remedies and so on. If you need help with technique, the hourly rate for lactation consultant is upwards of $100.

B) *It is convenient because the breast is available and doesn't need sterilising* – again technically true but the breast is also not an object floating in space. It is attached to you. If a baby feeds three times a night for one hour at a time, then guess who needs to be awake for every one of those feeds. You! There is no tag-teaming feeds with your partner to get some extended rest.

C) *It provides contraceptive benefits* – yes but only if a woman is breastfeeding exclusively day and night within the first six months. I'm guessing this would provide even more protection since the woman would be too tired from being the exclusive provider of food and her boobs too sore to even think of engaging in extracurricular activity.

D) *It quickly soothes a fussy, unhappy baby* – yes if said baby is a willing participant. Some babies refuse the breast, others don't know how to latch on, and others still have colic or other ailments that prevent them from gaining the benefits. I've also heard that hugs and humming are great at soothing an unhappy baby.

E) *Breastfed babies have smell-free poo* – if this isn't the ultimate in Shit Don't Stink then I don't know what is. I'm sure the nappies of breastfed babies smell like roses but that still doesn't make the business of wiping brown goo from someone else's butt any more palatable. Even if said butt belongs to your little darling.

These digs are not designed to say that breastfeeding is too much of a hassle to bother but rather to point out that a healthy dose of reality should be injected into the selling of breastfeeding. The benefits are based on the ideal of a mother producing the perfect amount of milk for her keen and latchable baby. It is complete and utter la-la land.

Perhaps it is just the mummy-circles I mingle in but I have met dozens of new mums and between us only a few have spoken to a woman who has had a dream ride with breastfeeding. The rest have struggled in some way to either make their milk happen, stop their milk from happening so much or to attach the baby. And then there are the ones with physical side effects like cracked nipples, mastitis, and engorgement.

These are all a normal part of the breastfeeding spectrum so why not tell women these things? It's not like those prenatal classes held back on the realities of labour and birth.

Yes, breastfeeding is an incredibly natural thing but it is by no means a snap. It is hard, monotonous and at times physically and emotionally demanding work. To pretend otherwise to the uninitiated is nothing short of misleading and sets women up for feeling like failures when they're anything but.

Crossroads

Little Old Man is three months old. He still looks little but not as old as he did at the start. His eyes sparkle as the light of recognition slowly flickers on. He knows there is a world around him and he is furiously trying to understand how it all works. It is a marvel to watch him grow.

The milestone also means I have been trying to breastfeed on some level for three months. I have reached the crossroads where many women have already turned back. I know I shouldn't compare myself with others yet it feels like a small victory to have persevered so far despite all the obstacles. So now I have reached it, how much further down the breastfeeding track do I go?

I keep wavering on my next move. As with all things motherhood, it seems to be a heart versus head decision. The longer I can provide up until that six month mark, the more the long-term health benefit to him. I imagine giving up and then cursing myself for not trying harder every time he gets an ear infection or cold. What kind of horrible mother would I be if I didn't do everything in my power to give Little Old Man the best start possible?

The mummy guilt trips I enforce on myself are grossly unfair on paper but emotionally hard to get around, even when I know the statistics on breastfeeding rates.

On the more practical end, I also need to factor in that pumping takes up three hours a day. This is a lot when you don't have that much spare awake time to start with.

To make the process harder, I gave back the electric pump after the first month because I get more milk with manual pumping. Yet manual mostly requires two hands, which means for those three precious hours I sit and stare at all the things around the house that I could be doing if I had a spare hand and the time. I make mental lists of housework, ordering by priority, and then rarely get round to doing any of it. By the time I'm finished stealing the time needed to pump, Little Old Man has grown bored of his play mat or is hungry and requires some attention.

The only thing I have been able to do while pumping is write this. I have taught myself how to use voice recognition software that The Hubby downloaded after the birth when I couldn't sit on the computer chair. Like pumping, typing is a slow and at times frustrating effort but it sure beats watching daytime television. And being able to write has kept me sane since the birth. It reminds me that I have a brain and, rather ironically, I have written more with less time than I used to because the luxury of procrastination is gone. Either I type now or forever forget the thought, it's that simple.

So what to do about pumping. I first raised the prospect of giving up a few weeks after the birth. The Hubby said he would support my decision any which way but seemed relieved that I raised the topic of giving up. He has seen what an enormous pressure I have placed on myself to make milk happen and has gently asked before whether the effort is worth it.

But, like me, he seems to waver too. He later asked whether it would be possible to continue pumping just twice a day before quickly adding that it is my decision.

When I think I am ready to give up, I feel a sense of relief that all this pumping will soon be over. I grow impatient to reach the latest deadline that I have set myself. I daydream while pumping about all the things I could be doing with an extra three hours and two hands.

Then the deadline gets closer and I realise I have to start weaning but can't. Something stops me from putting my plan into action and I delay once again with a new deadline.

The result is a sense that I am endlessly waiting for an end that never arrives. And it never will as long as I keep pushing it away.

Spilt Milk

When I can't quite reach a decision in motherhood, either Little Old Man or my body provides the answer. This time it is my body.

It started with a sniffle, then a sore throat, and then full blown flu-like symptoms. In the weeks since, I have coughed and hacked my way through sinusitis in the hope it would magically disappear but it did not. When all the signs were there that it had turned into infection, I still ignored it. Too busy, too tired, too whatever to go to the doctor. There was always an excuse.

Then it got to the point where my throat was so irritated that I dry-retched and gasped for air when I got into a coughing fit. I couldn't sleep properly and neither could The Hubby. My coughing was constant and spreading deeper into my lungs, despite me wishing it away.

"You are going to the doctor this afternoon."

"But there's only the medical centre open today. Can't I wait till next Wednesday when my normal doctor is on duty?"

"No, because she may be fully booked already. You are going to the doctor today."

The Hubby isn't usually this bossy but he had had enough of my delay tactics. He didn't know why but had suspected correctly that I was avoiding the medical profession.

I have had sinus infections before and know the drill. Antibiotics, steam inhaler and rest. When I had the infected stitches after the surgery, I was prescribed antibiotics that didn't pose an issue through transference in the milk. I didn't know if I would be as lucky this time with the antibiotics needed to treat another body part. Turns out the answer from Doctor Random was no.

"Yep it's a sinus infection alright."

"So…can I get a puffer or spray or something?"

"You'll need antibiotics for five days."

"I'm breastfeeding at the moment."

"Oh…well you can continue with this type of antibiotic but your baby might get diarrhoea. If this happens, you have to stop breastfeeding immediately."

"Can't I just use a puffer?"

"No because the underlying infection will remain."

I consider my options. For a nanosecond I consider whether diarrhoea is really that bad but then realise how insane I have become. I was not risking dehydration in my baby or dealing with explosive nappies. The puffer wasn't an option nor was just leaving it. So there was only one option left; take the damn antibiotics.

And that is how my body gave me the nudge to wean. I am on the antibiotics and have cut down my pumping to only two hours a day. I am waiting to see what happens with supply. If it goes down dramatically, then I will continue to wean down to no pumps. If not, I will see how I go at the lighter load of four pumps a day for a while. Despite it all, I'm still lingering at the crossroads.

After each pump, I tip my efforts straight down the sink and try not to dwell on the action. As I tip though, I can't help thinking of all the times I held onto the express bottle for dear life so as not to spill a drop. Yet I resist the urge to get upset because, true to the saying, there is no use crying over spilt milk.

Good Grief

The few people I have spoken to about my breastfeeding problems have all said the same thing. Little Old Man is healthy and I did my best, that's all I could have done. More pointedly, I've been told that if I went to a nearby school and looked at the children in the playground, I wouldn't be able to tell the difference between those that were breastfed and bottle fed. They are all healthy children. We don't have a nation where only 14% of children are able to go a week without sneezing.

I know all this but logic is not what upsets me. Rather, it is the inability that upsets me. I keep coming back to the fact that this was not my choice. I wanted to breastfeed, I wanted that bond, and I don't have it. I can pump for as long as I like but it won't get me around this inability. Indeed, the longer I pump the more I feel like I'm actually avoiding or delaying grief over my loss.

Since I started taking the antibiotics, I have come to realise how much I clung emotionally to expressed milk. Without it, feeding Little Old Man has become meaningless. Try as I might to feel otherwise, there is no bonding moment. Feeding him formula feels like a chore just like any other. The moment has been hollowed out.

Perhaps this feeling towards feed time will change once I have stopped expressing altogether. I don't know if I'm doing the right thing and can't fully commit either way. My gut instinct is usually loud and on the money but this time it is noticeably silent.

Restart

"I'm sorry but I couldn't stop."

"It's ok, you don't have to."

The Hubby places his hand on my shoulder and I turn away. He must think I have lost my mind. Sometimes I think that about myself too. But I couldn't bring myself to do it. Not yet at least and certainly not in this way. The longer I tried to stretch out between pumps, the more my heart resisted what I was doing.

Milk is a funny thing. It is a delicate thread that continues from birth onward but, once broken, cannot be rewoven. By weaning, I can feel myself stretching apart that thin thread I have worked so hard to maintain and it upsets me to the core. I cry for hours over whether this is the right thing for me to be doing. I listen out for my instinct and finally it calls out yes, despite all my reasoning.

So I will continue on for a little while longer. The tedium of pumping is a small price to pay for not feeling like I did yesterday.

Sunriser

This morning Little Old Man woke me at 5 AM after being up with him at 2 AM. I struggled downstairs to feed him before placing him gently back in the cot and sending up a sleep prayer to the heavens. The baby gods must have been listening because he promptly started snoring.

I went back up to the bedroom and sat on the edge of the bed to pump. I would have preferred snuggling back down under the blankets and getting maximum sleep time but I knew now this was my choice. No whinging.

As I pumped, the sun began to rise above the crest of a nearby mountain. I watched as the morning grey turned golden and birds chirped from tree to tree. It was a beautiful sight, one I would have slept my way through in my pre-baby life. It wasn't the first sunrise I had enjoyed of late but it was up there as one of the most stunning.

I looked back across the bed at a sleeping Hubby and smiled quietly to myself.

Déjà Vu

When The Hubby and I first moved in together, I was a full-time student looking for work. We lived in a village near Hamburg, Germany, and had one car that he used to commute to work. If I wanted to visit civilisation then I had to catch a bus, train, bus, then walk.

I couldn't afford or justify the cost of commuting into the city every day when I had a perfectly good desk at home. So I sat at that desk – for months on end – dividing my time equally between writing uni assignments and job applications. I made a rule to go out at least once a day for a walk regardless of the weather or my mood. I also developed a rather unhealthy habit of visiting the bakery underneath our apartment most mornings to give the day a rhythm and practice my German. Well, those were my excuses for buying Danish tarts and donuts.

About every third day I would go completely stir crazy and invest in a bus ticket to the city. When I got there I couldn't do much because I didn't have the money. I would go to the library and borrow some books, meet up with a friend for lunch at the student cafeteria and then walk around the streets just to be near people. Sometimes I went to the shops to try on clothes, as it was free to do so and I could daydream about what I would look like if I had a job. Yes, I was that tragic.

I always thought I was quite an independent type but the isolation of village life taught me otherwise. I felt like I was apart from life rather than a part of it.

And now here I am nearly ten years later and increasingly feeling the same. The initial panic and rush of the newborn phase has calmed down into routine and I'm starting to see similarities with my old student days. While we now live on the outskirts of a city in Australia, we still only have one car which The Hubby uses to commute to work unless I put in a request. And I still have the same starving student viewpoint that questions why I should go out and spend money when everything I need is at home.

Some things have changed though. I do have enough money in my back pocket now to afford a bus ticket or any clothes I may wish to try on. Yet, apart from being pointless, I don't think I have enough to go out spending money every day as a cure for my isolation.

Being with Little Old Man is fulfilling and I'm grateful that we have the financial luxury of me being able to stay at home in his first year. It's just that being at home can really cut you off from the world. I miss the office gossip, the morning coffee run and intelligent discussion about what's making the news that day.

My new workplace is solitary and the boss is at times a rather unforgiving and thankless soul. He doesn't give much back yet other than shitty nappies and the occasional cooing, which I lap up as a sad form of conversation. Sometimes I like to pretend his cooing is really baby talk for gossip and he's telling me stuff like what a bitch that teddy bear in his nursery is. Ahh, so sad!

I'm not sure what the solution is other than to start by going back to the basics of a walk each day just to get out of the house. I will forgo the bakery run though, as I learnt my lesson the hard way about the dietary pitfalls of that one. To rework a line from the Cookie Monster, pastries are a sometimes food.

Now that Little Old Man is mildly more sociable and can go out for greater periods of time, perhaps I should also try to build more structure into my week beyond the Mother's Group. Maybe take up some random hobby that requires me to go to a class once a week. Or go to a Mums and Bubs movie every week. Or perhaps both! Something, anything, has to be better than being couped up without end.

Milk and Cookies

I've succumbed to the madness of one more experiment to make my milk happen. I swore I wouldn't do it again after the galactagogue tablets but there is something about a good news story that I can't resist. It's like the lure of television infomercials, as I have discovered during late night feeds. I mean all this positive talk about products that are always so simple to use, there must be something in it – right?

One of the women from the Mother's Group swore by lactation cookies, which contain ingredients that apparently increase milk supply. A quick look on Dr Google confirmed they exist, with many women breathlessly discussing positive results in chat forums. I read on while trying to temper my enthusiasm. I had to be realistic and learn to accept that there is no holy grail for me. But perhaps, perhaps, there might be a way to bump up supply just a little.

While Little Old Man naps, I set to work in the kitchen. The Hubby wanders in on the way to bed and asks why I am baking at 11:30 PM. He seems concerned when I get random energy spurts.

"I'm baking lactation cookies."

"Can I have some?"

"A couple but they are especially for me."

"Will they make me grow boobs?"

"No honey, they won't."

"Ok. Good night."

He gladly retires to dream of cookies with the assurance that he won't be filling out a D-cup with moobies anytime soon. I wonder though whether the mix rather than the supposed effect will stop him eating them. They have the shape of a cookie but the active ingredients are relatively nutritional; rolled oats, brewer's yeast and flaxseed meal. There is also, however, some butter, sugar and choc chips thrown in (presumably to make the whole affair less barf-worthy).

To even out the more unhealthy aspects, I take out some of the butter and sugar and replace it with mashed banana. I want to increase milk supply, after all, and not the width of my backside.

The recipe suggests eating some of the raw dough, as it is more effective than the baked result. I munch away on the gooey concoction, which has a distinctly yeasty tang to it. It wasn't the best cookie dough but I reserve judgement until trying the baked result. Even if they don't have the desired effect, they would freeze well for a healthy snack option. Well, healthier than the usual snack options I reach for at 3 AM.

By the time Little Old Man stirs for his last feed, I am munching on my third cookie fresh from the oven. They turn out to be quite tasty and for a fleeting moment I worry if it is possible to overdose. I imagine being rushed to hospital with exploding breasts. I dismiss my worries. The thought is a bit far-fetched, even for me.

I feed Little Old Man his formula and go to bed, joining The Hubby in dreaming of cookies.

Hold On

Becoming a mother has changed my perspective and reaction to a lot of things in life. My sense of empathy has been sharpened in ways that I didn't expect. Tonight was one such occasion. I watched the news, which led with a story from the United States about a group of children who were killed in a school shooting.

Before, I would find stories about children dying very sad yet it was more of an abstract intellectual understanding. I could only imagine and suppose the depth of tragedy because I had never held a child of my own. Now though such news touches upon a maternal nerve and sometimes, like tonight, I find myself openly weeping at the news.

When I was pregnant it felt like I was mentally holding my breath until the safe arrival of our son. I figured afterwards that I could then exhale and go on with life as I did before. Yet when he arrived, I found that I was only able to half breathe out. The rest I still held in.

I don't think I will ever fully exhale again. There is a part of me that will always be watching out for his safety. With his birth, I experienced first-hand the fragility with which life is given and events like that shooting are reminders of how randomly it can be taken away again.

The death of any child is a tragedy beyond words and, as a parent, I am able to glimpse into that heartbreak on a deeper level. I know how the parents would have felt when that child was once celebrated, from pregnancy test on through to the nervous nine months wait and beyond. How every milestone in that child's short life was met with the joy, patience and love of their parents. How that child was the sum equation of countless hours of feeding, settling, rocking and guidance. They were somebody's child, the embodiment of somebody's hopes and love.

But now, through some twist of fate, they have been taken from this earth well before their time. Their parent's grief becomes a sound bite on the evening news. Other parents watch on and all they can do is guiltily thank God that it isn't them standing in front of the cameras.

For my part, I couldn't imagine being in that position. I can't even bring myself to entertain the thought for a moment. Little Old Man is a part of me and always will be. My mind, my heart, cannot perceive life in any other way.

The only consolation I have found in watching such horrible, senseless loss is in turning to my little family. All that is left for me to do is hold on to my loved ones closer. It doesn't make sense of the senseless but it reminds me that there is still good in the world.

The Hump

We went to a party and saw a couple we knew who have a two year old plus another one on the way. The Dad spoke about how things were going with them while Little Old Man tried his hardest to be part of the conversation. He smiled and cooed, reaching his hands out to be met by an appreciative audience.

"You guys are doing really well."

"Really?" The Hubby asked a bit surprised.

"Yeah, look at him. He's such a happy baby."

"Thanks, it's hard to tell sometimes. I mean, we're just making it up as we go along."

"Well, you must be doing something right. And hey, you've made it over the biggest hump in their lives. It can be tricky from here on in but those first three months are the worst."

"Really?"

"Really."

The last add-on was exactly what we wanted to hear. And we heard it no less from a seasoned parent. Sure, there will be many challenges ahead but it is good to know the most intense period of our baby's life has passed. We can face whatever lies ahead with some sleep. Everything is less desperate and easier to handle with more than three hours of sleep to your name.

The conversation confirmed what we were already beginning to quietly suspect –the newborn phase was over. Little Old Man's sleeping patterns had formed and the stretches between night feeds were getting longer. They weren't quite sleep throughs but they were pretty close.

The first couple of times this happened I woke up worried that we hadn't heard anything and checked in on him. I watched his chest rise and fall to ensure he was still breathing. I listened out for his soft grunts and snores. And then felt silly when I realised he was sleeping away contentedly.

The following nights after that, I relished the sleep-ins but figured they were a blip and would be cruelly snatched from us once more by grumpy baby syndrome. But the sleeping stretches didn't show any sign of going away. Indeed, the adage that sleep produces sleep seems to have kicked in.

As a result, he is a much more rested and contented baby when he is awake. And, in turn, we as the parents are also more rested and contented. The two counterpoints feed positively off each other and the house is a much happier place than it once was.

For the first time, there seems to be hope of a life after newborn. We are going out as a family more and enjoying playtime. It feels like the fun is just beginning after all the hard work to get here. It's still hard work but there are benefits now too. We really must be doing something right.

The Distance

Having a baby is what I imagine running a marathon is like. You start out quick, legs pumping hard and fast with adrenalin. The sidelines pass by in a blur. You settle into a comfortable pace and find your stride, feeling confident that the end will be reached. But then your energy begins to peter out and you wonder whether you really have the determination to make the distance.

In a marathon, what comes next is that your legs either cramp up and you falter or you dig deep into reserves you never realised you had and push on over the finish line. In parenting, however, there is no finish line. You just have to somehow keep on keeping on.

In my own parenting race, I dug deep early and grunted my way through until the third month. I burnt up all the reserve I had before I realised the absence of a finish line. And then, last week, I tripped up and my legs began to cramp.

It began with the thought that this is now my life – week after week, year after year. Being a Mum isn't a phase I'll go through and then move on from. It's for keeps. I will always hold a special place in Little Old Man's life, long after he has grown up and started a family of his own. How that place looks is largely up to me to shape through my level of engagement and endurance.

Perhaps it sounds strange to only realise this when my baby is three months old but it was the first moment I stopped running at full stride and had a look around. The responsibility I felt at the endless track before me was crushing. Do I have it in me to keep going like I have been? What if I don't? What if I fuck it all up?

My pace faltered under the doubt created by these questions with no answers. And I haven't fully recovered speed. Perhaps I won't. And perhaps this is not necessarily a bad thing. I'm beginning to see that I need to find a new, more sustainable, pace. Otherwise I won't be able to go the distance.

Sliding

Lately I have been gravitating towards depression and haven't been able to slow the movement. The walls around me at present are pretty slippery and I can feel myself sliding into a place I don't want to go.

All the things that once protected me are not there anymore. I don't have a rhythm to my days or weeks. The centrepiece of my old life is gone. I have a job but it's not the old desk job that I used to go to. This means that I don't get to pick out something nice to wear each morning, catch the bus, read the news relevant to my job, have an intelligent conversation about said news, go to lunch with a colleague, and carry on email conversations with friends while pretending to be furiously busy. Individually all these things sound trivial but they make up a life – my old one.

Beyond not having a conventional job, the adrenalin and steep learning curve of having a newborn has given way to the monotony of feed, play, sleep ad infinitum. If you asked me what I am doing next Tuesday afternoon, I can guarantee it will be making one of those three activities happen. Even in sleep there is little rest for me. Little Old Man doesn't sleep long during the day and what little naps he has are usually had on me or in the cot after an extended crying fit.

Other than feed-play-sleep, there are only two things that give my week a structure at the moment. One of them is the Mother's Group on Wednesdays, which I attend religiously since it gets me out of the house and socialising. The other, sadly enough, is my pillbox that I store my vitamins in. Every morning I open another day and get closer to the end of the week, where I refill and start again. Getting to the last day gives me a strange sense of achievement, like it's a visual cue that I've managed to scrape my way through another week.

These two things are not enough to sustain me. It's not good enough to say I'm bored and need a hobby. There is more to this feeling than that. I need tangible purpose to my days beyond parenting. For, while this is perhaps the most important task I'll ever perform as a human, it only represents part of who I am. I am a mother but I was also many other things beforehand.

If these other parts of myself are not part of how I fill my days, then what I am able to offer as a mother is one-dimensional and limited. This won't change unless I change my approach. I can only ever give more of myself when there is more of me to give.

I understand how I got to where I am. Caring for a newborn is a full-on and full-time job. You literally are lucky to be able to scratch yourself in the early days. Yet Little Old Man has moved on. It would be unfair on both of us to continue to parent with the same level of intensity as at the beginning. He needs guidance and nurturing but he also needs a little space to explore the world on his own terms. As with every other aspect of parenting so far, I need to follow his lead and shift to where he is at developmentally.

So what to do? As strange as it feels, I need to put myself first for a change. It's time to put some grips on those walls so I have something better to hang on to. I will begin by listing the feelings that have been dogging me of late and put in place one activity against each to act as a counterpoint. Since I feel isolated, for example, I will borrow the car twice a week from The Hubby so I can get out of the house. I can pick him up from work and he can catch the bus one way. This is a fair compromise on a shared resource.

I will also try to stop feeling guilty for taking time to pursue my interests, like writing, when there is a spare moment to be had. Housework is always there and can be chipped away at more slowly than the current rate. It is more important to keep me happy than to have a smaller pile of ironing. Well, at least that's my excuse and I'm sticking to it.

These are good starting points and I will build on them further. I am nowhere near back into a place where I feel comfortable but at least I am pointing north.

Christmas

I hate Christmas. Actually, let me rephrase that. I hate the expectations and assumptions placed upon me by Christmas. With a baby, these are all way more intense.

"Ohh baby's first Christmas, you must be excited!"

"Errr, I suppose…"

"Have you had a photo with Santa yet?"

"Umm no…it costs fifty bucks"

"Oh, but you have a Christmas bauble with baby's name on it?"

"Uhhh…"

"Oh…"

I've had this conversation with a former colleague, a checkout chick, a couple of strangers, someone from the Mother's Group, an old friend (who should know me better) and my own mother (who *really* should know me better).

I don't do Christmas. To be frank, I am neither religious in a traditional sense nor particularly prone to fits of sentimentality that would see me buying engraved baubles. And I find the playing out of north European traditions silly in a hot Australian summer. A couple of times I celebrated Christmas in Germany and actually found myself excited about the holiday. The Christmas markets, the mulled wine, the gingerbread, chopping down your own tree – it all made sense. There is, however, no sense singing about dreaming of a white Christmas at 35 degrees plus.

I also don't do Christmas because my family is quite fractured due to a number of intertwining feuds. Joining the family Christmas lunch is like willingly stepping onto a battlefield. Given that I go out of my way to avoid conflict with certain members of my family on the other 364 days of the year, this is not my idea of a good time.

People have a tendency to assume everyone comes from a harmonious family and ask questions accordingly. I usually gloss over what I'm doing for Christmas before quickly turning the conversation back onto them. For The Hubby, life is easier. He does come from a family that can sit down together without the issuing of apprehended violence orders but sadly they live in Germany, which is quite the commute.

So Christmas day is usually spent with both of us sulking and wishing the day to be over. There is no picture-perfect dinner round the family table or gift giving under the tree. In fact, we don't even bother with the façade of a tree anymore. The reality of the day is the emotional equivalent of a yearly punch in the face. It reminds me of all that my family lacks and will never have. Nothing that I really feel like celebrating.

And now a baby has been added to the mix. At first I thought this would make the holidays even more complicated and sad than they are now. I know in a couple of years' time there will have to be a rethink of my approach to Christmas. He will pick up a belief in Santa from somewhere and we will have to run with it.

Perhaps surprisingly, I do actively want to encourage this. I want him to believe in the magic of Christmas. This is the gift belonging to all children, regardless of their parents' beliefs or membership of psycho families.

Maybe for Christmas, like in so many other ways, a new baby can herald new beginnings. Perhaps it doesn't have to be more complicated but instead be reborn from its current state into traditions that this family of three chooses and forges as our own.

Wet Patches

We've been through a few rough patches with Little Old Man but now we are going through some wet ones. It feels like a giant snail has moved into our house given all the drool trails over the furniture and carpet. I am continually covered in mysterious wet patches, some of which I only discover when standing in a breeze.

Little Old Man has found the joy of drooling and eating his hands, arms, toy rings, towels, and anything else he can grab to shove into his mouth. Preferably all at once.

When I pick him up, he extends his hand out from his mouth to touch me and a trail of drool follows. I hold him against me and he takes this as an opportunity to gum at my neck and eat my clothing. The world is there to discover with the mouth. So much so that it seems his current motto is: When in doubt, stick it in the mouth.

The Hubby is trying to work with this new wet patch after picking up and floating him above his head to encourage a smile. Big mistake. He got the smile but he also got an entire mouthful of drool in his eye. I burst out laughing and threw a towel his way, which Little Old Man promptly grabbed and shoved in his mouth.

He may be too small to talk but Little Old Man has also become an expert communicator. He loves to have conversations and doesn't like being kept out of the loop when others are talking. He can smile, grizzle, show happiness or displeasure and yawn in boredom. Above all, he can drool. I'm not quite sure what the drooling says to us but he is saying it in spades.

One thing though is for certain; he is a long way now from that tiny, fragile newborn that we nervously took home from the hospital. My little baby is growing – fast.

Gear Change

Becoming a mother is an enormous change in any woman's life and for me it has taken time to get accustomed to this new way of being. I can still go out and do most of the things I used to but not as spontaneously as I once did. Not that I particularly mind this, it's just different. So long as he is a baby, he is highly dependent on me and the bond we share as mother and child. I accept this as a great responsibility and have shaped myself around it.

What has been harder to shape though is my perception of myself. Do I stack up as a mum? Am I doing a good job? From the hospital on, I have been thirsty for feedback and reassurances from experts and friends alike to these questions. It is like I want a report card of how well I am performing in my new role to quieten my doubts. Really though, the appraisal I so crave has been sitting right in front of me the whole time.

Little Old Man is a healthy, happy and normal baby. He shows no sign of slowing down his pace of growth or being any less curious of the world around him. He is going from strength to strength in a confident manner. So why haven't I been able to do the same?

Until this point I have been operating as a mother on the proviso that I am who I am because someone says so. If someone says I am a great Mum, then I think this must be right and continue on until the next bout of uncertainty. Yet this is a rather weak and dependent point from which to see myself. If I am to be truly confident in my role, I have to start thinking that I am who I am because I believe so.

And that is where I'm at – trying to change gears in appraising myself and being realistic in the process. I am a mother doing the best I can and learning quickly. If someone compliments me, I remind myself that that's great but it shouldn't really change my perception much.

Parenting 101

If I could distil everything that I've learnt in the past four months about parenting into one line, it would be this: You have to be the bigger person in the room.

There have been times when I've felt like walking away because things were tough or frustrating. Yet I knew that someone had to get us out of whatever dead-end we had reached and that someone wasn't going to be Little Old Man. He is too little and inexperienced to possibly even think of placing such responsibility on his shoulders.

No, the dead-end streets have been rightly navigated time and again by myself or The Hubby. Together we have led Little Old Man out of crying fits, immunisation shots, overtired tantrums, growing pains and tummy upsets. And all with a calm hand, patience and a bit of creativity. Some hugs never go astray either.

There will be many more lessons ahead but this one feels like it will stick with us for a while to come. I suspect it will be the litmus test that makes or breaks us as parents and will become more complex as Little Old Man grows. Will we remain firm and not cave to a toddler tantrum? Will we teach our principles and set an example by acting accordingly? Will we admit when we make mistakes and seek to correct them?

My aim is to try to be the bigger person in the room on the majority of occasions. This will hopefully give him a solid enough footing for the life he one day will choose to lead. But I also know there will be times when I will fail at this goal. Nobody is perfect, least of all me! The best I can do then is learn for the next time.

False Alarm

Little Old Man has taken to sleeping in longer and longer blocks during the night. This is very much appreciated but we are still trying to get used to it. For the past four months we have existed on sleep that is interrupted numerous times during the night. It has become our routine and the new normal for our body clocks.

We are both guilty of waking up independently of one another and going downstairs in a mild panic to check on him. I have repeated a few times my method of watching his chest rise and fall to check he is still breathing. The Hubby's preferred method is placing a finger close to Little Old Man's nostrils to confirm air is still coming out. When then reach the same conclusion that he is alive and happily sleeping away.

Sadly, neither of us has yet been able to take advantage of the sleep through. The Hubby can't help but wake up and I still need to express once in the middle of the night.

To make it worse, last night I came down to express and Little Old Man was tossing and making sounds like he was about to wake up for a feed. I returned to bed and told The Hubby of the situation, as it was his turn to feed and he had kindly made me promise not to express and feed in one trip because it took too long.

He went downstairs with the intention to do a dream feed. This is where Little Old Man eats while still half asleep. It is The Hubby's preferred method of night feeding because the settling time is nothing. The trick is to catch him before he has fully woken up to realise he is hungry. Until this point, the grunts and tossing were the warning signs that he was surfacing from a deep sleep.

For whatever reason that wasn't to be. The Hubby attempted a dream feed but Little Old Man was too deeply asleep. He lay him back down, where he promptly started to toss and grunt again. He figured it wouldn't be that long until he was awake enough to feed and decided to wait Little Old Man out. Two hours of not being able to fall asleep on the couch later, The Hubby finally got the feed in that he was waiting for.

Meanwhile, I was upstairs unable to get to sleep because I felt terrible for waking him and didn't know what was taking so long. Yet I didn't want to go down in case he was asleep on the couch.

I later rang him at work and apologised for giving him the false alarm. It would seem that not only Little Old Man's sleeping patterns are changing but also his cues for hunger during sleep.

For the poor Hubby, my misreading of the cues led to us both having a pretty sleepless night. Ironically, the only one who managed to get a good night of sleep was the baby.

Perhaps we should ditch our clever strategies and simply wait for him to cry out in hunger. It is, after all, the only sure-fire method left.

Rollicking

Little Old Man is coming into his own. Gone is the passive newborn that lay swaddled in his cot or my arms, either screaming, feeding, sleeping or all three at once.

Awake time is now all about tummy time, rolling round on the play mat and sitting up. He has even started squealing in delight. Although I had to learn the hard way to check on what inspires his squeals after finding him rolling around in his own vomit, much to his own personal joy. The moment reminded me, yet again, that living with a baby is sometimes like living with a drunk.

To his growing repertoire of activities, he has added sitting in a highchair. We initially weren't going to set one up until he was ready for solids but changed our minds after scouting for one.

The Hubby did some research and we went along to the shops to try him out in our favourites. I half expected a loud protest at the strange experience of being placed in a chair but I underestimated his ability to surprise. As soon as we worked out how to lock him in place, we stood back and braced ourselves for screaming. Instead, we were greeted by a big gummy smile.

Little Old Man leant forward in excitement and slapped his hand against the table. He looked around the room from this new perspective in wonderment. There was no way the smile was going to leave his face.

"Excuse me, is this one part of the sale?"

"I'm afraid not. We also don't have any more in stock."

I looked back towards Little Old Man and his beaming face. For the first time as a mother, I felt the urge to indulge his whims.

"Is it possible to do a deal on the floor stock?"

"I suppose. I'll give you 10% off."

"Sold!"

The Hubby shot me his 'don't you think we should discuss this first?' look, which I duly batted off with a dismissive wifely smile.

Back home, we prepared dinner and sat him in the highchair to look on. He stared in curiosity at all the objects on the table that were previously a hidden mystery. It was strange to see him closer to our eye level, like he had made a milestone leap by moving from the bouncer to our table.

Little Old Man arched his back and thumped his fists confidently on the table as his legs swung freely underneath. The Hubby was amused by the dinner sideshow.

"He looks more like an El Presidente than a Little Old Man."

I laughed at the observation. It was true that his growing confidence and outlook were changing him. Maybe not to the point that he looks like a baby dictator but still.

The realisation that he was growing was bittersweet. I want him to flourish but part of me also wants to savour this age for as long as possible, even with all the work involved.

Different Strokes

I didn't cry when Little Old Man got his second round of immunisation shots. At first I was going to sit in the car while The Hubby went in with him but then remembered my goal of being the bigger person in the room. This wouldn't exactly work if I couldn't even bring myself to be in the room. No, I had to mum up.

We sat in the medical practice while the nurse prepared the needles. I stroked the downy hair on his head while he grabbed his shorts and lifted them up. Such a helpful little one, the nurse observed. Little did he know that he should be taking the opportunity to learn how to crawl, preferably to the nearest exit.

The nurse ran us through all the diseases he would be immunised against and the possible complications of the shots. My head exploded with red flags. It sounded like she was about to inject poison into him. I steeled myself by remembering that the pain and slight risk involved was far less than if he caught any of the diseases he would be immunised against.

She pinched part of his left thigh and pushed the first needle in. Like the first time round, his face almost went purple as he yelled out in surprise at this sudden hurt. Before he had time to truly protest, a second needle was on its way into his right thigh. This sent his screaming off the scale.

I held him to my chest and rocked gently.

"Shhh, shhh, it's ok, Mummy is here, shhh…"

It was no use. He was seemingly inconsolable. And Mummy wasn't far behind. His eyes flashed pain and anguish at me, as though they were asking why I had let that happen to him on my watch. I could feel my chin start to tremble. And then The Hubby picked him up and lifted him into the air.

"Whoooo! You're an aeroplane!"

I furrowed my brow in disapproval. How silly, I thought. That would never calm him down.

To my surprise though, it did. A kind of shock and awe tactic that wobbled us both off our distress trajectories.

"Wow…"

The Hubby grinned triumphantly and returned a quietened Little Old Man back down to his chest. I let him have his moment. He had managed to calm Little Old Man down from catastrophic to gurgling in less than a minute flat.

I hadn't really thought of it until then but our parenting styles and how we physically handle him are as individual as we are. Depending on his mood and the situation, Little Old Man can respond better to one over the other. Sometimes he needs to be gently rocked while other times he needs a solid hug or to be distracted from whatever it is that is upsetting him.

I felt bad for mentally crossing off The Hubby's tactic as silly. We both bring different skills and are learning new ones every day that add to our new role as parents. And, like our baby, these skills have the potential to occasionally surprise and make us see each other in a new light.

Fever Pitch

The nurse had warned us that one of the many side effects of the immunisation shots could be a fever for a day or so. What she didn't tell us is what a fever would involve. We had a bit of an inkling from the six week immunisations but that was nothing in comparison to this time round.

The morning after started quite peacefully. He had slept an incredible ten hours straight. I even had time before he woke to enjoy a leisurely breakfast using both hands.

He greeted the day with a smile yet this happy demeanour quickly crumbled the more he woke up. He was so hungry he couldn't possibly think of having breakfast. He took the bottle, he pushed the bottle away. He whimpered, turned away, took the bottle again before knocking it away once more and devolving into a screaming fit.

I felt his forehead. It was warm to the touch so I took his temperature. It was slightly elevated but nothing dramatic. I gave him some pain relief and dabbed his face with a wet towel. By this stage he was screaming without pause.

After thirty minutes of this, I remembered to put earplugs in to dull the noise. I wished I had thought of it earlier but the screaming had sent me into panic mode. I swear the heart rate and blood pressure of a parent skyrockets when looking after a screaming baby. Dr Google surely contains a study conclusively agreeing with me on that one.

The earplugs offer only mild relief but it is enough to go through every trick I have to calm him down. After one and a half hours though, I am at a loss as to what else to try. I grow increasingly worried about his pain levels and desperate to make it all better.

Little Old Man's cries grow in intensity. They don't sound like they normally do. There is something more high-pitched and sad sounding in them. I wipe away the tears running down his face. There is nothing of his usually chilled Buddha baby demeanour. He looks miserable.

I consider calling the nurse but she'd probably bat me away because his temperature isn't alarmingly high. Besides, as I was told, a fever is a good sign that his immune system is waking up to the immunisation. His unhappiness is a sign that the needles are working. Yet again in motherhood, I reach a point where I feel so helpless and unable.

The Hubby calls in every so often from work to see if things have calmed down. No we're fine, no need to worry. I'm a mother, I can handle this.

I look up at the clock and it is 2 PM. We have been going at it for a few hours with only a little reprieve. I did manage to get a bottle of milk into him and he crashed out in my arms for an hour. He has been on me all day. Every attempt to put him in his cot was met with howls of despair.

I know I need a proper break, I have nothing left to give. I place Little Old Man in his cot, turn my back to his cries and walk upstairs. I put on the bathroom fan and close the door to block out the noise and then have a shower. Normally I would have taken him upstairs mid-morning in the bouncer so I can shower but there was no such luck today.

I step out of the shower and assume he has turned purple from crying by now.

"Hello…?"

Oh God, it's The Hubby. He has called my bluff and come home early. I feel horrible, like he has caught me red-handed being a terrible mother. I hadn't even turned the baby monitor on because I knew he was safe and I needed the silence.

"I'm so sorry, so so sorry…"

The Hubby is holding a placid looking Little Old Man, which makes me feel like even more of a terrible mother. As though I couldn't be bothered putting the monitor on for a peaceful baby.

"Hey, I know he's been going all day. He was a bit whingey when I came in but seemed to calm down after I picked him up. Maybe you were both stressing each other out."

I switch from needing space from him to wanting to hold him. I reach out but The Hubby swings him away from me.

"I think you need to lie down for a while, you need a break."

"But…"

"He'll still be here when you come downstairs. You've done an amazing job, now rest."

I feel slightly buoyed by this assessment and try to remind myself that he is sick. I can't calm him down from everything. Sometimes all I can do is be there. Lucky for The Hubby and I, we have each other's backs when we can't go any further.

I lay down and instantly fall asleep. The fever passed later that night without any further intervention from me and the house calmed back down to its normal rhythm of ups and downs.

A Weighty Issue

I feel I might lose the plot if one more person tells me my child is well fed, chubby, big boned, a future rugby player, healthy, a bottle baby, well covered, advanced for his age, or just plain big. Yes, he is larger than the average boy his age but proportionally so and within range. His weight tracks well with his height and our family doctor is pleased with his development.

But that doesn't stop people from commenting. I wonder if they would be so quick off the mark if he had an unusually large nose or a weird growth on his head.

Mostly the comments seem well intended, like it's the first thing people can think to say when they see him and it pops out of their mouths like a bad dose of verbal diarrhoea. Sometimes though there seem to be undertones, which I don't really appreciate since I am not exactly petite myself. A worry about genetics does sit somewhere in the back of my mind but not as an active worry yet.

We run off his rhythm. He eats when he is hungry and I don't force the bottle when he gives us cues that he is done. Not to sound sarcastic but I don't think restrictive diets should be introduced before solids are. Let him grow in peace.

I will admit that I am somewhat defensive about this topic after growing up bigger than the average girl. I spent years hearing my mother bat off comments by saying I was merely big boned. I wasn't, actually, and needed nutritional help – the whole family did. There has to be an underlying problem in any family where every member, including the dog, is obese. But this is different, my child isn't even five months old yet!

While I get comments on an almost daily basis, one exchange retains the prize as most impolite. Recently we went for our first baby-swim lesson, as I was keen for him to learn as soon as possible how to be safe around water. Also, having grown up with a pool in the backyard, I wanted to share my love of water with him.

So there we were at the pool for his first ever lesson. I was so excited for him. I slowly walked with him into the water and let him slowly explore this new sensation. I swooshed him through the water with his head held high and cooed words of encouragement. My plan for his first swim was a gentle introduction to being half submerged in water. I wanted him to have a positive experience the first time in a pool.

The instructor swam over to us and asked what our names were. Her demeanour reminded me for some reason of the bossy I-know-better midwives at the hospital. I soon found out why. She grabbed Little Old Man out of my arms without asking and dunked his head under the water before flipping him over on his back.

"Babies who learn to be ok with swimming on their backs don't get the usual fears that older children do when they learn to swim late."

I look at Little Old Man. His arms and legs are flailing about and he looks panicked at the sudden change of pace. I want to reach out and grab him but sense the instructor would chastise me for, well, babying him. I stand by impotently and watch as she flips him over into another awkward position. Sorry baby.

"Oh you're a big boy aren't you?"

Oh here we go, I thought. Smile politely, grit teeth – she'll go away quicker then.

"But then your Mum isn't that small either!"

Oh. Wait. WHAT?! Did I just hear that correctly? Did she insinuate my son is fat through insulting me? That was quite some feat! I hadn't come across the double slap down before.

"I think I've got the hang of it now. Thanks."

I firmly grab a hold around his chest and pull him towards me. I am seething but, like a true former fat kid, I say nothing. I will surely think of some great comeback later but remain tongue-tied and embarrassed of myself in the moment.

I look at my son. He is batting the water with his hands and I return to our gentler introduction to the water. I am relieved he is too young to understand what was said. But that worry, the one I had earmarked in the back of my head for potential future reference, lurches forward.

Nobody wants their child to be overweight. There are serious health implications that could follow them through life. But for me, I also don't want my son to experience what I did growing up and then struggle like I do with standing up against rude people and bullies.

In a perfect world, all overweight children would be free to live without snide or even well-intended remarks. Such children need support from those close to them to help them back to a healthy weight, not running commentary on how they look. I can tell you from experience that such attitudes help nobody, least of all the child.

I hope my son doesn't grow up to be overweight but, after the run-in with the swim instructor, I realise I need to do more than hope. I have to set a good example not only through what I eat and how

I exercise but also by my reaction to uninvited comments. Only then will he stand a chance at not following in my heavier footsteps.

Public Property

Apart from comments on his size, the other main point of conversation I am greeted with is whether he is breast or bottle fed. My theory on why this comes up so often is that people are simply reaching for what they think to be safe baby topics to talk about.

While I know people mean well, it is still a topic I don't wish to discuss casually. The trouble is, nobody who talks to me knows that. They have no clue of the desperation and sadness involved in having failed at breastfeeding.

The bulk of questions are innocent chit-chat: breast or bottle? Oh, a bit of both. Ah ok. Nothing more said. Next topic.

And then there are the loaded questions, the ones that make it clear to me where the person asking stands on the issue. Have you tried to breastfeed? Have you given xyz a go? You know it's good for the baby to get some breast milk?

The easiest, most polite way to get is to brush over the details and change topic. Still, the fact that I am compelled by to discuss it at all is very grating. It is as though my very private wounds are opened up for inspection and general curiosity.

Perhaps I am overly sensitive about this topic (ok I am) but the most irritating reminder of breastfeeding are those stickers placed on the doors of public areas: 'Breastfeeding mothers welcome here'. I feel like buying a permanent marker so I can add 'and bottle feeding mothers too' whenever I spot one.

Yet my irritation at those stickers is nothing in comparison to a run-in I had with a slightly older tradesman who was doing a quote for some work on our ceiling. We were negotiating price and scope of the job at the dining table when Little Old Man started to show hungry impatience. I lifted him out of his bouncer and popped a bottle in his mouth.

The conversation about the work slowed to a stop. I could feel this man staring at me and looked up. I smiled politely and he continued to stare unapologetically back. I tried to get the conversation back on track but Little Old Man was fussing too loudly. And then he started.

"I can't help but notice you are feeding your baby formula."

"Uh yes…"

"Does he get any breast milk?"

What? Am I really having this conversation with someone who I want to fix some rain damage? I wasn't sure how to reply. The polite part of me reasoned he was older than me so I should be respectful but his tone and intrusion made my temper flare. I decided to try the cooler option.

"Uh, he gets a bit of both."

"Well, it really is worth giving it a try. You know, breastfed babies sleep better. All my grandchildren were breastfed and they are incredibly well behaved."

"My baby sleeps just fine."

It was a blank lie but a defensive one. I started to feel the sting of my own failure rise up. But then I felt something else – annoyance. I had taken the high road of showing him respect and he returned this by being even more insensitive.

Who gave him the right to pass comment? And what was the inference, that I was too ignorant or lazy to do the right thing by my baby? Maybe he can get back to me with his considered thoughts on breastfeeding when he has given birth, grown a couple of breasts and tried to get them to work.

I rose from the table and headed for the door.

"Thank you for your quote. We'll be in touch."

Clearly, we never were. Stupid arse.

Keeping Up

Before Little Old Man crash tackled his way into my life, I used to be quite socially active. I went out regularly to dinner with friends, was a member of a book club, went to the movies, loved to read or write at a local café and caught up nearly daily with friends for lunch at work.

I used to watch friends go off to have babies and, in the process, enter a social black hole that took them at least six months to claw out of. I would send them messages of support, only to have them answered three weeks later at some ungodly hour with an apology for the delay. I couldn't imagine how anyone could be that hard up for time that they couldn't send a text back.

And now I kind of know the answer. The newborn stage was a blur and I understood how it took three weeks to reply to anything. Since those early days, I've managed to keep on top of short emails and texts but the longer emails still languish at the bottom of my inbox.

If Little Old Man was more demanding during the day, then I doubt I would have had the time or impetus to have achieved as much non-baby stuff as I have. Thankfully though, luck and the baby gods have been on my side even if some days it doesn't feel that way.

Yet despite his easy going demeanour, I have let some things slide or have struggled when getting back into my old pursuits.

I set a goal of returning to book club next month yet I question my ability to commit to reading a book in one month. In an attempt to test the waters, I downloaded last month's book but only managed to read ten pages. If I have time and half a brain, then I'm writing. Reading anything more than the morning headlines or a few emails feels like a decadent waste of precious non-baby time.

As for catching up with friends, I still do but not as much as I used to. The Hubby and I have also been out for a few well-timed dinners where we've mostly had a sleeping baby. Although these trips feel more like an attempt to cling onto our old selves than relaxing evenings out. There is nothing more unsettling than being in a crowded restaurant with a sleeping baby. It is like trying to eat dinner with an unexploded ordinance parked at the side of your table. Even if you're pretty confident it won't go off, its presence does put you a bit on edge.

Then there are the things that have really been on the slide and are only now showing signs of improvement. Our poor pet fish have suffered greatly with the arrival of Little Old Man. It's awful to admit but we looked after them pretty poorly in those early days.

Deep in that black hole, we had mono-focus and couldn't see anything around the home that wasn't baby related. The tank had to turn green at one point before either of us remembered to clean it.

The first victim of our slack pet keeping was a rather high-maintenance tropical fish and then a bottom feeder. We have since made a more concerted effort to clean the tank regularly but some days remembering to feed them is struggle enough. A conversation had almost daily between The Hubby and I goes something like this:

"Honey, have you fed the fish?"

"Umm, I did it the other day…you?"

"I can't remember."

We both then look at each other then at the fish, who seem to eye us off with their disdain.

One weekend we went away and forgot to feed them before we left. When we came back, there was one less fish and no fishy corpse to be found anywhere. Our only conclusion was that their hunger turned to cannibalistic desperation.

We feel bad about the fish. Oh and the pot plants – they haven't fared well either. We try to keep up and remind each other of the things that need our regular attention around the house. It's so easy though to overlook things that don't make noise to get your attention, particularly when there is someone in the house who does.

Guilt Turtle

Before we became parents we tried to do as much of the baby shopping as possible. The idea was to avoid making emergency shopping choices under the influence a screaming baby. It seemed like a logical and very adult idea at the time.

I now see that the trouble with pre-purchasing was that we had no clue about what our baby really needed beyond the big ticket items. Even then we got it wrong in buying a bassinet that ended up being used for about a week before he took to sleeping in the pram.

And if you don't really know where the line is between need and don't need when entering a baby store, then you may as well hand over your wallet at the front register.

The Hubby took charge of preparing the nursery. With me busy baking the bun, he wanted something constructive to add to the baby-making process. He took a thoroughly German approach and researched product reviews, made a spread sheet of the best options, and sourced the best deals. We spent our weekends scouting prams, car seats, cots, baby monitors etc. The list of baby essentials seemed endless.

Undeterred by the hole this list was making to our bank account, we also picked up incidental purchases. These items are strategically placed in the way of would-be parents and priced so that you don't really think that hard ("Oh what's ten bucks for peace of mind on [insert imaginary baby problem invented by merciless marketers here]?").

Now I'm sure if The Hubby ever reads this, he would point out that the majority of these purchases may have been made by me. I would like to note though that my body was awash with hormones at the time and, well, actually that's not much of an excuse. I was excited and in the mood for nesting. Mea Culpa.

So yes, I bought a few things that turned out to be useless or counterproductive to their original purpose. High on that list is the Guilt Turtle – a turtle-shaped light that measures the temperature in the room and turns a different colour to tell you whether it is too cold, too hot or just right for the baby. Perfect, you would think, for those fretting parents who are unsure whether to add or subtract a blanket from their sleeping baby. After all, you don't want to overheat or freeze a baby.

For a start, if you do either of these things then a baby is going to let you know by screaming. They are pretty good at that. Secondly, if you don't want to wait for a scream then you can tell if the temperature of your baby is right by feeling their chest with your hand. If warm to the touch, then take off a blanket. If feels right, leave it.

So back to the Guilt Turtle. Because I bought it, naturally we felt we had to use it even after we'd worked the chest test out. While the original intended purpose was useless, the soft glow of the turtle has served as an alternate night light. We still fumble round but at least we can see our hands without having to turn on the ceiling lights.

The problem with the Guilt Turtle though is that it is permanently red, which indicates the room is too hot. If I turn the air con on for an hour I can manage to get it to flicker occasionally to green. I feel so guilty when I lay Little Old Man down each night and see the red turtle. It is like a blinking red neon sign hissing at me: *"bad mother!"* Well, maybe not. Maybe that bit is in my head. But still, I feel bad when really the room is at most two degrees warmer than what is recommended.

And really, what child in the history of mankind hasn't slept in a room that was too hot or too cold for them? It is only really the last couple of generations that have the technical option to acclimatise their house to a perfect 18 degrees Celsius year round. Given how carbon heavy babies are already, I'm not quite sure if this is something any parent should strive for.

Try telling that though to the Guilt Turtle.

Human

Babies are so incredibly human at the most basic of levels. There are no social mores or feelings of embarrassment built into their tiny brains yet. It's probably just as well because a day in the life of a baby would be pretty mortifying if they were aware of what they were doing and what we adults needed to do to look after them. But they're not so that's what makes it all so cute.

Take farting. If The Hubby farted on the couch, I would be pretty cross at his lack of consideration for those around him. If Little Old Man farts on the couch, we both giggle like schoolkids and gloat about the loudness or staying power of the subsequent odour. Well ok, maybe I giggle more than The Hubby but the principle is the same. A baby can do no wrong at this age because it simply doesn't know any better.

Likewise, burping provides loads of childish humour. There is something deeply funny about a small, seemingly fragile, being letting out a burp so loud that it can be heard rooms away. And they let it out with abandon. There's no trying to supress for the sake of politeness. It sounds like they are bringing it up from their toenails.

But for all their squishy grossness, babies are also human in other ways that many adults have forgotten and perhaps could learn from. They do not conceal their emotions behind a poker face or a fake smile. Whether they are happy, bored or upset, they will let you know. What you see is what you get, for better or worse.

One of the best parts of the day is in the morning when I know he is awake. I bend over his cot and say good morning. His eyes dart around until they lock with mine and then he wriggles in excitement.

The wriggle starts in his legs, works through his body and finishes with flapping arms reminiscent of an overexcited penguin. It melts my heart every time.

I know this age of absolute innocence will end when he becomes more socially aware. And there will be a time when I need to teach him that bottom burps are for the bathroom. But, for now, I'm quite content enjoying his humanness.

Complicated

"I think you've lost the ability to sit down and do one thing at a time."

"Huh? What are you talking about?"

I look up from my tab computer and over at The Hubby. He is staring at me in disbelief. I look down and see the tab on my lap, a piece of toast in one hand, the other controlling the breast pump, and my left foot pushing Little Old Man in is bouncer. I was also listening to the news in the background but don't admit to this one.

It seemed he had my number. I was so absent minded in my little beehive world that I didn't realise how ridiculous it may have looked from the outside. The truth was, there was no urgency. Little Old Man was quite content in his bouncer and The Hubby could have stepped in if he cried. I had the time to enjoy my toast, watch the news, read my favourite trashy gossip site and pump all at a comfortable pace. I even had time to talk with The

Hubby about his day or, God forbid, relax on the couch and stare into space.

Ok so I admit I may have become accustomed to doing everything at once even when it isn't technically necessary. I even multitask after Little Old Man has been put down for the night and I know he will be asleep for at least the next few hours. And as he gets into a daytime nap regime, there are more moments when I can slow down and take the time to enjoy what I am doing.

So why is it difficult for me to do that, even when I have the opportunity to? It's like some switch was flicked in my brain after birth and I can't help but multitask. I know there is some fear in me that if I don't do everything straight away, then perhaps I won't get another chance that day because a screaming baby could interrupt me at any moment. There is also an underlying sense of urgency left over from the newborn stage, as though the adrenalin of those early days is only slowly leaving my body or I'm so used to it that I can't let go of the pace.

Since The Hubby pulled me up, I have tried on a couple of occasions to do just one thing at a time. When I was out shopping by myself, I sat down for lunch and decided to do nothing else. I went to reach for my phone about five times before I finished the last sushi roll. It felt strange, uncomfortable even, to only focus on eating.

I haven't really taken the time to savour the food that I'm eating since the birth. The one exception to this is when The Hubby has cooked proper meals for us and insisted that we sit at the table and eat like human beings. At other times though, food has been relegated to something I shove in my mouth to stop the hunger pangs so I can get on with other things.

Whittling down to doing one thing at a time won't happen instantly. Perhaps it sounds crazy but I can't just stop and go back to normal. Actually, even pre-baby I was fond of multitasking but nothing as bad as I am now. It can save time but it can turn into too much of a good thing. You think you can do it all at once but end up doing everything half-arsed or not at all. Worse still, you develop the attention span of a toddler.

For now I am going to try doing a maximum of two things at once since the experiment of doing only one thing was a bit of a stretch. I have also set myself the rule of putting down whatever I am doing and actively listening when The Hubby is talking to me. I can't imagine how irritating it must be to have a partner who is constantly on the move and not paying full attention to any one particular person or task.

My new tactic seems to be working so far and I have already noticed a positive difference. The Hubby seems less exasperated with me and I find I enjoy things more. I still slip up and find myself on occasion doing four things at once but I'm getting better. I even managed to write this and only drink a cup of tea at the same time.

Now to pack the dishwasher and make dinner...

Puppy Love

I started my role as mother with zero experience with babies. The closest I had come to caring for a baby was coming from a family that always had dogs. I grew up happily looking after, training and grooming our puppies.

If you've never looked after a puppy, the analogy to a baby might seem a bit strange. If you have though, you will know how much time and attention is needed when you first bring a puppy home. They are just as helpless and in need of care as a baby. The only difference is that they grow out of that phase quicker than a baby does.

So with nothing else to draw on, I have been remembering tips from my puppy rearing days as a way to get my head around looking after a baby. As crazy as it might sound, it has worked really well so far. I knew how to make Little Old Man swallow baby pain medication and how to get eye drops in his eyes. I also felt more confident filing and cutting his nails. Dealing with the drool was easy. I knew what made for a great chew toy. And wiping in between all the skins folds on his legs was like the time I looked after a friend's shar pei for the weekend.

Seeing my baby as a kind of human puppy though does have limits. As he grew, I got excited when he reached milestones like grabbing objects. Then the fine motor skills continued to get finer and I realised he had overtaken even the smartest of dogs I've reared.

Nevertheless, I do find myself congratulating him by saying "What a clever boy! Who's a clever boy?" while patting his head vigorously.

I know I have to let go of the analogy in my mind. It was helpful at the beginning but he has outgrown the comparison. He is not a helpless puppy – he is an amazingly clever little human. But that doesn't stop me from wanting to house train him and get him to roll over and sit still on command. That could come in handy when he becomes a toddler!

A Touch Too Much

At the end of the day when The Hubby and I fall into bed, he crawls across to my side of the bed for a cuddle before sleep. It's our tradition and I love it. Yet at times a cuddle is the last thing on my mind. When Little Old Man has been clingy all day, all I want to do is curl up into an autonomous ball and recharge.

It sounds horrible when I put it like that. The Hubby is, well, my husband. Spending time with him each day is important too. It's just hard when someone else has been on me, at me, and all kinds of grabby and demanding to then turn around and fulfil someone else's request to be held. They are both my family and I love them dearly but there are still limits on how much I can give of myself. I feel like setting up one of those ticket systems they have in supermarket delis and yelling out "get in line, people, one at a time!" Perhaps though this would lack some sensitivity to my loved ones.

I have tried to work out why I feel this way. At first I worried it may have some deeper meaning but I concluded it is simply a physical thing. After so much contact, my body goes into a kind of sensory overload and needs to calm down. It's a bit like going to a loud concert and needing to sit somewhere quiet afterwards.

Thankfully the feeling is short-lived. I am able to recharge overnight to the point that I am almost in withdrawals by the time I pick Little Old Man out of his cot in the morning. And I'm equally as fond of giving The Hubby a hug on his way out the door if we're up at the same time.

Baby Shower

When I was pregnant my friends asked if I wanted a baby shower. I didn't really because I never liked people making a big fuss over me or being the centre of attention.

Rather than explain this, I conceded to an afternoon tea and requested no gifts or games. My logic was that I didn't want to celebrate what I didn't have in my hands yet, which was also true yet harder to argue against. The afternoon tea was more of a catch-up with friends before I entered the unknown foggy world of parenthood. In hindsight, it was a good move – even if some of my friends thought I was a little strange for ditching the baby shower concept.

Fast forward six months to last night, where I found myself in the middle of a friend's baby shower. She is the complete opposite to me and loves all the traditions around life's big events. As such, we had games, balloons, present opening, party favours and baby paraphernalia strewn across her apartment. It was like an explosion of all things baby.

I found it interesting to sit for the first time on the other side of the fence looking over at a mummy-to-be. My friend spoke of being nervous about the birth yet countered this with her faith in the obstetrician she has chosen. She was sure of how she wanted the birth to go and assumed she would be a breastfeeding mother.

As she spoke with equal parts nerves and excitement, I looked at her and found myself smiling. I could see her mind trying to give some kind of order to the chaos that was about to be unleashed upon her. Six months earlier, that would have been me talking. I would have been saying those words as a means of comforting myself from the great unknown. Now I know. And what I know from experience is miles apart from the anticipation beforehand.

But I wasn't about to dismiss her perceptions and come off sounding like a know-it-all. In truth, I don't know it all. I know the baby experience only from my perspective. Perhaps she will have a dream run in the delivery suite and a dream baby who sleeps through from hospital on. Even if the road is a little bumpier, maybe she will react in other ways to me or will be able to go through it all without much afterthought.

Still, at the risk of really sounding like a know-it-all, it was fun hearing the almost innocent views of her friends gathered there. Only myself and one other woman there were mothers and it showed in the conversation. Their banter reminded me in a good way of where I once stood.

Oh that birthing stuff, it's not that hard – you take an epidural and it's all good.

Babies only cry every couple of hours for the first two weeks and then they are fine.

Babies are soooo cute! They are just like little dolls. I want to have five!

I want a boy, then a girl, and then maybe another boy. I can't decide.

I can't wait to visit you in hospital and hold the baby. I'll have to sit down though to hold it.

Your Mum will help you out so it will be easy.

I spoke with a friend after her waters broke and she was so calm. I thought that's when you get rushed to hospital, like in the movies.

Then there were the gifts. As my friend opened them, I couldn't help but tick off in my mind whether they would be useful or not. Some gifts were great, like a musical mobile and bamboo cotton swaddles. Others not so much, like a newborn onesie with fiddly press-stud buttons on the back and a wrap so small it could double as a handkerchief. I could see which gifts were destined for a useless pile like the one we have gathered in our spare room.

As I left, I hugged my friend. It was the last time I would see her before she entered the mummy club. There were so many things I wished to say but knew not to. I remembered my anger at not being told what would happen to my body after birth, like the boab tree legs. I could now see why though these things were not said and didn't feel angry anymore. It's all so individual. I'm sure there are a thousand different things that could potentially happen to a woman's body.

Nevertheless, my mind still flicked through all the advice in an attempt to find that one piece which would fit her perfectly. But I knew it was of no use.

If I told her all the things I knew that could happen during and after the birth, it would freak her out completely even though one, maybe two, might end up happening. Besides, whichever way her birthing experience goes, the road ahead is hers alone to discover. No amount of advice will alter this.

"Good luck. I'll see you on the other side."

"Thanks. I can't wait!"

Pumping Along

Little Old Man is almost five months old and I am still hand pumping five times a day like a crazed loon. But, unlike earlier, I am a crazed loon with a set goal now. No really truly this time. I want to reach six months and then start to wean as I introduce solids to his diet. I am comfortable with this plan. It doesn't upset me in the way my first failed plan to wean did.

Pumping has become part of my daily routine. It's something I do, like brushing my teeth or combing my hair. The only time I find it annoying is when I forget the last pump of the day and remember just as I'm slipping into bed.

I have given breastfeeding the best shot I could. I will walk away safe in the knowledge that I provided what I could of that precious liquid. I still feel sad sometimes that I wasn't able to share the special bond of breastfeeding with him but the main thing is that he got the milk.

And I still have my special bonding moments with him. Like when he has his bottle and rests his head against me as he falls asleep, drunk on the feeling of being full. Or when he nuzzles his head into my neck and breathes out a huge sigh at the end of a crying spell.

Regardless of how a baby is fed, there are going to be deep bonds formed in the first six months. I've been told by several women that the bond between mothers and their sons is particularly special and I can see now what they meant.

No matter how big Little Old Man grows up to be, I will have nursed him through the most vulnerable period in his life and helped develop all sides of his personality. When he is older, I plan to tell him there is strength in being able to cry and ask for a hug sometimes. With any luck, he won't lose this part of himself in the process of becoming a grown bloke.

Perhaps I am aiming for the stars but I hope one day if he ever reads this, Little Old Man will appreciate the reasoning and efforts I took to breastfeed him. I half suspect he might say "ewww gross out, Mum!" until the point he becomes a father himself and sees the bond firsthand.

At any rate, I hope at some stage in his life he will appreciate what his old Mum did for him way back when.

The Betty Homemaker Test

As I learnt from the Guilt Turtle, buying baby products can be an experience that often leaves my wallet empty and my spare room full of useless things. The unfortunate thing is that I haven't become some kind of guru of all things baby.

With each stage that Little Old Man enters, a new plethora of baby products open up as options for me to purchase. And I am left standing in the baby store feeling as clueless as I was at the beginning of the previous stage.

At the moment I am deliberating over the need for a baby food processor since he is set to start solids soon. Like most other baby-related purchases, they hover around the $100-150 mark. But is a processor really necessary? Will it become indispensable or simply clutter my kitchen?

I recently devised a test to apply to such purchases and it has guided me well so far; did a mother in the 1950s use one?

If the answer is no, then the obvious question is what did they use as an alternative. Maybe their alternative was terribly time consuming or not age appropriate. Maybe though, our grandmothers knew better than we give them credit for. Without a machine for every function in their lives, they learnt how to make do and get creative.

In the case of the baby food processor, I imagine that the average 1950s housewife did not have one.

What they had though was ingenious in its simplicity. They had forks. With a bit of effort, you can mash and puree the hell out of any boiled fruit or vegetable using a fork. If I wanted to be a bit more thorough, I could also get out my stab mixer that I use for making smoothies. Problem solved! And no need to fork out $150, if you pardon the pun.

Manicured

Before I had a baby, it's terrible to admit but I used to look at a mother who had recently returned to work in my office and wonder why she couldn't make a little bit more of an effort. I mean, how hard could it be to put moisturiser on those flakey hands more often? Or at least make a bit of effort with a touch of makeup or perfume? And while she was at it, maybe get rid of those weird white patches on her clothes? I felt compelled almost on a daily basis to give her a makeover. Yes, I can be a bitch sometimes but a helpful one at heart.

Now all those questions are coming back to haunt me. I have the answers because I live the answers. That flakey skin is the result of good hygiene when handling a baby. If you wipe away poo or vomit or pick their tiny nose with your fingernail, you need to wash your hands. If they are formula fed, you need to clean the bottles and sterilise them. If you handle raw food and then need to tend to your baby, you need to wash your hands beforehand. And the list goes on.

At the end of the day, I find myself washing my hands possibly more times than the average person suffering from obsessive compulsive disorder. Even if I went to the effort of putting moisturiser on between each hand wash, it would be on for only an hour or so before the next hand wash. And while I'm not a dermatologist by trade, I can only imagine that the moisturiser offers little barrier to the depletion of natural oils in my skin from all that antibacterial soap.

Apart from the technicality, my mind doesn't think of details like hand moisturiser anymore. Even if it did, I don't have the time to give myself a twenty minute mini-manicure every time I wash my hands. The closest I get these days is wiping the excess baby oil on the back of my hands after Little Old Man has his bath.

Sadly, having a baby is precisely the time when I most needed to pamper my skin more. Nothing makes my hands look more haggard and damaged than when I hold onto his flawless baby skin.

As for the makeup and perfume, these come with their own challenges. At the beginning I kept the makeup regime going and found concealer to be a godsend for those sleep bags under the eyes. But now Little Old Man has grown a bit, the makeup has mostly been given away, except for the concealer. I'd look scary without it given the amount of sleep deprivation I have!

Part of my lack of commitment to makeup is being time poor but the more major part is the physical realities of a baby. When I pick him up, he likes to bat at my face with his hands. For a better cleanse of my makeup, Little Old Man turns to his favourite sport – climbing me like a mountain while I'm sitting. His little legs pump up and down until he manages to reaches the summit of my head. Once there, he grabs at my face or swipes his open drooly mouth across it. After a few rounds of playing Mummy Mountain, there is very little makeup left.

Perfume has proven trickier from the start. I used to wear it on my belly because I didn't like it rubbing off on the collars of all my shirts and smelling stale. But then post-partum I started to wear a muscle-holder-in-thing to help bring the abdominal and pelvic muscles back into shape. They are like a massive pair of Super Granny pants made with fifty layers of Lycra that go over my normal undies and cover from my knees up until under my Girls.

My pants are great at giving shape at a time when I feel and look like a deflated flesh balloon. Not so great though for wearing perfume, as I ended up with a similar problem to the collar since it rubbed off and smelt stale. So I took to wearing perfume on the back between the shoulder blades. It was the only part of my body left to avoid it rubbing off on the baby or clothes.

Perfume, in case you haven't noticed, is something I'm quite particular about. I love it but only when I put it on myself for my own personal pleasure. I prefer subtle and avoid the lingering or overpowering scents. One of my pet hates is hugging another woman and ending up with an uninvited drenching of her perfume on me.

Worse still, as I have discovered, is a woman asking for a cuddle of Little Old Man. If she wears perfume on her neck, as most normal women do, then it will rub off on him when she holds him over the shoulder. I cannot stand receiving my baby back covered in someone else's random perfume choice. I don't even want my baby to smell like my perfume, as seen with the shoulder blade trick. Maybe I'm being picky (ok, I am being picky) but a baby should smell, well, like a baby rather than a musky oriental scent bomb. I haven't quite worked my way round the social etiquette of this one and I have been caught out many times.

Finally, there are the white marks on the clothing. I now know this is baby vomit and overflow from feeds. Try as I might, I can't really avoid the appearance of these marks on me. Little Old Man is crafty in his ability to do a sneaky side vomit when I turn away for the slightest of moments. And once the vomit has made contact, it is very hard to scrub completely out.

So one day in the future when I return to work with my dried out skin, bare face and white marks, I fully expect to be judged by some childless woman for my appearance. And perhaps I deserve it a little since I was once in her shoes. But what I know now is that I probably wouldn't even care about being judged. If I am there, awake and able to function back in the adult world, then I've already won.

Oh, you're such a Teethe!

"I thought we were over this bit. I thought he had learnt to sleep."

The Hubby sounds mildly annoyed, like Little Old Man had reneged on a business deal and was taunting us over the fact. Actually, he was doing just that – even if he had no awareness of his actions. Between us we got up to him five times during the night instead of our usual one. On the last call of duty at 4:45 AM, he woke up after his feed and laughed, cooed and blew raspberries. Anything to try to make me engage eye contact so he could wake up fully. But Mummy doesn't play ball at that time of morning. Ever. I have learnt the hard way that, once you engage, any hopes of further sleep vanish.

Things did not improve during the day that followed. Little Old Man grizzled and generally seemed out of sorts. His cheeks were also flushed red but weren't hot to the touch. A check with the thermometer confirmed that he did not have a fever. I turned to Dr Google to get a diagnosis.

"Hmm, I think he might be teething. Well, it's either that or he has rabies."

"I'm going to go with the more likely option."

Silly Hubby, always going with the most sensible solution. What if one day Dr Google was right and one of us was suffering from some highly exotic ailment? It can happen, you know. I mean, someone in the world has to have rabies otherwise the disease would be extinct. And what if we ignored all the symptoms and Little Old Man turned into some kind of wolf boy as a result? Who would be laughing at their wife then?

Ok, given his age and that he hasn't been in close contact with wild animals frothing at the mouth, it did seem more likely that Little Old Man was suffering from the age-old problem of teething. But still, you never know!

"...so what can we do then?"

"It says on this site that our options are to give him cold wet towels to suck on, buy some gel for his gums, hold him when he's upset and give him Panadol when he is in lots of pain."

The last bit tugged at my heart. "Lots of pain"? My Little Old Man? I would suffer pain a hundred times worse if it meant I could save him from feeling the pain himself. As a mother, I want him to live a life free of pain and hurt but know this is not feasible. It is simply not the human condition.

We began our regime of handing him wet face towels to chew on and giving him extra cuddles. As with everything else so far, we follow his lead. By the time bed time rolls round, he is in need of long cuddles and singing. Sometimes when he is inconsolable, we give him the drops and gel before gently rocking him to sleep.

I was warned beforehand by other parents that teething isn't an easy or quick process. They weren't kidding. The first tooth hasn't even broken through despite all the grizzling. The goal of a full set of fangs seems very, very distant.

Welcome To Pluto

"Did you know that Pluto is not a planet anymore? It got reclassified in 2006 and is now a dwarf planet!"

The Hubby looks at me strangely, as though I have been rifling through the drinks cabinet for an extra kick to my housewife existence. He closes the door behind him and loosens his work shirt.

"You've been saving up your words all day, haven't you?"

"What? No, Pluto is very interesting! You know, it was only discovered in 1930. That's quite late, isn't it? And..."

And so I went. I was a one-woman science show with a complete run-down on the greater debates of 20th century astronomy. The fact that I had never previously showed the faintest interest in astronomy was not lost on The Hubby. His natural curiosity for science has always been met by yawns and me stubbing my toes on the carpet like a five year old with ADHD.

"This is all very interesting but why are you telling me this? You think astrology is a science because it refers to the solar system."

"That's not true! I know the difference between astrology and astronomy. I'm not stupid!"

The last bit is true; I'm not stupid, I just happened to have a baby. That is precisely the problem. Even though my time is mostly taken up with the physical demands of looking after Little Old Man, my brain is still ticking over.

With not much to think about and little opportunity to discuss, it has started to latch on to random stimulation. A chance flick of the television over lunch led to my latest obsession with Pluto. My mind spent the rest of the afternoon thinking of Pluto and I was ready to pounce as soon as The Hubby opened the door. I went at him like the intellectual equivalent of an overzealous Labrador.

Unfortunately or fortunately, depending on the viewpoint, The Hubby already gets plenty of mental stimulation at work. By the time he comes home, all he wants to do is play with Little Old Man, have dinner and enjoy a beer on the couch before bed. Yet for me, the evening is the first chance to engage with an adult. The result is that our minds are operating in different time zones.

Since the Pluto Incident, I have twice more ambushed The Hubby with random documentary finds. He has received two comprehensive history lessons – one on the life of Bennelong, an Aboriginal interlocutor between the British settlers and aboriginals in the 1700s, and the other on the Long March that led to the communist revolution in China.

I have chosen the timing of my lessons a bit better though and have allowed him to come in from work first. The compulsion to talk to him about random factoids has underscored that, yes, I really do need to get out and use my brain more. Thankfully, I do get out now after I felt myself slipping into a kind of cloistered funk. And the start of book club again has given me an additional intellectual outlet – if I ever find the time to read in between all my docos, that is.

Being housebound for days on end is not fun and enough to do anybody's head in, even with the busy distraction of a baby. I do, however, find it relaxing to be at home if I manage to get out a couple of days a week. And that is exactly the balance I am aiming for since making the decision to be more proactive. I now plan my social calendar a week in advance, booking in two days where I have lunch with an old colleague or friend.

Plus I have swimming lessons for Little Old Man and the Mother's Group.

The more structured approach to socialising has worked well so far. I feel more content and less desperate for conversation at the end of the day. Hopefully for The Hubby too, it will also mean less talk about Pluto and Communist China.

The Well-Dressed Octopus

I heard that dressing a baby is like trying to put an octopus in a string bag. Then I had a baby and thought this was a slight exaggeration. Save for their awkward bobble heads, newborns are quite straightforward to dress. They lie there passively and you can move their limbs in whatever direction you want. Infants, on the other hand, not so much.

Little Old Man has made changing him easier by developing his neck muscles. On the downside, he has also discovered he not only has hands and feet but can actually use them to influence the world around him. This has given him great pleasure and aided his inquisitive nature. It has also left me laughing and at times exasperated. The octopus is well and truly out of the bag.

Changing a nappy has become hazardous, particularly if a Number Two is involved. If it's a Number Three then I can forget it, the whole thing is a lost cause and we may as well jump in the shower together. But a Two? There is still a chance of getting the area clean and a new nappy on without us both wearing poo.

I start by undoing the old nappy, surveying the damage and folding the front back up to avoid any spontaneous leak onto my shirt (occupational hazard of having a boy). I quickly move my hand across to grab the number of wet wipes I predict I'll need. At this point, Little Old Man registers that it's game time and rolls his legs up into the air. He then either manages to grab them, making a nappy change impossible, or let them flop down and up a few times more. In all this movement, it is possible that the loosened nappy falls back down and he literally puts his foot in it.

If I manage to keep the nappy front up, then I gently but firmly move his feet back down onto the mat. Ever so eager to oblige, he then stretches his legs out straight and pulls them together. I counter by trying to jiggle his legs about to get him to relax them enough that I can wipe and get a nappy on. This then sends him flying back into the previous position of legs in the air and heading for his mouth. We usually have to repeat this a few times before we get there.

Dressing Little Old Man is no less tricky. In addition to his leg acrobatics, there are also his arms and hands to contend with. First there is getting the shirt over his head, which can involve him trying to gum the shirt, push at it with his fists or kick off my chest as I am leaning over him. Once I get past the head, I have to put his arms through the sleeves. A little tricky if he has grabbed the shirt from around his neck and shoved half of it in his mouth.

Once I've managed to dislodge the onesie from his mouth, he likes to flail his arms or legs about while I'm trying to do up the little press stud buttons. I focus intently on the buttons as the change table jolts around. Invariably, I come to the end of a row of these buttons and find one spare. Depending on my mood, I may undo all the buttons and start again or let him go through the day wearing misaligned buttons. A massive concession for an erstwhile perfectionist.

The creativity of Little Old Man's moves is incredible given that only weeks ago he lay there so placidly. I have been caught out many times while trying to learn how to work around his latest tricks. I've managed to put his swimmers on with one leg poking out an arm-hole and have given up completely on any clothing that has more than three buttons. It is basically now a case of throwing clothes at him until something sticks.

My little octopus may be a handful but at least I still manage to keep him kind of well-dressed. Actually, that's not always true. Ok, at least I manage to keep him dressed full stop!

Grizzly Bear

The teething continues. Some days he is unhappy no matter what position you put him in. I imagine he is grizzling from the low-grade pain of teeth pushing through his gums. The noise is constant and, although it is not quite crying, it is close enough to register in my brain as such and cause me to be on constant high alert. I've started to refer to him as Grizzly Bear but I hope this is one nickname that is temporary.

The teething has resulted in more daytime sleep and less play. This may sound like I have an easy task but getting him to sleep or eat requires truckloads of patience and some earplugs. At times it feels like he is another baby to the one I once knew. Gone is his usual bubbly smile and determination to roll and crawl. They have been replaced with sleepy indignation and a zero tolerance threshold.

The change has made me aware that, despite his age, Little Old Man has already developed quite a distinct personality. He can make his wishes and emotions clear through body language and differently pitched squeals. I know very well when he is happy, curious, bored, tired, wanting to be picked up, finds something funny, and is keen to hold an object. All these nuances have mostly been replaced by the interminable grizzling. I am lucky now to get a few smiles during the day, which is the hardest thing of all to deal with because I know this means he is unhappy.

Like all phases, I know this phase will also pass with a little patience from me and some pain relief for him. It has to. I want my Little Old Man back.

The Smiling Assassin

"I've already dealt with two today, no way!"

Little Old Man has just made an unearthly sound from his highchair. It was so loud it reverberated on the plastic seat below. He looks between us both and smiles one of his big gummy smiles. It's as if he knows what he has unleashed.

The Hubby looks at me in desperation. He knows I mean it. He has dodged the bullet twice today and I am in no mood for negotiation.

Resigned to his fate, The Hubby picks him up and heads over to the change mat. He sprays some pre-emptive lavender oil round to mask the impending stench. The only thing this trick of his has managed to do is make me associate the smell of lavender with baby poo.

"I wish we could buy that stuff they use on crime scenes, the one they use to cover the smell of week-old corpses."

"What? Chloroform?"

"Nooo, chloroform makes you faint."

"Oh you don't need any of that, just open the nappy and breathe in deep!"

I conveniently find an urgent reason to be in another room. There will be no mercy from me. Earlier in the day I had to leave a café urgently to deal with a borderline Number Three. With no parent room or horizontal bench in sight, I resorted to rolling out the change mat in the boot of the car. It was public and not pretty.

Little Old Man has become cleverer in sharing his bodily functions. The grosser it is, the cuter the face he pulls afterwards. It is a perverse correlation that makes me question if he has inherited my family's warped sense of humour. From sneaky side vomits to explosive Number Threes, he goo goos and gaa gaas his way through with unnerving cuteness.

I am sure one day we will look back at all these incidents and laugh. We already kind of laugh now even when we're dry-retching at the same time.

He is a smiling assassin, seemingly unaware of his actions but with a cheeky grin that belies his innocence. I don't particularly believe in God but someone must have been thinking when they designed a creature so helpless and demanding yet so utterly irresistible and cute at the same time.

The Hubby ties off the nappy bag, places Little Old Man on the floor and begins to breathe again.

"Your turn next!"

The Longest Night

I knew I had to but was avoiding it. There was always an excuse not to weigh myself. Wrong time of the month, too soon, too much water the day before, and the list went on. But then one Saturday morning I hopped out of the shower and decided it would be the day I found out the truth.

I hadn't known the truth for quite a while. After my first weigh-in at the obstetrician, I managed to avoid getting weighed again for the rest of the pregnancy. At the hospital they had to weigh me for the epidural and I told them I didn't want to know the result. I figured the day was going to be hard enough without having to be confronted with my own weight demons.

But those demons weren't going away with me simply ignoring them. I had created a vacuum by not knowing the total damage. In this vacuum those weight demons multiplied and hissed my worst fears back at me. I had to face them by stepping on those scales. And face them I did.

I gingerly hopped on the scales and breathed out, hoping in some faint desperation that the lack of air in my lungs might somehow help the final figure. It didn't. The number was scary. Far scarier than I had imagined.

Turns out, when it comes to post-pregnancy weight, the truth hurts. A lot.

How could I possibly weigh that much? Surely the number was a mistake? I hopped off and on again to confirm. The number was accurate alright. Not only that, it was close to the biggest number I've ever weighed in at.

I began to panic at the enormity of the task ahead and felt like such an idiot. How could I have let myself go like that? How did I not notice? What had I been thinking?

Now was not the time for recriminations though. I was on the way out the door with The Hubby and Little Old Man to go to a festival. I tried to shove the demons back and hold in my despair all day. It was a hard task. I smiled and walked around the festival, talking to people we knew and chatting with The Hubby. All the while a gnawing ball of anxiety ate away at my stomach and made me feel ill. How could this have happened? How? How?

By evening The Hubby had grown suspicious despite my best efforts to hide my panic.

"Is something wrong?"

"Nope…"

"Something is wrong. Is it something I said?"

Those demons wouldn't be held back anymore. I broke down and told him all – well, except for the actual number. No woman fesses that up to her husband!

"Well, what are we going to do?"

"I don't know."

"I think you do."

"Yeah, I do. I'm so sorry."

I kept apologising like I had no other word in my vocabulary. Sorry, sorry, sorry. And I was sorry. Sorry for putting myself in this mess. Sorry that I didn't pick up on my obstetrician's gentle suggestions that maybe it was a good idea to keep a track of my weight. Sorry that I used the pregnancy as a calorie free-for-all. Sorry that I blithely ignored that none of my pre-pregnancy pants went past my hips. Sorry I ate all those damn lactation cookies. Most of all, I was sorry for letting myself down in such a way.

Twelve years ago I had lost a big chunk of weight. When I say big chunk, I mean the kind of weight loss that companies like to advertise in magazines to spruik their product. The kind that other overweight people hear and dream one day it might be them. And, unlike the almost total majority of people who pile it back on in the first five years, I also managed to keep that weight off. Well, I did until pregnancy came along.

I thought about the girl I was before I lost the weight – socially awkward, shy, isolated, no boyfriend, no life, no perspective on the future, no nothing. And now she was back, or at least her frame was. The memory of her sadness draped around me once more. I had come so far and yet it felt I had ended up nowhere. I didn't want to be her again. No way, now how.

In my upset, I reached for the phone and for Sans in Perth. She has had her own fights with weight and I needed to hear her view.

"Meags I have been there, you know I have! Give yourself a break though, you've had a baby for Christ's sake. Giving birth is one of the hardest things you will ever ask of your body. It is a mess right now but you can get it back."

"I don't know if I can…the number is awful."

"It's a number. A number does not define you."

I wasn't convinced.

"Meags, listen to me. It is just a number. Think of it as a starting point."

"Yeah, I'll try."

Despite the upset, I knew she was right. It was just a number – albeit a terrifying number but a number all the same.

Losing weight had always been primarily for me about improving my health and longevity. I was beginning to realise though how much the number on the scales had also been about defining me. At the same time I lost my chunk of weight, I gained the confidence to get my life back. The two had become intertwined. I knew it was wrong but I could see now how I used my weight to judge my baseline value as a human being. Putting back that weight made me feel like my value had plummeted through the floor.

After I hung up from Sans, I knew I had to shift this perception just as much as I had to shift the weight. Happiness should be defined by so much more than a number.

I went to bed in the hope of sleeping away my upset. It wasn't to be. My mind raced with criticisms and disappointment. I couldn't switch it off. All the while, that sick feeling in the pit of my stomach churned along. I tossed and turned and tossed again. Nothing.

In total I slept an hour and another half hour towards daybreak. It was the longest night.

The Perfect Storm

In the middle of me hyperventilating about my weight, Little Old Man decided it was time to ramp up his night-time efforts. His cries broke the night and sent us running down the stairs several times. Gone was his much-appreciated routine of waking once a night for a feed. In its place, random sleep spurts. It felt like we had been thrown back into the newborn phase.

The Hubby and I struggled in our own ways with the situation. He found it hard to understand why the baby wouldn't stop crying despite having been fed, changed, given pain relief and lots of hugs. I found it hard to get myself back into a sleeping pattern after my sleepless night of worrying. It took me two hours to get to sleep and then, just then, Little Old Man would scream his way through the baby monitor and wake us.

To add to everything, he developed diarrhoea and was averaging about a dozen nappy changes a day. All the wiping quickly took their toll on his sensitive skin. His bottom was red raw and he yelled out in pain whenever we tried to gently dab away another mess.

As I took a bag of nappies out to the bin, I remembered my original promise to plant a few trees to neutralise the carbon footprint of having a baby. The number of trees to be planted had grown along the way to the size of a forest. Surely a few more trees would be added with all the nappies Little Old Man had gone through with his bout of diarrhoea.

I wondered whether there was a program somewhere where you could buy a tree planting for each bag of shitty nappies you threw in the bin. Kind of like those carbon neutral options you can opt into when buying a plane ticket, only this scheme would be for guilty parents.

My space for non-baby thoughts came to an end when I returned to the front door and heard screaming. I re-entered our little world of pain and closed the door behind me.

By the time Monday morning rolled around, it was clear that The Hubby would be unable to go to work and pretend to be a normal well-slept human. More than that, he was very much needed at home. There was no way I could have dealt with this on my own. We decided things had to settle down first before he started his work week.

It was only two days later that I felt ok enough to be at home with Little Old Man on my own. His crying fits and constant whining have shaken my confidence. I wondered if I was only a good mum when the going was good. In that moment, I second-guessed myself and folded under the pressure of sleep deprivation and stress. It was only with The Hubby's help that I was able to get some rest and perspective.

The situation reminded me that, for me at least, the true test of motherhood comes when I'm operating on three hours of sleep and have to keep my cool in the face of an inconsolable baby. In those moments, I have to remember to breathe and take time out when all I really feel like doing is punching a pillow or smashing a plate in anger and frustration. It sounds awful like that but it is probably only human.

The week inched on with us lurching between the extremes of his moods and sleeping. There were mild reprieves here and there but the storm doesn't feel anywhere close to easing. No teeth have emerged, despite my obsessive checking of his mouth. I know there is little to do but be patient and wait it out. Even the darkest clouds pass eventually.

Step One

There is a saying that the longest of journeys begin with the smallest step. I always found it kind of corny but annoyingly true.

With that thought in mind, I took the first and smallest step into the local branch of the weight loss company I had successfully used twelve years prior. I joined up, got the instruction pamphlets and weighed in. When I saw that number again, I tried to remind myself of what Sans had said. It was just a number, a starting point.

I took a seat among the other members for the weekly meeting. Looking around the room it was like a trip down memory lane – albeit a lane you would prefer to sidestep. I remembered how much I hated the meetings. The woman who ran them was holier-than-thou thin and had a patronising sing-songy voice that made me want to slap her silly. In a perverse way, having to listen to her pep talks every week did inspire me to lose the weight but only because I knew the longer it took, the more I'd have to listen to her.

A woman stood up to run the meeting and I braced myself for the onslaught of cheesey quotes. But they didn't come. Instead, she spoke of how she had fallen off the wagon in the last couple of weeks and how easy it was for her mind to think of excuses for doing so. She listened to those excuses until she realised her pants were feeling a bit tighter and she checked her weight. That was enough to refocus her. The candour was an unexpected relief.

She handed out cards and asked people to write down their most used excuse for not watching what they ate. I looked down at the card and remembered all the excuses I had used when pregnant. I thought hard about my present situation to see if any of those excuses still held. Nothing came to mind. It was then that I realised I had no excuse.

I handed back the card blank. It was time.

Change in View

When I first went along to my Mother's Group, there were only a narrow range of topics that people discussed. Week after week we circled around breastfeeding, formula feeding, nappies, contents of said nappies, sleep patterns and signs of development.

With a couple of the babies now nearing eight months, the topics have broadened considerably. Baby topics still feature – like crawling, teething, solids, weaning – yet other topics have also crept in. Some mothers have begun to talk of their impending return to work and others about what they used to do in their former lives pre-baby. There is also talk of return to part-time study and resuming hobbies given away.

One by one, it seems that each mother has slowly lifted her head up to see there is a life outside of the intense first few months of babyhood. For me, that first head lift was realising that I needed to get out more, followed by the more painful realisation that a weigh-in was well overdue. The idea of me returning to work, however, remains far off in the distance.

Even so, the increasing chatter about returning to work and childcare at the Mother's Group has bothered me. At first I couldn't work out why. If women feel ready to go back to work, good for them – I really have nothing against it. So why does it annoy me so much?

The more it gets talked about, the more I realise that my own far-off horizon of work is inching closer as the weeks go by. I still have another seven months of maternity leave but it doesn't really seem like six months since I had my last day at work. In some ways that time feels like aeons ago but in other ways it has flown by in a blur.

I guess I should be happy at the prospect of returning to work. I will get my wish of being part of society once more and enjoying my morning coffee while it is still hot. I could even go to the toilet without the action causing hysterical cries of abandonment. And yet, the idea of work leaves me a bit cold. The truth is I actually have grown to mostly like being at home with Little Old Man, even if it is sometimes painful and isolating.

Despite all the obstacles though, we have built our daily routine. And I now find the solace of being at home enjoyable as long as I get a couple of days out a week. But would I want to do this stay-at-home-mum gig full-time until he is in school? While I cherish this time, I must admit that I'm comforted by its finite nature. I am a mother and a wife first but not to the exclusion of all other aspects of myself.

So what is it then? What bugs me about returning to work?

While the idea of sipping coffee in peace sounds great, I also need to remember the less than ideal parts of my work. Ah yes, that's right. I have a couple of great colleagues but there are also those annoying ones plus the office politics and those interminably long meetings about nothing in particular. Then there is the work itself.

The career I have built up is ok but nothing I've ever really felt challenged by or like it was what I was put on earth to do. Work always felt more like something to pay the bills and fill in the time. I quickly grew impatient and agitated in different jobs but, thinking on it now, it was not because of the work. Rather, it was because I knew on some level that these jobs were taking time and energy away from what I really wanted and needed to do.

And what was that, exactly? If I ever stopped long enough to listen, my heart would always tell me the same thing. All I ever wanted to do was to write and connect with people through it. Now that I am actually squirreling out non-existent time from my day to at least fulfil the first part, I find it hard to conceive of giving that up.

Perhaps that is the underlying reason why I am uncomfortable with the prospect of work. It reminds me of my return to getting my thoughts caught up once more in the everyday.

Having a baby and the emergency surgery really sharpened my mind on what is important and what I would like to achieve in the short time afforded to me in this life. I have learnt painful yet ultimately invaluable life lessons along the way, ones that I fear losing sight of only to wake up in twenty years with no idea of what the hell I've been doing all this time.

The Hubby and I are fortunate and prudent enough to have been able to afford me being at home for so long. Yet money doesn't grow on trees, as my mother used to say. Short of winning the lottery, I will have to return to work eventually to help pay the bills. There is no solution to this other than to write while I have the space and use this time to the fullest with Little Old Man. He is, after all, the reason for this all.

Weaning Times

As if I wasn't facing enough challenges with my weight and teething, I also decided to throw weaning into the mix for good measure. I half figured I was upset anyway so what did it matter if one more thing was potentially on the list.

I know I wanted to reach six months and, ever the perfectionist, I was really focussed on reaching that mark. Yet, as usual, my body had other ideas. An old back injury was playing up and I knew I needed medication for it – medication that was a no-no with breastfeeding because it would pass through the milk.

The choice before me was to continue on to my goal with limited mobility or to wean early. I thought back to the benefit equation. Did the benefits of breastfeeding outweigh the deficits?

Looking at the situation logically, the answer was clearly no. As a full-time carer, I had to be able to move and function. Little Old Man wasn't going to lift himself out of the cot and change his own nappies. Moreover, I had to start thinking more of my own health. If I could barely move then exercise was not possible. This meant exercise couldn't aid my weight loss attempts.

I thought of the stop-gap solution of continuing to pump while taking the medication. There was no way though that I was going to pump and tip again. Spilt milk was too much to handle. Besides, I would need this medication for a couple of weeks until my back settled down. By that stage, I would have almost reached my goal in any case.

It was at that point of bargaining with myself that I realised the situation was ridiculous. Little Old Man had grown past the vulnerable early stages and so had my thinking. He was almost ready for solids and I was ready to move on to the next stage with him.

Without telling The Hubby, I started the medication for my back and began to wean. I didn't want to announce it with fanfare, only to find myself once more backtracking in tears. I took out an express, then another one the next day, and another – tipping out whatever was collected. I waited for the same sense of desperation and sadness that drove me back to expressing the first time round. It didn't come.

Instead, I felt relieved to be free of the pumping regime. There was some sadness but it was like I had already done the grieving the first time round. Now all that was left for me to do was to let go of that final physical part of me holding on. The remaining grief was manageable.

Once I knew the weaning was going to stick, I told The Hubby what I had been doing. He gave me a reassuring hug but by that stage I didn't really need it. I was confident that I had finally made the right call.

My back felt better than it had done in months and, without the direct reminder of expressing, I was beginning to see a way forward from the sense of failure that had dogged me.

Even if I didn't meet the self-set target of six months, I could see a path through which to hopefully see my efforts as more success than failure. I did all that I could to provide for Little Old Man with what my body allowed me. I am positive that in time I will come to see this as an achievement in itself.

Stillness

I know I have been in the house too long. I can feel the creep of isolation and sense that I am slowly drifting away from the world. I also know I've been couped up too long when a major excitement is discovering that The Hubby has bought a new brand of nappies.

When I'm at home for long stretches, the days become so similar that they seem to meld into one continuous stream. I wake early and have my breakfast before Little Old Man stirs. A couple of hours and bottles of formula later, we go for a long walk through the neighbourhood.

I trail through streets previously unexplored, like a suburban pioneer out to map the surrounds of my limited existence. When I return, the sun is sitting high above – I guess it is midday, I don't even bother wearing a watch anymore. The sun eventually sits over the back terrace, leading me to close the curtains in the living room so as to block out its heat. And there we stay, playing and resting in that artificial darkness until The Hubby comes home and the day can wind down into the night.

It sounds a bit lame when I write my days out like that. In a sense they are but in another way the stillness and predictability is comforting in light of recent illnesses and the weigh-in shocker.

I just want to hide under a rock until I lose all the baby weight. I'm so embarrassed by it all. I still can't believe I couldn't see how my figure had changed to accommodate such an extra load. How? How? Try as I might, I haven't been able to get past this question.

But at least I am beginning to focus on other things and block out any criticisms that pop into my head. The journey of weight loss I have embarked upon is going to be long and hard enough without me beating myself up every step of the way. I have to find a way to draw a line underneath what has happened and get on with reclaiming my health.

I don't think I'm the first mother to step on the scales post-baby and freak out at the number and I definitely won't be the last. It's no excuse but hormones, babies and sleepless nights do exact a price upon a woman's body. If I had my time over I would have watched my diet and weight like a hawk. Who knows, maybe even this wouldn't have made much of a difference. At least though I would have known what was happening and could have been prepared when the total price was tallied up neatly into one awful number.

While all this makes me feel like I want to continue in this hermit pattern, I know logically that it is not a good idea. As comfortable as it is, staying at home all the time makes it all too easy to start sliding down into a hole again. I have already noticed that slide starting to happen. What is scary this time though is that I don't particularly seem to mind. And I should mind. I really should.

Like it or not, it is time to go out again and be a part of the world.

Belly Up

Little Old Man has learnt how to roll over from back to tummy in his cot but is yet to master the trick of rolling back. He is also not yet used to sleeping on his belly either. This means that every time he lands on in his belly, he wakes himself up and screams for help. After a couple of weeks of teething, this new way of depriving us of sleep has not exactly been welcomed. Our old sleep routine has well and truly gone belly up, or belly down as is the case.

The first few times Little Old Man rolled over and woke himself, I came down to settle him. I stumbled through the living room in my usual 3 AM daze only to be awoken quickly by the sight of him unsettled and struggling on his belly. I had visions of every sudden infant death brochure and poster thrust my way since conceiving; *don't let them sleep on their belly, don't let them sleep them on their belly.* Argh, he's sleeping on his belly and I don't know for how long! I am a terrible, neglectful mother and my baby is going to die because of it!

Well, not quite. While the SIDS advice is to be taken seriously, they should also caveat the time in which it is dangerous for a baby to sleep on its belly. When the baby has learnt to roll over and chooses this position of their own accord, then it is not such an issue.

Unfortunately for me, I did not know this the first few nights I found him on his belly. I flicked him over onto his back and watched him roll right back on his belly and call out for help again. You would think if something upsets you, then you wouldn't do it. Babies though are a different breed. I have to remind myself that they have not quite worked out the cause and effect thing in their tiny baby-sized brains.

When flicking him over didn't work, I paced around trying to think up an alternative. It seemed wrong to go back to bed and leave him to struggle alone on his belly, grizzling the night away. What if he got to a point where he could no longer keep his head and face-planted? What if then he couldn't breathe and I was asleep upstairs blissfully unaware of the danger unfolding?

I flicked him onto his back once more and placed the palm of my hand over his belly while I tucked him in super tight. There's no way he could get out of there, I thought proudly to myself. And then he did – in less than one minute. I resigned myself to his new sleeping preference and let him stay on his belly. I patted and shh'ed him back to sleep.

I checked his airways to make sure they were clear and returned to tempting thoughts of my own bed. Yet the SIDS mantra ran through my head again. I couldn't leave him on his belly like that. I gently lifted him back onto his side, thinking this was at least better than nothing. He didn't seem to agree and promptly awoke screaming. I picked him up and we began the settling process all over again. Thirty minutes later, he was sound asleep on his belly once more. I returned to bed and spent the rest of the night straining to listen to any untoward noises through the baby monitor.

By dawn, I was tired and not looking forward to the day ahead of me. I was used to not sleeping but this wasn't something I was going to accept lying down, so to speak. I looked up the number for a sleep hotline (yes, it exists) and rang for advice. I ran through the issue and the woman on the other end said I had done exactly the right thing by settling him on his belly.

"But what about SIDS?"

"That is when they are younger. If he has strong enough neck muscles to hold his head up, then the risk is far less of him face-planting and being unable to move. Basically, this is a normal stage that babies go through. He has learnt how to roll one way, you just need to have the patience until he learns to roll back the other way."

I wasn't overly impressed by the free advice. Did she want to do a few night shifts at my house and then talk to me about patience?

"Well, what do I do about his grizzling and crying? He can't sleep if he's unhappy and if he can't sleep, then nobody can sleep."

"I understand it's tricky. You should also be trying to teach him to settle when on his belly. He has learnt how to do this on his back and now has to learn it again for his belly. When he is able to self-settle in the new position then he won't grizzle as much and can sleep."

Hmm. Sounded logical. Or at least logical enough to give it a shot. What other option did I have? Clearly Little Old Man wanted to be on his belly and no amount of flicking, tight blankets, bumpers or other restraints were going to work. He had a stubborn streak as strong, if not stronger at times, than his mother.

I realised then that we both had to learn how to be comfortable with his new sleeping position. And the only way we were going to get to that point was by starting with me being comfortable.

Sleep, Poo, Sleep

As if it was obvious enough by now, life has been dominated by sleep and poo since Little Old Man came along. At times these are the only two topics I can think of and talk about with The Hubby. The baby's poo, the baby's sleep, our sleep or lack thereof. These are the greater tides that wash over all our actions and ultimately influence how our days turn out.

I think of my life before I had a baby and laugh. Before him, I used to be an absolute baby myself about sleep. It was a precious time for me, one that could occasionally be interrupted by stress but mostly worked fine. The night was a welcome part of the day, a time to wind down and cuddle in bed with The Hubby before lights out. I would classify any night that I didn't sleep more than seven hours straight a bad night. If it was under five hours of sleep, I would call in sick the next day at work and snooze away. Ha! I used to do that, I really did!

Cut to now. If I get four hours straight, I'm having a good night. Three is pushing the boundaries of do-able but I know I will still be able to charge on through the next day. I learnt early on how to suck it up and get on with the day. Having a baby has taught me the outer limits of my tolerances in many areas with sleep being no exception. Sleep deprivation has become like an old war wound although it is not one worn entirely with pride. More like tired resignation.

As for poo, pre-baby it was a bodily function that I knew everyone did but never spoke of. Now though, it's an open topic. Our interest in talking about poo, however, does vary wildly depending on what is happening with Little Old Man. If he is fine, then a cursory acknowledgement is shared between The Hubby and I. Poo done for the day, it was green, let's all move on.

If his health is not so great, then the topic is discussed at great length. Nappies are divined like tea leaves, with different colours or textures used to predict future moods. Little deposits might mean some more crying to come until he works whatever out of his system. An explosion could indicate a happier and more relieved baby.

Thankfully, our newfound openness with talking poo does have its limits. We haven't devolved as functioning adults to the point that we also talk to each other about our own personal poo efforts for some comparative analysis. That is not to say I haven't been tempted.

Then there is Little Old Man, who seems far too comfortable with the concept. He still insists on staring at us while he shits in our lap, much like dogs do when you pass by them mid-business. The Hubby pointed out that he prefers to stare at the bookshelf than at us except for when he is about to do the deed. We just don't get it.

A few times he has done this during the last feed of the night. He has screamed and kicked his way through his last bottle before turning calmly to look me in the eye. Finally free of the pain and with a full belly, he has then promptly drifted off to sleep in my arms.

Even with the risk of a Number 3 increasing as the time passes, I can't help but watch him. I smile as his perfect pout makes sucking actions and I gently stroke his oversized hamster cheeks. Just one more minute and I'll change him, I keep saying to myself despite the growing stench.

At some point the smell fades into the background as I focus on this vision of peace and absolute contentment before me. I know in the years to come, it is this image rather than the smell that I will remember and cherish. In those moments, I realise this must really be love.

The Communist Bloc(k)

In politics there are many beliefs but I have learnt that they are all essentially underpinned by two types of people; realists and idealists. The realist will look at a situation and question what can be done with what is in front of them. The idealist will look at a situation and question what could be done if something was or wasn't in front of them. For my money, the perfect politician would be a schizophrenic able to swing between these two extremes in thinking.

In parenting, there is a similar divide between realists and idealists. Although I aspire to loftier ideals, I know my feet are firmly in the realist camp. The Hubby, on the other hand, is an idealist longing to have realist tendencies. Whenever he surrenders one of his ideals, he looks at me for a compliment on how flexible and reasonable he is. I do the same in reverse.

So far, our differences have had a positive effect on our parenting. When a dilemma arises, we vigorously discuss the merits of one solution over another. We spar off each other and end up with an agreed approach that has been rigorously thought out.

That said, our fundamentally different perspectives can also a pain. Take toys. Toys to me are for learning and having some fun – yes, even the noisy blinky ones. We were gifted a few such toys along the way and I accept them as an inevitable fixture in any parents' house, like the bag of impractical clothes or raspberry leaf tea gathering dust in the kitchen cupboard.

I don't mind letting Little Old Man have a couple of plastic toys but I wouldn't want my house overrun by them. I see the merit in letting a child explore at their own pace without a shrill toy overstimulating every sensory organ in their tiny bodies. On the other hand, I also think there must be some worth to these toys since they hold some inexplicable hypnotic draw over babies. They can't help but be mesmerised by the flashing lights and a woman with a hokey American accent singing about Old McDonald and his farm. Nobody said babies have taste.

In contrast to my position, The Hubby has essentially issued his own personal fatwa on plastic toys. In his perfect world scenario, our child would sit quietly on a play mat with his wooden blocks. Day in, day out, Little Old Man would play with those wooden blocks blissfully unaware that even kids in the former east probably had more awesome toy choices.

But The Hubby is not a Stalinist dictator in disguise. He has granted Little Old Man the right to drool over plastic chew rings, which somehow snuck their way into the toy box. But these do not blink nor do they make noise so their corrupting powers are limited. This makes them kind of ok. Annoying to his vision of our child bathed in the light of parental righteousness but ok.

Apart from the sneaky plastic, the one great exception to The Hubby's fatwa is his beloved Lego. He reasons that it is educational and entertaining enough to neutralise the plastic aspect. I find this hypocritical. Either you ban plastic on idealistic grounds or you don't.

There appears to be no end in sight to the debate in our house over toys. I doubt we will ever reach a perfect agreement on what our child can and can't play with. The tricky part will come when we both have to bend towards the middle and provide an agreed united front. There is no point having different rules for different parents. I remember learning pretty young how to sniff out the weak points between my own parents and use them to my advantage.

It would be stupid to think I can put aside the debate comfortably for another while yet. Little Old Man is already sizing us up, of that I am sure. Even at his tender age I can see his mind ticking over as he works out what toys and games each parent play with him. One day, perhaps sooner than we realise, he will turn the discord to his favour and have us scurrying for cover. And let's face it; I will be the weakest link.

Little Old Man already knows that with me he can play on the magical illuminated square after I recently downloaded a baby app on my tablet computer. I must admit it did feel slightly wrong doing this so soon. I thought the debate over screen time would come much later yet this changed when he pawed excitedly at my tablet whenever I turned it on.

In a nod to idealism, I have set a limit of five minutes a day on baby apps. I have also justified its use in my mind by figuring some exposure to technology can't be a wholly bad thing. Maybe it might even give him an edge in an increasingly wired world. Although I suspect other parents also use the same justification while their children hijack their smart phones and accidently change the language setting to Korean.*

I can't imagine what The Hubby really thinks of this latest development in our toy debate. At present he seems to be biting his tongue in an attempt to appear like a realist. So as not to incite him out of the silent truce, I make our five minute play time during the day when he is at work.

The worst part is, the app blinks and makes noises – for shame! And you know what? I bet every kid in communist Russia would have given their last wooden block for just one go.

* This has already happened to me, twice. Hours of entertainment trying to navigate the settings by memory back to English have ensued.

Ships in the Night

"I've missed you."

"I've missed you too."

The Hubby and I are standing in our bedroom. He is behind me with his arms wrapped around my waist. We linger for a moment, enjoying the feeling of being together.

I remember back to The Hubby's attempts to make us eat a meal together at the table. I must admit that it ultimately proved to be a smart move on his part (even though I'd never admit that to him!). Our dinners are one of the few communal moments we have as a family.

You would think if two adults live in the same house, there would be very little to miss. But while we inhabit the same space, we still operate in different time zones. The continued sleeping difficulties of Little Old Man have locked us into tag-teaming to ensure a chance of some sleep for both of us. My ability to use those chances has been limited by biting insomnia, which doesn't seem to let go. It seems months of interrupted sleep have taken their toll on my body clock. I wake at random hours, alert and ready to go.

When I do manage to get to sleep, The Hubby sometimes takes an extra shift so I can function the next day. When he returns from work, he trudges up the stairs for a rest so he can do it all again. We both know this situation is only temporary. Neither one of us, especially him, can continue on like this. The teething, the belly sleeping dramas and my insomnia have to leave us at some point. This is not sustainable.

Feeding Time at the Zoo

Little Old Man has started on solids. When I first thought of him eating, I imagined he would be enjoying a miniature plate of lamb chops, mash and peas. Well, maybe not that extreme but I did imagine that solids meant food that somehow resembled what I recognise as food.

Instead, he is eating rice cereal – a sticky paste with no discernible flavour. It looks like the contents of the pots of glue that used to sit in the middle of classroom tables at school. All I remember of those pots was the weird kid who couldn't resist sticking his fist into them and licking the slop off when the teacher wasn't looking. Perhaps he was just reliving babyhood.

Despite its bland neutrality, Little Old Man has been slow to warm to the idea of rice cereal. He pulls faces and juts his bottom lip out in disgust at the abomination in his mouth. I can hardly blame him, it does look unappetising. But I say that as someone who has tried real solids.

Just like the pots of glue, I have discovered that rice cereal has an incredible sticking power once dried. When Little Old Man attempts to feed himself, the spoon invariably flies through the kitchen or gets whacked against his tiny head. I later find crusty spots of beige on my tiles, cupboards, fridge, and microwave as well as on his ears, eyebrows, arms and tangled in his fine hair. I once found it on his neck and ran to Dr Google fearing it was some kind of flaking skin disorder until I worked out it rubbed off with effort.

Out of mild boredom on my part, I tried to introduce other flavour sensations into his diet. We have given carrot, banana and avocado a go but to no avail. He was particularly averse to avocado, which is strange since it is so bland and apparently closest in taste to breast milk. I spooned some of the mashed green goo onto his top gums and he pulled a face like I had shoved cat poo in his mouth. Actually, he probably would have preferred cat poo. At any rate, his tongue thrust forward and his hands collected the avocado just in time to flick it across the room. I tried a few more times till the white tiles resembled abstract art and gave up.

So we are back at rice cereal. I will try again with some fruit or vegetable but will bide my time until he is more confident with the idea of eating. While it only looks to me like slop, I know it is a big step up from formula and has the potential to fill him up enough to stop some of the night feeds.

Mutual Appreciation Society

When I am out and about with Little Old Man, I often notice I am the recipient of sideway glances or people turning their heads back as we pass by. Sometimes these looks are accompanied by a comment about how beautiful or peaceful he is. Mostly though there are just smiles accompanied by the occasional knowing nod.

I have grown used to being the object of attention even though I used to fly happily under the radar. A baby is a positive thing, everyone wants a piece of the action. It's just human nature.

I have come to believe that the looks I receive are looks of longing and daydreaming. They are not about me as a person but rather what I represent – a young mother carrying a healthy baby brimming with life and promise.

The majority of these looks come from two types of people: pregnant women or women with older children. To the pregnant women, I imagine they are looking at me as someone who has crossed the finish line and flourished. One day they will be me with a bit of luck, pain and endurance. All their anxieties around the birth will be replaced with carefree strolls down the street. Little do they know the effort it sometimes takes to put on a respectable front in public.

To the women with older children, I think I remind them of those days where life was more innocent. They look back through heavily tinted rose-coloured glasses to a time when they too pushed around their cooing baby. Perhaps they think of it as a time when they were their child's world rather than a source of perpetual annoyance and boundary setting. If they stop to remember the hard work involved to get to the insolent teenager stage, then I figure that is when I get thrown the knowing nod.

Yet what I wish I could say to these women is that I give sideway glances too. I remember being pregnant and looking at other women with babies, hoping that I'd make the transition as smoothly. And now that I am that woman, I find myself looking at pregnant women and imagining their life of nervous anticipation. There was something magical in the not knowing and the desire to hold your baby and study their face for the first time.

Likewise, I look at women with older children and think that they really have made it. For while a pregnant woman might look at me and think I've crossed the finish line, I can see that I've actually just crossed the starting line. The path from baby to adulthood is very long and pot-holed.

Mostly though, I find myself looking at pregnant women and asking whether I could ever do it all over again. Could I be in those shoes once more? I'm still not sure on whether I have it in me to create and nurture another life. I like to think so but then I have a rough day with Little Old Man and can't imagine ever going through it all again.

And then I find myself giving sideways glances to a newborn and their mother. My heart aches with the memory of the intense love in those first couple of months. I look down at my own baby and see him smiling in his proper pram chair, having graduated from his bassinet.

I remember being told in the early days that the hours pass slowly but the years go by so very quickly. I see time starting to quicken and, in that moment, feel I could do it all a thousand times over again.

The Littlest Mutual Appreciation Society

Before I had Little Old Man, I had no idea how much children love to see babies. Now that I cart around a baby all day, I am very aware of how the sight of a baby is enough to send even the most laid-back toddler into a fit of excitement.

"Baby! Baby! Look Mum, a baby!"

I can't help but smile whenever I hear these exclamations when we're in public. For the toddler, it's like they have seen one of the Seven Wonders. Perhaps they have. Babies are incredibly wondrous beings when I pause long enough to pull my exhausted head out of the nappy trenches.

But why are toddlers so universally excited by babies? Like adults, no two toddlers seem the same. Some like cars while others are more interested in butterflies or collecting snot on the back of their car seat. Yet they all, without fail, love babies. The only thing I can put this universal interest down to is the recognition that there is someone on this earth smaller than them.

For their part, toddlers are perceived as similarly fascinating creatures by babies. Little Old Man could look at things with only fleeting interest. Yet put a toddler in the same room and he is a captive audience. Get that same toddler to talk and he will laugh at every syllable.

The only reason I can surmise for this is that babies can see toddlers don't yet belong to the larger people that rule their lives. They aren't babies yet they aren't adult-sized either. There seems to be an instinctive mutual fascination with the special in-between place they inhabit.

Whatever the cause, it is beautiful to see each side look at the other in awe. It is one of my favourite unexpected pleasures since becoming a mother, particularly since I had no idea before.

Teeth, Teeth, my Kingdom for Some Teeth!

"Hey guess what, my baby woke up this morning and had teeth!"

"Oh wow! That's great! Did he have any teething beforehand?"

"A little bit over the last couple of days but that's it really."

I bite my lip. I am genuinely happy for my friend. And no teething beforehand? Half her luck. I wouldn't wish teething on my worst enemy, let alone a friend. But the ease of her child's teething really rubs my own frustrations in.

It has been a month since teething entered our lives. I'm beginning to doubt he is teething. Perhaps it's just some developmental phase he is going through. Whatever it is, Little Old Man continues to moan and occasionally scream the house down in pain. He bats at his mouth and chews at anything he can reach. As much as I try to avoid the analogy, he really reminds me of a teething puppy. Thankfully though my shoes have not being a target of his overzealous gumming.

I keep waiting but his old sleep pattern hasn't returned and, in my darkest moments, I think that it never will. Maybe the time when he woke once a night was just a blip – a golden age we will look back on fondly as the years pass by in a sleep-deprived blur.

No, things surely have to get better. This cannot last. I consult my *Baby Bible*. I have flipped through it in times of crises and have found it informative on some issues yet dubious on others. Like when it advised me to have a cup of tea to relax when the baby wouldn't attach. A. Cup. Of Fucking. Tea. At the time I would have needed a shot of tranquiliser to relax and come down from my stress high.

I flick through the book to see what it has to say about teething. Use the gum gel – tried that, made him scream louder. Use a teething ring or refrigerated wet rags – yep, used those but with limited interest. Pain relief – oh yeah, thank God for pain relief. Lots of hugs – ditto. And finally, patience – patience?? The Good Book is offering me patience?! Some babies teethe on and off for months before anything happens.

It goes on to say that teething can be a testing time for some parents. Hmm, true. And many parents find it a joyous moment when they discover the first two white stumps in their baby's mouth because it marks a significant milestone in their young life. Yes, I can well imagine. Yet my joy would have little to do with the milestone bit since I am quite fond of a gummy smile. No, after a month of this hell, I will surely be cracking out the champagne at the sight of teeth.

I have been told by some sympathetic Mums that the first teeth are the hardest. Here's hoping that, for once, the old wives tales prove true.

Olympic Performance

If I'm out and about with Little Old Man, my parenting skills are guaranteed to be tested. When he starts up, I feel the glare of onlookers and imagine what they are thinking as I move to react. Will I rise to meet the challenges and discreetly move through life with a baby? Or will I have to deal with death stares from members of the public as my beloved son throws a wobbly?

Some places are more forgiving than others. If I'm in a café with other parents, the tolerance levels are higher and the vibe more relaxed. In those situations, Little Old Man and I usually fade into the background as screaming toddlers take centre stage. I sigh in relief that he can't possibly match their pitch and decibel. Then I remember not to get too smug because such joys are yet to come for me. While his alternate nickname of Buddha Baby may bode well for the future, I am all too aware that even the most serene toddlers can have the occasional shit hair day.

In trickier settings, such as restaurants or our experimental family outing to an art exhibition, The Hubby and I have been ultra-considerate to the needs of others. If Little Old Man so much as whines once, then one of us takes him for a walk till he returns to Buddha Baby mode. This has worked well for us and we haven't felt stressed when the situation occurs.

The real test comes, however, when we've been somewhere we can't easily walk out of.

Maybe it is just me (ok, it is just me) but sometimes I like to imagine that I am being assessed by those Olympic judges that sit beside the diving pool. The ones that hold up white cards with their scores for degree of difficulty and performance. I like to imagine their presence when I've done a good job in a tricky situation. I guess it's an elaborate form of patting myself on the back for a job well done.

When I have found myself in an inescapable situation, I imagine the degree of difficulty scores skyrocket. The judges hush and watch on keenly as I go for gold.

Today I gave a gold medal Olympic performance. Little Old Man and I had drawn the short straw of taking the car for a service. The last time the car was serviced I also drew the short straw, which has me wondering if this is a pattern. In any case, the last time I was heavily pregnant and couldn't move beyond some awkward chairs in the showroom. I beached myself there for two hours watching the same morning news repeat itself over at half-hour intervals.

To avoid a repeat of boredom, I packed the nappy bag full of formula and toys. I knew there was a café about a twenty minute walk from the car yard. What's more, it was always empty since they do terrible coffee – a small price to pay for a relaxed atmosphere.

My perfect plan, however, was dashed by the overnight arrival of rain. I checked the car in for its service and took a seat in the waiting area. The television was gone, replaced by a vending machine that hummed along almost as monotonously in the background. I looked at the other people stuck there waiting and then out the window. There was no way the rain was going to clear up enough for us to go for a walk. I would have to wait it out again.

At first Little Old Man was amiable. He bounced frenetically up and down on my lap while staring at some fine print on the wall behind me. Perhaps he would become a lawyer, I thought to myself. When he got bored of this routine, he began to twist and contort his body against mine. He managed to turn to the other side and reach out towards some brochures. I picked one up and he started to scrunch the pages up. A sales employee walked by and gave me a disapproving stare. I gently wrested the brochure from his grasp and neatly patted it back into form on the table.

Bereft of his brochure, Little Old Man then cranked it up a couple of notches and began to squeal in protest. The noise reverberated off the tiled floor and up into the high ceilings of the show room. His voice travelled around the room like an audible ping-pong ball.

In an effort to calm him down, I bounced him back on my lap but it was no use. Figuring he might be hungry, I popped a bottle in his mouth and he started sucking vigorously. Phew, maybe that was the problem. He gulped the bottle down and gave a small interval in noise before returning to his squealing. Damn.

I got up and walked around with him, ohh'ing and ahh'ing at the new display cars like a ham actor. I put his face up close to a tinted window, hoping his own reflection might distract him. If it did, the effect was only temporary.

Then I had a horrible thought. Maybe he was squealing because he was working on something. I looked at the clock on the wall. Oh dear, he was overdue for his morning poo. I looked down at him squirming in my arms and, as if he read my mind, he returned my gaze and became still.

In the noticeable silence created by the absence of his squealing, he squinted his eyes. Oh God, it was coming. I knew it. And then it happened – one of the loudest poo-farts I had ever heard from him. The noise was underscored by more silence. If the moment wasn't so awkward, I might have marvelled at his genius use of comic timing.

The hand cradling him felt warm and I prayed that it was not a Number Three. Please no, I couldn't handle a Number Three with an audience of onlookers and no change table in sight. Such horrors should be confined to the home. There has to be some Geneva Convention for parents stipulating this.

I stood still, thinking fast on my next move. Luckily, a salesman appeared to inform me my car had been serviced and was ready. I grabbed my nappy bag and pram and headed to the door without looking up once at my audience.

Outside the rain was still coming down. With one hand, I flung open the boot and put down his change mat on the flat surface. I placed him gently down on it and huddled over to avoid the rain getting on him. My back soaked through, making me keen to work even faster. I took a deep breath and opened the nappy to begin decontamination. It was a doozy. Not the Number Three I feared but generous in proportion and smell.

Job done, I safely pack Little Old Man away into his capsule and fold the soaked pram into the boot. As I drove away, I imagined those judges holding up scores of 9.5 for difficulty and performance. They were impressed and one even gave me a standing ovation.

I could have nabbed an extra half point if my car wasn't ready with such perfect timing. If that hadn't happened, I would have been forced to get creative by testing out the boot of a display car. Maybe the salesman had sensed that too.

Priorities

Some days the baby gods smile upon me and Little Old Man takes the unusual step of having an extended siesta. When it becomes clear that he has no intention of waking, I start to imagine what I could do with all the free time opening up before me. It is a dangerous line of thought, one that could jinx me in five seconds flat.

Yet I accept the possibility of extended sleep and prioritise what needs to get done in order of importance. I then set about doing these tasks in the set order, hoping to get through each one in time before Little Old Man wakes up.

High on my list is going to the toilet, showering and eating lunch, all of which sometimes go on hold depending on how demanding he has been that day. Then I focus on cleaning up a bit around the house before The Hubby gets home. Maybe I give us a head start into the evening by unpacking the dishwasher or doing the washing. I don't go too nuts on this priority though. I have little patience for housework. Near enough is good enough in my view – a rather different view from my neat German husband.

After the token clean-up, I move on to the computer and check the headlines to ensure I am aware if something major has happened in the world. I also check my favourite trashy gossip website for similar reasons although the term 'major news' is highly relative there. Then I might write a bit and, if he is still sleeping, play a few rounds of online scrabble. And then, only then, might I think of perhaps laying on the couch and trying to have a nap myself.

It is a bad habit but I always put my own rest way down on the list of priorities. I know I need to be able to function but the small windows of opportunity to get non-baby things done are so very tempting. They make me feel human.

The nap times remind me of when I was sitting tests as a student and I could see the clock ticking down. My handwriting would turn into a scrawl as I furiously tried to write down every last point I could possibly think of. When a teacher said, "Finish your last sentence" I went into overdrive and stretched the time out as much as possible until they said, "Pens down" and glared at me.

If I try to rest regardless of my urge to do things, then I usually end up tossing around on the couch feeling stressed about all the things I could be doing instead. I have tried to stop feeling this way, particularly on days where I haven't slept well the night before.

My gold standard for whether I need to make rest the top priority is the question: if he woke up right now, how would I feel? Would I be ready to go for another couple of hours or would I feel annoyed and tired?

If it's the latter, then I need to put down whatever it is that I think is so urgent and focus on resting. Even if I can't sleep, I know how helpful it is to close my eyes. As with the multitasking, I have found it hard at times to just slow it down and only do what is necessary – like breathe at a normal pace. If the kitchen isn't cleaned or I have to wait for another day to write then that is the way it goes. The perfectionist in me must stand down.

With that in mind, Little Old Man is presently fast asleep in his cot and I am going to join him in an afternoon nap.

Same Same but Different

When Little Old Man was a newborn, we were paranoid about hygiene. We went out of our way to ensure his formula was made exactly to instruction, at the right temperature and served in sterilised bottles. I do remember wondering why the water needed to be boiled given that we live in a country with fresh drinking water on tap. Yet I boiled away diligently for months.

Fast forward half a year and The Hubby is standing in the kitchen reading the fine print on the back of the formula tin. I watch him in half amusement. I don't ask why he would do something so pedantic as to read font size 2 printed on corrugated tin. In another lifetime he could have been a lawyer or an auditor.

"Hey, did you know we weren't just meant to boil the water but boil it for five minutes?"

"Huh?"

"Yeah, says right here on the tin."

I launch across the couch and grab the tin from his hands.

"Bullshit. Where?"

"There…!"

He is right. There in impossibly small print in a pale font colour it says: *"Tap water must be boiled for five minutes and cooled prior to use with formula."*

"Argh, we've been doing it wrong all this time!"

"And he's still alive, see? Nothing to worry about! You know, I don't think we need to fuss so much about sterilisation anymore. The other day I caught him licking one of the pram wheels and look at him – absolutely fine!"

I shoot The Hubby a look. Licking a pram wheel? Really? Not on my watch, buddy.

Surely he can't be so casual about the mistake or the licking for that matter. He is an absolute pedant for following instructions. In his whole life, I doubt he has ever jay-walked on an empty street or put together a piece of furniture without reading the instructions.

It was then I realised how much parenting has changed him. While he still maintains his Germanic love for order and punctuality, he has learnt to relax quite a bit along the way. Being ten minutes late is ok now if the trade-off is that we arrive with a well-fed and clean baby. His previous insistence on having exclusive packing rights over the dishwasher has also fallen by the wayside. It doesn't matter anymore if it is packed perfectly to take the maximum load. As long as we have something clean to eat off then it's all good. He is even learning to live with crumbs and toys strewn all over the house. Slowly but surely.

The Hubby is not alone on loosening his grip on previous obsessive quirks. Becoming a mum has obviously changed my life and outlook massively yet only in the quieter moments do I realise the many almost imperceptible ways it has changed me too. As much as I love to pick on The Hubby, I know I have been just as guilty of the same level of fastidiousness on certain points.

Pre-baby, both my handbag and wallet were impeccably neat. I used to order money in my wallet by colour and paid exclusively in coins when the purse was more than three centimetres thick. Otherwise, you see, the overall aesthetic of the wallet would be ruined. I also neatly ordered lip balm, lipstick, gloss, hand moisturiser, cuticle cream by ascending size in the side pocket.

Yes, it's all sadly true but I loved the order in my handbag. No matter how stressful my day was at work, I knew I could reach into it without looking and find exactly what I needed. It was a portable oasis of order.

And now?

Now I barely use a handbag. It is merely a junkyard filled with months of receipts and scraps of paper that I never get around to cleaning out. The previous neatness of my twice-daily beauty regime lies untouched at the bottom somewhere.

On those rare occasions that I do go somewhere without Little Old Man, I usually end up toting the nappy bag anyways. Transferring my wallet, keys and mobile seems like too much of a hassle. Besides, the two bags probably weigh the same when the accumulation of crap in my handbag is taken into account.

Underlying all this is the truth that I can't be bothered anymore. I have given up on my love of neatness wrapped in soft leather. Perhaps it will come back to me but right now I am strangely ok with battling to find my keys or phone in the black hole that is the nappy bag. It is just the way it goes. Life has changed and so have I.

Accumulation

Speaking of changes, our house used to be stylish and understated. We had what we needed as a couple plus a few personal knick-knacks and a wall-length bookshelf filled to the brim with snooty literature and old uni books. When Little Old Man was still just a thought on the drawing board of life, I considered our home cosy but not crammed. We comfortably filled our living space.

Now our home is like our other previous neatness obsessions. The style guide has fallen by the wayside. The muted earth tones of our living room have been overpowered by a garishly loud bouncy jumper that was a gift (read: I would never have brought such an aesthetic abomination myself). Because of our now crammed quarters, the bouncy jumper sits awkwardly in the way of everything and, despite its size and colour, is virtually impossible not to trip over.

Underneath the bouncer is a quilt from my mother that had previously been shoved at the back of a cupboard, deemed out of whack with the rest of our interior decorating. But it gained a life when the carpet proved too rough on Little Old Man's skin as he attempted to roll and hone his crawling techniques.

To top off the mismatched explosion in colour, the quilt is covered with toys (not all wooden!), baby books and multi-coloured face towels.

Against one wall is his cot, change table, clothes drawer and our computer desk. The change table is overflowing with spare nappies, formula and every other baby accoutrement possible. If an outsider looked at our change table, they would conclude we live on the tundra of Outer Mongolia and have to stock up for the harsh winters. In reality, we live five minutes from the supermarket. Better safe than sorry though, I suppose.

On the other side is our bookshelf, a point of continual obsession for Little Old Man. I am convinced that he is eyeing it off for destruction when he finally masters the art of crawling and eventually walking. I can see when he stares at it exactly how his mind is ticking over various methods for pulling it apart, book by book, before finishing the job off with copious amounts of drool and vomit. There is German precision in those eyes and sometimes, like when he looks at that bookshelf, it scares me.

But when the time comes he will be lucky to even reach our bookshelf. Shoved right in front of it is our couch, which is as far back as possible in the room to allow maximum play space. The fish have also been moved to the kitchen for the same reason. Lucky for them, this has also meant that we tend to see them more and therefore remember to feed them on an almost daily basis now. There is even talk of replacing the cannibalised fish lost during the early days. We almost feel redeemed as fish parents.

At the other extreme, the rooms upstairs are mostly filled with boxes and piles of ironing. Our living space is downstairs and we only use upstairs to sleep and store stuff until it is needed downstairs. This means our contents are not evenly distributed throughout the house, making it both crammed and empty at the same time.

When Little Old Man was about six weeks old, The Hubby and I got into some weird nesting phase where we were suddenly obsessed with buying a house. Because looking after a newborn is a perfect time to go house hunting, finance a mortgage, exchange deeds and move. We went out a few weekends to look at properties before realising the lunacy of our ways.

Yet the desire for a more permanent housing solution remains. There is an accumulation of things that goes along with having a baby and this can't be avoided, even if you are ultra-efficient at selling or storing the things you don't need anymore. The end effect is the sense that we are outgrowing our home just as quickly as Little Old Man outgrows his clothes.

Butter Up

I don't go on diets – I go on weight-loss regimes. I like to call them regimes because it reminds me of a dictatorship. The cruel tyranny of calorie counting and denial need to be called out for what they are. When I am on a weight-loss regime, food loses all spontaneity and mindless enjoyment. Instead, every last morsel is planned and monitored with military precision. Food becomes serious.

For all my sacrifice, I demand a high performance result from my body. I expect a loss each week of between 500 grams and 1.5 kilos. In reality I am lucky to minus 500 grams off and, barring perhaps a bad dose of gastro, I never get anywhere near the upper loss ideal.

Over the weeks, this makes me impatient. Then I calculate how long it will take me to get to goal weight based on previous losses and get disheartened. If I combine this with a loss plateau, this usually is enough to make me quit altogether.

In the past, my impatience and desperation has seen me running towards the less sustainable end of the spectrum, where diets are advertised based on my desperate thoughts. 'Lose weight now!' 'Melt those kilos!' 'Lose a dress size a week!'.

These sorts of diets are really weight-loss regimes in the true dictatorship sense of the word. I once lost 5 kilos in three weeks eating only 800 calories a day. I also ended up stopping the diet because I got viral infection that led to tonsillitis and two middle ear infections. I was so sick I couldn't work for weeks. The diet had run me down to the point of being vulnerable to illness.

This time, I was determined not to repeat such past performances despite my desperation. If it was to be done, then it was to be done properly. I don't have the luxury of being able to throw away my health or energy for rapid weight loss. It's hard enough to look after a baby with sustained sleep deprivation, let alone adding starvation to the mix.

The only problem is that I haven't learnt the patience needed for sensible weight loss. I found myself falling into the frustration trap again. Since starting my latest regime, I have been averaging the perfectly acceptable loss of 500 grams per week. Except for tracking my food intake and the occasional denial, I don't really feel that deprived. And the exercise is something I am doing in any case. I walk about an hour a day with the pram in the hope of calming Little Old Man and myself down after a few rounds of screaming.

So I should be happy with the results from minimal changes in my lifestyle but I haven't been. I keep focussing on the bigger goal number than the smaller numbers that bringer me closer to it.

Instead of getting locked into my old patience problem though, I set about devising an alternate way of viewing it. What if I could get around measuring my success with the almighty number?

With that in mind, I copied and pasted a picture of a block of butter four times in a line. I made six of these lines on a page, printed it out and stuck it on the fridge. A block of butter is 250 grams so each line represents a kilo.

I looked at the page and crossed out the weight I have lost so far. This translated to ten blocks of butter. That's a lot of butter off my backside! The result is that I am pleased, far more so than thinking that I had lost 'only' 2.5 kilos.

The Last Straw

I just yelled at The Hubby. Not a snap or a snide comment. A yell. And he yelled back.

We don't do yelling, it's not our style. We prefer to discuss an issue at length since we're very adult. When that doesn't work, we stomp around in moody silence like children until one of us offers a way out. In our ten years together, we have never yelled at each other once. Until now.

The tension has been building in me all day. Little Old Man is still teething. It feels like the longest, most drawn out teething in the history of mankind. Every afternoon he works himself up into constant half-crying. I put gel on his gums, rock him, attempt to distract him with the bouncer or tummy time but all to no avail. Given this has dragged on for almost two months, I use pain relief only when absolutely necessary. I don't want to drug him up on pain relief and have him end up in baby rehab.

The result is a baby where nothing works to calm him down. The closest to calm is sitting on my lap, which stops the constant half-crying yet results in him thinking it is time to play jumping castles on me. Trying to contain nearly eight kilos of wriggling and kicking baby is an intense physical workout that literally leaves me bruised. After about half an hour of this, we're both a bit over it. I put him back in his cot to hopefully have a nap since he has expended so much energy.

All I want to do at that point is lay on the couch and stare at the ceiling in silence. But then the screaming starts. He is indignant that I have put him in the cot and sets about telling me so. He worms his way up to the end and starts butting his head against the board, sending him into even more desperate screaming. I pick him up, try to calm him and then place him back in his cot for another go. No luck.

By this stage I am pretty worked up myself. It is so disheartening to try everything to soothe my baby and fail miserably. What's worse, I know it will happen every single day. It starts every afternoon at around 2 PM and goes until he finally fills himself with formula and crashes in exhaustion at 9 PM. It is crushing to have to deal with this day in and day out with no end in sight.

And that's where The Hubby comes in. He has been working back a bit and I have been left holding the baby for an extra hour. An hour doesn't seem like much but it is an awful lot at the end of a day of child care when we're both really tired. The edge I operate on at that time is fine. An hour can be the difference between mild irritation and complete meltdown.

By the time The Hubby arrived home today, I had tripped over into the meltdown category. He walked in and picked up Little Old Man from the cot. He was crying inconsolably and I get a look from both of them like I have been neglectful in my duties. Or at least that is how I interpret it.

With a new audience to hear his woes, Little Old Man increases the volume and urgency of his screaming. The ball of frustration in my stomach begins to rise. I can't handle the sound any longer. I have to get out.

But I'm also aware that I'm hungry. I can't just go upstairs and close the door because there is no food up there. I will have to sort my dinner out. I go into the kitchen and get an attack of the guilts for putting myself first. I head over to the formula tin and start making up a fresh bottle just in case the screaming is because of hunger. It shouldn't be, he fed an hour ago. But it's worth a shot.

The Hubby follows me into the kitchen. He can't see what I'm doing on the bench and asks me to make some formula up. I sigh and say I'm right on it but he doesn't hear me over the screaming. That's when I crack it.

"I AM MAKING THE FORMULA NOW!!!!"

"OK, JESUS! SORRY!"

He retreats quickly out of the kitchen and into the garden. The change of scenery momentarily distracts Little Old Man from his crying. Every fibre in my being is bristling with anger. Why the hell did he bring the baby into the kitchen when he knew that I was a spent force? There was a reason I walked out of the living room and into the kitchen. Yet he thinks it wise to follow and stand right behind me with Little Old Man inches away from my ear?

I have the instant urge to apologise to make things right but I also don't really feel like I would mean it, so I say nothing. I put the formula on the bench and make a sandwich to quieten my hunger.

"I'm going for a walk with the baby."

"Good."

"Do you want me to lock you in?"

"Yeah, doesn't matter. I'm going upstairs anyway."

And really, truth is, it doesn't matter if he locks me in when he goes out. I already feel trapped in this daily cycle of teething hell. A locked door is neither here nor there.

I suppose I will calm down eventually and feel like saying sorry and mean it. But I know myself well enough that I will be inclined to sulk first even though I know it is unfair. Apart from the tactical error of coming home late a few days in a row and following me into the kitchen, The Hubby hasn't done much wrong. It's not his fault that our baby turns into a screaming teeth banshee every afternoon like clockwork. It's not Little Old Man's fault either. It's nobody's fault.

I try to remain upbeat but this is grinding me down. If someone could tell me that he would have his blessed teeth by next Tuesday then I would be able to handle it a lot better. But the endless waiting and tantrums is too much at times.

The Unspeakable

I phone a friend the next day for some sympathy. Instead, I am invited into her world of pain. I don't particularly mind though because it is a relief to not have to think on my own lot in life. Plus her lot sounds worse and I find it weirdly inspirational that she seems to take it all in her stride. If she can endure all that she has and still be sane, I figure, then I can definitely get through Little Old Man's teething antics.

Her baby is six weeks younger than mine and has been a handful since the day he was born. He still wakes up hourly between midnight and 6 AM for a feed. She sneaks in sleep between 7:30 PM and midnight then again when he goes down for an hour nap here or there during the day. This has been going on for six months.

I have no idea how she is still standing, let alone able to string sentences together. When she worries about the impending teething, I tell her she could be lucky and her baby might grow teeth overnight. I have heard that happening to a few babies now. Not many but a few. Perhaps the baby gods will show some mercy since she has had such a rough start.

"Oh no, the baby gods hate me."

"Well, even if his teething is bad, how much worse can he get? He already wakes hourly. What's he going to do? Not sleep at all?!"

"Maybe. He is a dodgy baby."

I laugh. The idea of a baby being dodgy is a funny one. Babies are too young to realise the chaos and stress they mete out on their parents. There is innocence in their maddening ways.

And then she says it – the unspeakable thoughts of frustration and rage that every parent probably has at some point but never freely admits to. And with it, my image of her as an unflappable Supermum gives way to a more realistic view.

"Sometimes, I swear, I feel like I could put him in a box with air holes and post him to Somalia."

"Why Somalia?"

"They have lions there."

I laugh again. Not at my friend but with her. Aware she has said something mothers don't normally say, she quickly tries to retreat.

"Oh you must think I'm an awful mother to think such things. You know I would never do that really. It's just that he gets on my nerves so much sometimes."

"No I don't think you're awful at all. At least you thought of the air holes!"

"I'm really not a bad mother"

"Hey, to be honest, sometimes I imagine throwing Little Old Man out the window but then I take a break and everything is fine again. I think it's just normal if you are sitting at your limits with little sleep, you know?"

"Yeah I do."

And I knew she knew, all too well. The first six months of a baby's life are enough to test even the most patient of parents. I don't care how chilled you are, if someone screams in your face for a good couple of hours then you are going to have a brain snap at some stage.

I explain to my friend that I would never, ever lay a finger on Little Old Man but there have been times when I too feel myself being pushed over the edge of what I can handle.

My creativity when frustrated doesn't stretch as far as shipping him in a box to Somalia. But all the same, when I start thinking along these lines, I recognise in myself the need for a time out and take it. I phone a friend, scream into a pillow or occasionally put Little Old Man in his cot and dance around like Peter Garrett from Midnight Oil. I don't, as we have already established, drink a cup of tea to calm down.

Regrettably, like with the yelling incident, I have also at times dumped on The Hubby. But let out my frustration on the source? Never, touch wood.

"Oh thank goodness! I thought it was just me."

"No, I don't think so at all."

"Sometimes I say to him that it's a good thing that he is so cute. I can't tell you how many times he has reduced me to tears and then smiled and everything was ok again."

"Yep, those gummy smiles have a purpose."

We wind up our chat and I hang up feeling less frustrated at my situation. I am also relieved. Through her raising the unspeakable, I know now that my friend and I share a common and all too human side of ourselves. Even she, the gold standard Supermum in my mind, feels the stress a little too intensely at times.

Mending Fences

After talking with my friend, I reflect on the yelling incident. A couple of days have passed and I know I need to patch it up with The Hubby. While the yelling hasn't been mentioned, it stands between us like a proverbial big white elephant.

I waited for The Hubby to come home and took my chance when Little Old Man was being peaceful. I approached the topic with care, making sure that he knew I was not looking for another fight but to make amends.

We talked about the yelling, I apologised first since I was the one who started it. I explained why it had happened, how I was at the very edge of my patience with Little Old Man, and that following me into the kitchen had tipped me over. I was cautious not to make this sound like I was blaming The Hubby but rather just giving an explanation so we didn't have a future repeat.

The Hubby apologised for following me into the kitchen and said he understood what I was saying. He added that he just wished I had said it earlier rather than choosing to give him the silent treatment, which made him feel unwelcome in his own home. I feel horrible for making him feel this way, as that was not my intent.

We hugged an awkward truce and the elephant exited the room. I felt mildly annoyed by his criticism but mainly because I knew he was right. I shouldn't sulk – it's a bad habit that helps nobody. For his part, he seemed mildly annoyed too by my explanation but accepted that if I ask for a time out then he has to let me have it in peace.

Little Old Man screeched us apart from our hug. He was rolling around on his play mat and seemed mildly miffed at being left out. I picked him up and we resumed our hug, this time as a family.

Say What?!

At the start of our journey, Little Old Man had some distinct cries that I had deciphered and associated mostly with barnyard animals. Those cries are mostly gone save for two, including the leftover strangled cat and the newly arrived Little Lamb. In their place are more abstract imaginings.

The new cries all have a common theme – they are loud, extremely so. I used to think a newborn cry was loud but it is mild in comparison to an infant. High-pitched sure, but not nearly as loud.

After some research, I found out exactly how loud an infant's cry is. If you were to line up noises in increasing intensity, an infant's cry would sit at the louder end of the scale at 110 decibels. This is about as loud as a concert, ambulance siren or train. It isn't as loud as a jackhammer or an airplane taking off but way louder than a hairdryer, vacuum cleaner, air conditioner or fridge. For the record, I don't hug any of these things close to my head like I do a baby.

The crying is annoying on many levels, not least of all because I have permanent damage to the hearing in my right ear. Whenever it gets too loud, a crackling sound starts and I can't hear much else. There is nothing that can be done about this other than to avoid loud noises – something I was quite good at until I had a baby.

I am loathe to say why I have permanent damage to my right ear but I guess there is little humility left after having given birth. So…whew, here goes. When I was a teenager, I stupidly stood in front of a massive amp at a Hootie and the Blowfish concert. I know now on many levels the wrongness of that sentence. There is nothing cool about damaging your hearing in such a rookie way at, of all things, a Hootie and the Blowfish concert. Nothing.

Rest assured, I have been punished for my poor choices ever since. If I go to a concert now, I am forced to wear earplugs. I can't hold extended conversations on a mobile using my right ear and I avoid parties like the plague. It is as though I have been forced into premature middle-age, where I find myself grumpily complaining about how unnecessarily loud the world is.

And now with a baby, the punishment for my past misdeeds has gone up thousand fold. I have to always remember to dive for my earplugs first when Little Old Man needs settling. If I don't, then I will enjoy the full aural assault of his many cries. After half a minute, they begin to sound like a crackly old record on a gramophone.

I suspect my hearing has suffered further for having a baby. Whether this is permanent or passing only time will tell. Perhaps in a few years I will wake up and discover the hearing completely gone in my right ear. At this point, I will devolve into my mother and be forced to begin each sentence with, "Hey? What did you say?" while looking vague because I continually mishear the punch line.

When I was younger I used to speculate why my mother was half deaf. She never went to concerts or listened to music at full tilt. During my slightly narky teenage phase, I put it down to the fact that she wasn't deaf but rather she simply preferred not to listen to me.

Now, in my more forgiving thirties, I assume she needs hearing aids because she is old and has had children. Maybe it was my own crying as a baby that is to blame. Perhaps I wore down whatever remained of her delicate inner ear after my older brother had had an earnest go at it. Or maybe she just had bad luck with her hearing for whatever reason. Who knows?

All I know is that I predict an entire generation of mothers are going to start wondering in a few years where it all went wrong. They could blame the concerts or the MP3 players they had permanently stuck in their ears during their twenties. I suspect though it will be much easier to point the finger at their children.

Like blaming your mother, I have discovered it is much easier as a woman to blame the baby than yourself. It's an unexpected bonus to have another person to pass the buck onto. My butt is now the size of a small planet? Blame the baby! I have rings under my eyes? Blame the baby! I don't call my friends as much as I used to? Blame the baby! Ahh, it's a wonderful catch-all.

Even when babies grow into teenagers and argue back, it's not as though you will be able to hear them in any case. So, with that in mind, bad baby! Now pass mummy her hearing aid…

Exit the Barnyard

Since I'm on the topic of Little Old Man's crying, here is an updated list of my interpretations of his infant cries:

The Whistle – This squawk comes out of nowhere and can be a cry of acute joy or pain. I never know until I have picked him up for a closer inspection, which carries the inherent risk of a repeat whistle in my ear. Sometimes I suspect he does the whistle to test out his ability to magically stop everyone around him in their tracks.

The Glass Breaker – When I first heard the whistle, I thought that was as high as a baby's octaves could go. And then I heard The Glass Breaker. It is a screeching crescendo that usually comes at the end of a long screaming session. I don't mind The Glass Breaker so much because it signals the end is nigh and he will calm down soon. The cry remains a curiosity though. I'm sure if the wind was blowing in the right direction, the pitch and intensity would be enough to shatter eardrums or thin plates of glass within a two kilometre radius.

The Obliterator – This is the evolution of The Strangled Cat. When Little Old Man feels like he needs to ramp it up a notch, he will breathe in even deeper and fulfil the promise of The Strangled Cat's last gasp. The sound that comes out is otherworldly. I imagine this cry is the hearing equivalent of ground zero, where all trees and light poles bend back into the ground in reaction to the crushing wall of white noise. Like The Whistle, it has the capacity to stop people in their tracks but, by that stage, Little Old Man is too far gone to notice.

The Heartbreaker – Before I had a baby, The Hubby used to get me without fail by holding up a stuffed toy and stretching out its arms out to me for a hug. He would add "mummy!" or a little cry to this lame act if I didn't take the bait. I knew he was manipulating me for his own warped amusement but I couldn't help myself. I'm unsure whether Little Old Man has inherited this manipulative gene from his father or is purely acting on instinct but he now does a similar thing. He will half-cry and pout with his bottom lip while looking at me. If I don't react, which is rare, he will add a few sniffles and cry "baa waawaa" while his bottom lip sticks out even further. I firmly believe "baawaawaa" is baby-speak for "Pick me up now!" and I comply every time, feeling like the meanest mother in the world but not quite sure as to why.

The Scream – This is not so much about Little Old Man but about me. At about forty-five minutes into trying to settle an overtired baby at night, I start to picture in my mind Edvard Munch's painting *The Scream*. It encapsulates perfectly what is going on inside my parent-brain at that precise moment.

The Surprise! – At 4 AM in the morning, just when I have trusted the silence enough to lull myself back to sleep, along comes The Surprise! Little Old Man will scream through the baby monitor and startle me back into consciousness. I race to see what the matter is and find him blissfully asleep. There is no explanation for this cry into the night and he usually happily sleeps on until daybreak. The same, unfortunately, cannot be said for his mother.

The Half-Arsed – I'm sure the technical term for this cry would be something like grizzling. It is the sound of a baby that is kind of upset but not so upset that they feel the need to ramp up. As such, I usually don't react to the Half-Arsed. If I reacted to every noise Little Old Man makes, then I would be running after him all day. No, if you want my attention then you have to work for it!

Little Lamb – Little Lamb signals the last throes of protest before falling into a sleep. Much like the Half-Arsed, it isn't a full cry but it isn't whiney one either. It is a vocal protest, flat and dispassionate. The sound escapes almost involuntarily from Little Old Man with each breath out and is similar to the bleat of a lamb. Often heard coming from the backseat of the car or cot after a long day.

The Piggy Squeal – Finally, a cry that is borne out of delight rather than pain, teething or tiredness! When Little Old Man understands or finds something amusing, he will let out a squeal not far off in sound from an excitable pig. Again, it is all about the pitch, which is permanently set to ear piercingly high. Sometimes it makes me wish I gave birth to Barry White's lovechild but still, there's no complaining about piggy squeal!

Cool Down

The summer that seemed without end has finally started to fade around the edges. Red leaves have sprouted on the tips of trees and a chill has entered the night air. It is a reminder that the year is well underway and those endless months of maternity leave aren't so endless anymore.

The change in season has also heralded the turning of the Guilt Turtle from red to yellow. It is still not the perfect guilt-free green but the change from red has made me feel less, well, guilty. It has also marked the time where Little Old Man's upstairs nursery is no longer deemed too hot for him to sleep in.

The Hubby accordingly moved his cot and furniture from our living room and into the nursery. It was time that he had his own space and we reclaimed ours. The move graduated him to feeling like a fully-fledged child rather than a noisy camper in our living room.

The cooler days have also marked a change in Little Old Man's wardrobe. Gone is the simple singlet and nappy outfit of summer. Getting dressed in the mornings is now a much more strategic affair. I have to be mindful of the varying temperatures and dress him in layers to take on or off. Not an easy task with my little octopus.

Overall the change in seasons has not created too many adjustments. I imagine those will come with the winter, which is just around the corner.

Smug Sharks

I have discovered there is a lot of opportunity in motherhood to take the low road of smugness when interacting with other mothers. Thankfully, I have also discovered that the difference between feeling like a natural born earth mother and a hopeless vomit-covered train wreck is very fine. This has tempered any wish in me to glower in smugness at another mother's bad hair day.

Motherhood is hard – yes, it is also has many beautiful and amazing points but, at its core, it remains a tough gig. Anyone who says otherwise is either a liar or drinking way too many cups of tea. Either that or they gain some warped sense of happiness from wiping bums and can be excused from my clearly scientific-based statement on the grounds of insanity.

I've lost count of the number of times I have been down on my knees, begging to the baby gods for mercies both big and small. Nothing has made me more desperate and dependent on the support of others than giving birth to and caring for a baby. Needless to say this has left me feeling far more humbled in the past seven months than in my entire life beforehand put together.

And just when I get through a rough patch and start to think that surely must have been the worst of it, along comes something even worse. The main thing that keeps me going then is my unending love for Little Old Man and The Hubby. That and those brief sweet patches in between, when the sleep patterns settle into something manageable and he is being particularly amiable. Those glimpses into the future beyond babyhood offer me enough hope to hold on to during the trickier times.

Those glimpses also ground me enough to realise that any positive developments are random and can be taken away just as easily as they are given. If Little Old Man outgrows his dummy or rolls over earlier than the developmental standard, there is no reason to be filled with smug mummy pride. These are merely points he has reached and by no means indicate any superior mothering skills. Babies develop at different rates, all you can do is support them with hugs and love while they busy themselves with the business of growing up.

Perhaps I am lucky but I have surrounded myself with mothers who seem to follow a similar philosophy. I have yet to meet one of those mythical smug mummies or felt like Little Old Man has been looked down upon from on high by one. Before I had a baby though, I was wary of the concept. I imagined these women would circle me like sharks, sizing up my flabby non-yogafied body and drawing conclusions based on the amount of snot hanging out of my baby's nose. They would then go in for the kill, openly comparing their genetically blessed arse and baby to my own relatively meagre offerings.

Yet my interactions with mothers so far have revealed not even one shark lurking among them. The women at my Mother's Group are diverse and great at different mother things in their own ways. We all bring our own perspective to the group. I love the fact that we come from different walks in life yet have been thrown together by the common bond of motherhood. I now count on women as friends that I otherwise never would have previously come across in my old life.

When we meet, topics will invariably be raised and discussed. Someone will ask another mum about whether their baby has reached a certain developmental milestone too but only as a gauge or to gain some practical advice. There is no boasting or chest-beating about how their baby has done xyz when nobody else's has. We all cheered recently, for example, when the first of the babies in our group crawled across the rug at morning tea. It was such a happy moment for everyone, as we have all watched these babies grow from newborn on.

Outside the group, any friends with babies have been similarly humble in their approach. Perhaps it is because I have been upfront that I'm flying blind in this crazy job of parenting and doing what I can. I make no pretences of being perfect, let alone smug in any victories. If I am able to help out, then

I will offer advice. Likewise, if I am in need of advice, I will seek it out.

While I don't have smug mummy friends, I have come across plenty of smug grandparents. Some even in my own family, who shall remain nameless. Smug grandparent types are only too keen to compare Little Old Man's development with that of other babies. The extra degree of separation from direct parenting coupled with their own foggy memories of raising children, conspire to them questioning my parenting approach or inferring that my baby is falling behind milestones.

Your baby is still drinking formula? My David was on pure solids by five months.

You shouldn't hold your baby so much, he is far clingier than my grandson who is only six months older than him.

You're making a rod for your back there by spoiling him with so much attention!

My grandson had teeth at six months!

My grandson was already crawling at seven months!

My grandson could <insert whatever Little Old Man is not able to do > by that age!

At first I was annoyed at this rolling uninvited commentary but, as in pregnancy, I have learnt to smile and nod vacantly. Maybe it was the run-in with the elderly tradie who fancied himself as a lactation consultant on the side. If people want to bask in the reflected glory of their offspring or their offspring's offspring, then they can go their hardest. I won't be sucked into their smug comparisons that use my own offspring to highlight the fabulousness of theirs.

Without my willing participation, it turns out that the smug sharks I feared are more like misguided piranhas. In my experience, they are usually also ageing with a few teeth missing. Yet even if they were fellow young mothers with shiny new teeth, I still wouldn't be intimidated. Nobody can nip at my ankles unless I choose to dip my feet into the murky waters of comparison.

Smug Karma

Perhaps I was being too smug in congratulating myself for not yet mingling with any smug sharks. Whatever it was, the universe decided to teach me a lesson on smugness.

I have a friend who has two kids. I used to think that we were on pretty much the same wavelength in terms of parenting. She's practical, spendthrift and very direct. But then she forwarded an 'open letter' email originating from a blog. It was electronic smugness en masse, neatly delivered to the inboxes of myself and her other mum friends.

The letter was addressed to "Dear Mom on her iPhone at the park" from a 'fellow Mom'. It was crushingly patronising and laden with guilt-trips.

Play with your children at all times, seize every moment with them before they grow up all too quickly! Tell them about the clouds, about the creator who made those clouds! Your behaviour shows them your phone is more important than they are! Pay more attention!

I was annoyed by the assumptions made on a mother's parenting skills based on a snapshot of her behaviour. I know myself that I check my smartphone when I'm out with Little Old Man. Does this make me a neglectful mother? Does one email check observed by a judgemental eye wipe away the hours that I spend rolling around with my baby on the floor? I like to think that our relationship as mother and son is made of stronger bonds.

I also like to think that I am developing a sense of independence in Little Old Man by not obsessing over him every minute of the day. I purposely give him his own play time on the floor, allowing him to discover alone for five or ten minutes before joining him. If he needs me earlier, of course I will respond.

He always has my attention if he needs it but I don't believe it's healthy to watch him at all times just in case I miss a memorable moment. Besides, micro-mothering him into the ground is not going to help when I go back to work and he has to find his way in childcare. How will he cope when there is a ratio of four toddlers to one carer's divided attention? I'd rather teach him gradually to be independent-minded rather than have it forced upon him suddenly.

Needless to say, I deleted the smug delivery in my inbox. It was sneaky in nature because the first reaction is to point out how judgemental and corny the premise is. Yet it is also based on a niggling truth – parents do juggle time and socialising with their children. all do it yet there seems to be an undercurrent of guilt about this juggle which enables such claptrap to bounce round the net.

And where there is guilt, there is invariably smugness. The letter reminded me that nothing makes some people feel better than lauding their parenting choices and skills over others. I guess it is only human nature to compare yourself with how others are travelling in similar circumstances. Yet it is another thing altogether to make the leap and use that comparison to actively make others feel bad for taking time out for themselves in order to feel holier-than-thou. That isn't human nature, that's the work of a smug shark.

Car Wreck Inspections

The birth of Little Old Man seems like a lifetime ago. So much has happened in between that I barely even give it a thought these days. That is, until I find myself knee-deep in another conversation about the topic with a fellow mum and wondering how I got there again.

When newish mothers meet, there seems to be some irresistible urge to talk birthing stories. It's like a tipping point in the conversation, where the trust is judged high enough to start sharing the most intimate of medical details. When the point is reached, birth stories are brought out as easily as snapshots tucked away in a wallet. Gory details are swapped around casually and, occasionally, even photos of the birth shown for good measure. I've heard and seen just about everything. And not free willingly either, I should add.

Sometimes the overshare happens with little warning beforehand. Some women see a baby and think there's some insider's club that enables one to skip social niceties and enter some imagined realm of universal motherhood. I once had a waitress ask how old Little Old Man was and then added she has a five month old. I thought the chit-chat would end there and I could get down to the business of ordering. Instead, she then asked whether I had a "natural or a C?" Erhm, actually I was kind of hoping for some chicken soup rather than a full gynaecological discussion.

I try to be understanding and tolerant of this tendency this seemingly universal topic of discussion. I'm not a prude – nobody can be after giving birth – yet at the same time I just really, really don't want to know. To me, birth stories are akin to changing nappies. I don't mind dealing with my own son's business but gag when changing another baby's nappy.

Unfortunately, there seems to be no way to avoid the conversation once I find myself in one. So instead I nod in the right spots and give the appearance of listening attentively while trying to simultaneously block out the mental images assaulting me.

I find these tactics the quickest way to skate through yet they are not fool-proof. At times conversations have veered so left of centre that they slam right through all my carefully crafted defences. This can be confronting but also at times unexpectedly funny. Like the time a woman told me about the many attempts to get an epidural into her. The doctors took over two hours to get it in and she said she was practically begging for relief in the end. When the epidural finally worked, she described the physical relief that followed as like her vagina was yawning open.

Ever since this uninvited analogy, whenever I see someone yawn, my mind performs some Salvador Daliesque leap of imagination and visualises in place of their head an over-sized yawning vagina complete with full bush. I think I've been scarred for life.

The only conclusion I can reach on what inspires this level of overshare is that giving birth is a massive life event. It is the emotional equivalent of being involved in a car crash and winning the lottery all in one day. I'm guessing that is why the topic is returned to over and over again. If something that big happens, there seems to be a natural tendency to want to talk about it.

For me though, I've done all the talking I wish to do on the topic of Little Old Man's birth. I don't wish to rehash the day nor do I want to share the details of why I wasn't able to sit properly for weeks afterwards. These are things I talked about at the time before neatly burying the car wreck of my birth story under a nice patch of lawn in the back lot of my mind.

I see no point in revisiting that lot at every opportunity. The neatly manicured lawn there is flat and nondescript for a very specific reason – so I can walk straight over it and continue on in life. If I keep digging it up, then all I end up with is a pothole that I fall into every time. For the way my mind works at least, talking and dwelling on the same event isn't going to achieve a lot.

As such, I rarely speak of my own experience in these imposed discussions. Even when prodded, I keep it to a minimum and say enough that most can read between the lines that I don't wish to say any more. I've only rarely been pushed by those who cannot or will not read my cues, at which point I have to be blunt and say I don't wish to discuss it further.

In a way I don't mind that women feel the need to share with me, even if the stories are at times quite confronting. I can see that for some there is a need to dig up their birth traumas on a regular basis. It is almost as if doing so gives them a sense of safety in the familiarity of retelling.

Perhaps also it helps them to reinspect the contours and jagged edges of the wreck, to see that it is still the same and hasn't with time morphed into something scarier. Still, I really wish they wouldn't share the birthing photos. Some things really are best left private!

Nasal Retentive

I have been giving a lot of thought lately to a question I never imagined even existed before I had Little Old Man. Namely, how do you blow a baby's nose?

For adults, there is an easy solution. You have a stuffy nose, you blow it. Yet training a baby to make the same logical movement? No chance.

So for weeks I have listened to Little Old Man's endless sniffles and grunts. Drinking a bottle can be tricky if he is really blocked up because there is no way for him to drink and breathe at the same time. Then there is the snoring. He is worse than The Hubby right now (of course, I don't snore so no direct comparison can be made there).

I check in with Dr Google. I confirm that he hasn't got a cold, as there's no temperature or cough and the gunk has thankfully not spread to his lungs. It seems to me that he is just in need of a really good nose blow to clear out whatever is stuck up there.

In my internet searches, I come across a product that promises to do what Little Old Man can't. Instead of encouraging him to blow it out, a specially designed bulb syringe can suck it out. I rush out in my excitement and buy the product. The action reminds me of my mother and her habit of buying quick and easy solutions to all her woes. But this is different, this will work. It said so on the internet.

I unpack the bulb syringe from the packet. On one end there is a plastic bulb, on the other a small valve. I have since learnt that it is commonly referred to as a snot sucker. Nice. As long as it does the job, I don't care.

I watch an instructional video on the internet and am immediately suspicious.

"Simply depress the bulb and insert the valve into the infant's nose. Slowly release the bulb, allowing the excess moisture to be released."

Simply. If one word makes me suspicious of a baby product, it is simply. The use of adjectives in the marketing of baby products is akin to those used in the real estate game. If I see 'renovators dream', I can read between the lines that the house is a cess pit in desperate need of a wrecking ball. In the same way, the use of 'simply' in a baby product can be read to mean way too complex or impractical to ever work on a real live baby.

I watch the video again to get the technique down pat. I pray to the baby gods that the product works despite my scepticism. Then I notice something in the video which makes me even more doubtful – they are using a sleeping newborn as the test snot bunny. Yes it takes them a while to get there but, once asleep, a newborn is practically in a coma. When Little Old Man was that young, I vacuumed round his head and played music without fear. I could have easily stuck whatever I wanted up his nose without a flinch.

I pick up the snot sucker and look over to Little Old Man. He is playing innocently in his bouncer, unaware of his mother's fiendish plans. Part of me feels bad but another part knows I am doing this for his own good. And who knows, maybe it is just a case of simply inserting a piece of plastic in his nose.

I approach him, imagining the moment ahead to be like those stories of injured wildlife that let humans get near them because they have some innate understanding that the human is trying to help them. Or maybe not.

Turns out, Little Old Man is not that keen on random objects being stuck up his nose. He arches his head back as far away from me as possible. I recruit The Hubby to hold his head still while I try to edge closer. It's no use. Every limb is wriggling about in protest. As soon as the syringe touches his nostril, he convulses into a screaming and wriggling mass of angry baby. There is no way that The

Hubby can hold him still. It takes us ten minutes to calm him down and we both feel like the world's worst parents for trying. So much for simply.

Since the snot sucker incident, I have tried a saline spray and managed to get it up the nostrils on two occasions. I don't push the matter though, as I don't want to upset him to the point that he doesn't trust us whenever we are near to his face.

Someone suggested taking him for a swim in the sea to get salty water up there. As desperate as I have been at times, I doubt I will embark on the two-hour drive to the coast. Besides, I'm not convinced. I suspect the exercise would involve simply inserting his head into the cold ocean to effortlessly clean out his nose.

No, as gross as it is, I think the only way for him to unblock his nose is simply with time.

Stuff

"I know I don't want any more children after this one but sometimes I'm a little sad. Like, I know this is the last time I will ever be pregnant and go through this."

I am having lunch with a friend who is 36 weeks pregnant with her second child. Her words come from a place far more advanced than where I'm at but I do know what she is going through, kind of.

I had an inkling of that feeling during an earlier visit to a baby store. I went there to look at some specials and walked past the cot showroom. I saw a couple there, the woman absentmindedly patting her rounded middle while the husband ran a tape measure over a cot.

I felt a pang of sadness at the scene. Even if we eventually were insane enough to consider another baby, there would never be another cot because we already have one.

My reaction surprised me. When I was pregnant, I was pretty detached about it all. I knew there was this life growing inside me but I felt an abstract kind of love towards it. I had never held a baby for more than a minute, let alone held my own. I could look at the grainy scans and feel the baby turning inside me but I could not truly grasp at what was not yet in my hands.

Only in hindsight was I able to see how special the time was. I had been through birth and felt those feelings of motherly love, the ones that strike to the core. I understood then why a colleague of mine was so excited over each big baby purchase I made. To me at the time it was just stuff but to her it was what that stuff represented – the start of a new life, the fledgling of a young family.

I could see my friend's sadness along the same linear. Even if she had ended up having five children, the entrance of the last for her would nevertheless be bittersweet. For it is the passing from one phase in her life to the next, where she will watch her children grow into adults. And although she is happy with the size of her family, there is a finality and sense of completeness in having her last child. The boundless potential of her life is beginning to shrink.

Carousel

Little Old Man is so tantalisingly close to crawling. He teeters back and forth on his knees as though he is trying to rev his inner engine into the right gear. When this doesn't get the desired effect, he commando rolls across the room to get the feeling of movement. It is a feeling he seems to be in search of at every possible occasion.

Dressing him or changing his nappy has become for me a test of endurance – both physical and of patience. I can see now that the octopus was just a warm-up. Now he flails his arms and legs about, his torso is in constant rotation, he pushes against my every pull, and any spare piece of material is grabbed at or shoved in the mouth. It is like trying to dress a carousel.

The obvious danger in dressing a moving target is that you have to balance between trying to get clothes on and stopping him from falling off the change table. I have considered changing him on the floor but suspect I will end up chasing after a half-naked baby commando crawling away. Such a scenario can only end in carpet burns and tears for all involved.

Instead, I have chosen distraction. He 'helps' me by holding his pants or a toy while I change his nappy. This may hold his attention just long enough for me to get the legs of his pants on. It doesn't work all the time though.

I have also chosen, as usual, to daydream of the perfect product solution. I want a change table that is made of the exact opposite material to Teflon. Or, failing that, Velcro strips I can attach to the mat and his back at change time.

The situation is a reminder of the challenges being set by his increasing mobility. I can't contain him with distraction forever. Soon those engine revs will turn into a roar and he will be off and crawling. And then the real fun will begin.

Demotivation Central

As it turns out, that period where Little Old Man slept through night after glorious night was just a blip. It has longingly been dubbed in our house The Golden Age of Sleep.

There have been good nights here or there but no return to this time, not even close. Instead we have endured months of suspected teething, extended tantrums and interrupted sleep all round. And still no teeth to show for it. My earlier fears seem to be coming true of us having one of those babies that teethe endlessly while their teeth realign in their gums. Either that or I jumped the gun a bit on my diagnosis.

Or perhaps he doesn't have any teeth in his head at all. Maybe he is destined to look like a Little Old Man for the rest of his life, complete with gummy grin and bald head. It fits the bill. When he is focussing, he sucks his bottom lip up underneath the top one and it disappears into the toothless hole. He looks like a miniature grandpa with his dentures out.

While he looks like a little old man, his behaviour of late is more akin to a grumpy old man. Whether it is down to teething or not, who knows. All I know is that our current relationship seems to resemble that between a disgruntled customer and a service representative who can do nothing but smile as abuse is hurled forth. Smile, smile, in training they said the customer is always right. And even if they're not, a smile might make them calm down or walk off in disgust. Since Little Old Man can't yet walk off, he stays put and scowls in indignation.

The grump factor starts first thing. During The Golden Age, he awoke smiling and gurgling sweetly. Now the days start with him startling from sleep with a loud cry or grizzle. The mere suggestion of a bottle sends him into rage. How could I possibly dare to think of food at a time of such hunger? Then, after a while of screaming, I manage to get the bottle in and he sucks furiously as though he had not been offered food for days.

At this point, he may continue until he is full or stop midway and pout his lips high into the air.

There is no way to sneak the bottle past this fortress and any attempt will invoke a further screaming. So I put him in his cot or continue to hold him or put him in his bouncer – all of which encourage, you guessed it, more screaming.

I wait the tantrums out and offer the bottle again, hoping his belly will fill sufficiently this time. If I'm lucky, after this extended performance he may do a Number Two and return to slightly normal baby until mid-morning. Screaming and a big shit – that is how I start my mornings.

This goes on every day at the moment. It's like he has regressed to newborn but with all the strength and escape artist abilities of a toddler.

All these are hardly compelling reasons to spring out of bed when the baby monitor flashes back to life. Some mornings when he starts, it feels like he has only just finished from the night before. It reminds me of the beginning, when time was one long continuum. Like then, I find myself awake at all hours and have gone back to drawing a line between the days with the sun rather than clocks.

My only slight consolation is that others in the Mother's Group are having similar troubles. I am hoping this means it is some developmental stage he is growing through.

I know it is not intentional on his part but it feels as though he is running the ultimate demotivation program, just to see how much I can take before he has completely worn me back to nothing. And some mornings he gets his answer. I tuck my head under the pillow to mute the sound of the monitor and cry a little before getting up. When this happens, no matter how well the day might pan out in the end, I feel like I've lost before I even started.

Run on the Board

"I can feed him. You rest."

"No, I can do it. I need a win."

The Hubby pauses to look at me. He can see by my face that I am serious. Little Old Man is half asleep and only needs a little more formula to knock him completely into the land of nod. It won't be a struggle, just a pro-forma of formula.

But I need to get him there. I need to have the feeling of an easy win, to get him into bed without a screaming marathon. It's been a while since I have got a run on the board and it is starting to wear on my mothering confidence.

I look down at him cradled drowsily in my arms. He sucks half-heartedly at the bottle until he reaches his fill. His body relaxes further into me and he begins to snore. I enjoy the moment of peace. It is like we are sitting in the eye of a greater storm raging all around us.

All I want is just one day, one day, where he is halfway amiable. At the moment though this is a lot to ask of him and I know that.

I place Little Old Man gently down in his cot and he turns over to sleep. I may not have a day of wins but at I least have one night.

The Land Before Time

"Can you still remember the time before you had a baby?"

"Yes, vaguely…I remember at least that there was a lot more sleep!"

I am talking with a friend's mother, who herself probably can't remember a time before children even if she tried. She raised four children herself, two of which still live in her home with their children. On top of this, she works in childcare.

Life before and after children is difficult to describe to someone who hasn't had any themselves. It is like trying to explain a foreign country to someone who has never been there. You can describe the buildings and landscapes but you can never really capture the sense of what it is like to really be there – the smell of cafés, the snippets of passing conversations and sense of being a part of the scenery.

My life pre-Little Old Man is beginning to feel equally foreign to me. It is a distant place I vaguely remember inhabiting. I still have remnants of that time around the house though to remind me.

My handbag collection sits proudly on top of my wardrobe, mostly unused since I rarely go out without Little Old Man and the gargantuan nappy bag. Even though I'd never admit it to The Hubby, I sometimes stare at my collection and ponder why it was once so important to me. It seems so wasteful now.

Inside the wardrobe itself are clothes for work that are now hanging unused. It seems silly that I spent entire pay packets on work clothes given that I hold an office job in an industry not even remotely creative or fashionable. I doubt very much that some of the clothes would fit at the moment but, even if they did, I have nowhere to wear them.

I haven't quite slid down the sartorial scale to daggy housewife but I do have a more casual collection of clothes to choose from. Alright, maybe I do slide that far at times. As much as I deny this, my yoga pants are really just dressed up tracksuit pants given that I have never done a downward dog pose in my life.

Every so often when I'm at home I do like to dress up a little - maybe not to office level nice but smart casual. If I go completely wild, I may put on makeup even though I know Little Old Man will wipe most of it off by mid-morning. The effort in itself reminds me that I am human. Plus, it lets me enjoy the stockpile of clothes and accessories I barely used due to too much choice. I love hunting through drawers for these little finds and using them here or there. And my awareness of how many things I have has killed off in me any desire to go on a spending spree.

Beyond the clothes, there are other smaller reminders of my previous life. One day Little Old Man was pulling apart my wallet and my old coffee club card fell out. I picked it up and saw I was almost due for a 'free' cup. Did I really need to spend four dollars a day on mochas though? They didn't even really taste that good. I only went as a thinly veiled excuse to escape my desk for twenty minutes and bitch about office politics.

I think back to the question originally posed to me. Yes, I do remember the time before children but it doesn't seem as important as it once did. Perhaps my attitudes will shift back towards where they used to sit when I eventually return to work but I doubt they will ever go back completely. My life exists in another land now.

Le Smug Shark

I finally came across a smug shark! Well, at least I think I did.

A school friend of The Hubby came to Australia from Germany on holidays with his French wife and two year old daughter. I had met them a few times before and we all got along really well.

The wife has a quirky sense of the world. She's the kind of person that you need to talk to a few times before you understand how her thinking works. She is sharp, very sharp, and has a keen eye for observation. And she likes to fully think over her thoughts and construct them into carefully plotted arguments and counter-arguments before sharing them. As a result, whenever I speak to her I feel on the back foot and mildly stupid.

It came as no surprise then that she had spent her holiday dissecting the parenting skills of Australians and comparing them with what she knew and practised. The aspect that shocked her the most was how much Australian parents talk with their babies.

"It is unbelievable! This constant chatter. It is like verbal diarrhoea."

"Well, I wouldn't go that far…"

"No? Do you think that the world needs a constant dialogue in order to be understood? That your child must be entertained by your observations at all times?"

"Well, I…"

"Children do not need you to explain the world to them."

"Huh?"

"They can see it for themselves! It is so Disney, so *American,* to chatter chatter chatter. Like your every thought matters and your baby must hear it. We are not actors in some great movie. Life does not need a soundtrack of words."

I was lost and unsure. Was she smug sharking parents or Americans? Or American parents? Or Australian parents who she thinks act like American parents? Or could this conversation be written off as some weird French thing?

"Well, how do you talk with your child?"

"I talk only when necessary, when I need to communicate something to her."

"Ok, but what if you want to explain to her that a bus just went by and it is carrying people to work? Or that you are just popping into the shops with her and need to buy some dinner?"

"She can work these things out for herself. I don't need to infantilise her."

"But, but she *is* an infant!"

"Two year olds are smarter than most people give them credit for."

I'm unsure of what to say. I don't want to agree simply to be polite but I also don't want to disagree because she seems so strident. In truth, she kind of scares me! And I feel judged, even though she has no clue about how I am with Little Old Man.

If she spent a day with us, she would see I am a very active member of the chattering masses. I have made up dozens of songs since he was born for all sorts of activities. I have a theme song for changing his nappy, when we're cuddling, when I'm trying to distract him, when we're playing with The Hubby, when I'm settling him, when we're in the car…ok, you get the picture. But making an idiot of myself is all worth it – he pays me back tenfold with smiles and hugs.

I also talk to him constantly. I used to be quite introverted in my thinking but now I am selectively extroverted. When it is just me and Little Old Man at home, most thoughts big and small pass my lips uncensored. I like to show him my serious side as much as my silly side. It does not surprise me that things evolved like this as I am much the same with The Hubby. Well, except perhaps for the unfiltered thoughts bit.

I know one day I will have to be more selective in what I say in front of him and teach him there are times for silliness. At the moment though I am not at all concerned. He is discovering the world and I am shaping his observations with words. I'm not an expert but I can't imagine this to be a negative thing. Certainly not on the grounds that it is supposedly a thoroughly American thing to do.

Our lunch date comes to an end and we wave goodbye to our friends for probably another couple of years. I remain unsure what exactly the encounter was but I resolve not to be bothered by the feeling of being indirectly judged. Like with many things in parenting, I have gone with what I think is reasonable. And I am happy with this.

Strengthened

With dogs in the family growing up, someone needed to take them for a walk every day. Since I was usually the one who begged the most for a new puppy, the task always befell me.

Even after I moved out of home I still went for these afternoon walks. It was partly habit and partly a guilty sense that I should move in an attempt to keep my weight at an even level. Either way, it was usually out of a sense of what I should be doing. Walking was just one of those necessities in life.

Then I fell pregnant. It started out well enough. I could still move about pretty freely until about halfway through the second trimester. From there on in, my world got smaller and smaller as pelvic girdle pain took over.

I was told by my obstetrician that my pelvic bones were bending under a mix of pregnancy hormones and the weight of the baby. I found 'bend' a strange term. To me, bones can break or splinter. Bend just seemed wrong.

The further into pregnancy I got, the more wrong that bending feeling became. In the last few weeks I was housebound and could barely make it to the post box. I would get up in the morning, have a shower then go back to bed to rest from that strenuous activity. Eventually I would get up, dressed, and gather up everything I could possibly need for the day downstairs. There was no way that I could walk those stairs more than once a day. Stairs and pelvic girdle pain do not mix.

And then the whole birth thing happened and, well, we all know how spectacularly badly that went so no need to rehash. Safe to say though that the birth took away what little physical reserve I had left. I lost all my strength and many of my muscles seemed to disappear overnight.

It was only through losing everything and then gaining it back by walking in ever increasing circuits near my house, that I have realised how precious my health really is. I now take it as a blessing rather than a chore that I am able to walk an hour each day.

I still have a long way to go until I'm back to my pre-pregnancy weight but somehow I have lost the sense of panic I felt when I first stepped on the scales. My goal is to be healthy and strong rather than to reach a particular number. I see this time as a second chance, complete with greater awareness of how lucky I am to be able to move myself in the right direction.

Quiet

When Little Old Man was younger, I used to relax when the house went quiet. Silence, as the saying goes, was golden. I knew that I could set him down in one place and, like the cute baby blob that he was, he would still be in exactly the same position when I returned. If he was happy to lay there, he would quietly entertain himself with a toy or staring at his hands.

With increasing mobility, he must now not only be within earshot but also my line of vision. If I hear no noise from him then I know it is the time to look up and check what he is up to. Odds on he is concentrating on something he has found while worming across the room. Only a quick quality control by Mother Central will determine whether that object of interest is really something Little Old Man should be getting his hands and mouth all over.

Even when he is in my arms the surveillance continues. He arches his back and reaches his hands out as far as possible in all directions hoping to latch onto a new point of interest. The world is there to be touched, drooled upon and then thrown on the floor at great speed. It feels like a full-time job keeping up with him and he hasn't even started crawling yet!

Mr Popularity

Little Old Man is gorgeous. Yes, I am horribly biased but he really is a genetically blessed baby. With his chubby thighs and easy smile, he is ridiculously cute. And his cuteness doesn't just end with his looks. Even at this tender age I can tell he has a kind and warm personality.

If I am ever in doubt of my ability to objectively perceive his cuteness, all I need to do is go out for a couple of hours. Strangers talk to him, others smile and some even congratulate me. Closer to home, family and friends are besotted by him. His grandparents cannot get enough photos of him.

Yet being cute does come with its downsides. All the attention is flattering but can get intense at times. There are the awkward conversations with strangers who ask for a hold or, even worse, hold their hands out to him and he reaches back in reflex. I then have to interject like an overprotective Mamma Bear and make some excuse that he has just eaten or is a bit tired.

Perhaps I am being a little overprotective but I am his mother and I respect that he is a person, albeit a little one. People wouldn't pass round an attractive adult like a prized turkey so why do they feel compelled to do the same with a helpless baby? They may not be able to speak but they have the right to be respected too.

The polite tension over this regular request was tested recently when my mother asked me to accompany her to the local bowling club. When we walked in about thirty grannies turned in unison and cooed at the sight of a baby. Many lifted their arms up in anticipation of a hold. I gulped and suspected that Little Old Man did too.

They were relentless in wanting to touch and hold him. I let a couple do so but then drew the line when he started to get upset. But that's not fair, a few cried out almost in unison; we didn't get a turn! I politely said he was tired and went into a corner to calm him down. Some grannies followed, poking at his feet and asking him if he was really tired. Subtlety was clearly not working.

I handed him over to The Hubby and went over to my mum to say we might take him for a walk round the block to calm down. And then I heard my husband's tone change into something I wouldn't expect to hear directed at a group of elderly women in a bowling club.

"Ladies, please! Please! He is not a toy! Leave him alone!"

I turned to see The Hubby gently batting away a very elderly and potentially senile woman, who was dancing around him and prodding at Little Old Man. Every time he swung round to get the baby away from her, she followed as though it was a game. Little Old Man was crying and over it.

All the polite tip-toeing around the point was gone. We were not going to be able to make a discreet exit. The Hubby was in the right – Little Old Man was overstimulated and overwhelmed by all the attention. It seemed these women were too excited to recognise this and back off.

We headed for the door, not before another granny launched herself from around the corner to wave her hands in his face. If their enthusiasm didn't press all my Mamma Bear buttons it would almost be comical.

I was positive my mum would later say we overreacted but she was surprisingly mute on the matter. Either way, it wouldn't have mattered. Sometimes I have to do what I think is best for my child regardless of what others may think, my mum included. I can do it politely or more firmly but the point is that I keep his best interests at heart. If that makes me a party pooper or overprotective or whatever, then so be it.

Growth

I know Little Old Man has grown since he was a newborn. I can see it in the clothes that he routinely grows out of and the leaps he makes in his development. Yet these changes can be so subtle that they are almost imperceptible on a day to day basis. There is no way to see how dramatic his growth has been over the past eight months other than looking at old photos.

That was, at least, until I met up with the friend whose baby shower I attended a while back. Her baby is less than two weeks old and I gasp when she is lifted up for me to see. She looks so incredibly tiny and on the verge of being subsumed by the swaddle wrapped around her.

"Is she premature?"

"Haha no, she weighs and measures pretty much the same as yours did at birth."

"Really?"

"Uh huh. Would you like a hold?"

I find myself surprisingly nervous about holding such a tiny and fragile being, even though not long ago I confidently slung my own newborn over my shoulder like a tea towel.

My friend gently transfers her baby into my cradled arms and I look down at her half-dazed face. She has just breastfed and is milk drunk. I smile and gently stroke her side. Was Little Old Man ever really this little?

I look over to him – he is attempting madly, as usual, to crawl. He has commando rolled his way over to a television cabinet and collected two remote controls on the way. Earlier in the day he managed to grab a brush on a chain at a cosmetics counter and swing it round wildly. It was the first time I realised I had to watch him in the pram, as he can now grab anything within striking distance.

I return my attention to the newborn. In truth, she is so tiny that I feel like I could hold her in the palms of my two hands. With her slight frame and ridiculously chubby cheeks, she strikes me as more of a hairless hamster than a baby. She seems otherworldly until she yawns and reveals herself to be so very human in her vulnerability.

I find myself saying to my friend all the things that made my eyes roll when Little Old Man was a newborn. She's so tiny! Careful, you'll blink and she'll be crawling! Enjoy these precious moments!

I know these are all clichés but they are also true. It was only with the direct comparison that I could see how much my baby had grown. He is a strong-willed giant, aware of his surrounds and going head-long after everything he wants. She, on the other hand, is still blinking in confusion at the light of life she has been given.

I continue to gaze down at this living miracle in my arms. When Little Old Man falls asleep in my arms, I still gaze at him in the same way and feel the same kind of giddy love of the early days. Yet these moments are becoming rarer. I now mostly get my kisses and hugs on the fly while trying to prevent him from launching across a room. It takes all my strength to hold him back.

My moment of reflection is interrupted by the sound of paper being scrunched up. Without even looking up, I carefully hand the newborn back over to her Mum and run over to save whatever it is that he has decided to destroy. Oh, how fast they grow. They do, they really do.

Afterthought

Like her daughter, my friend was still in a daze at this new life she has found herself in. Her coffee table was littered with nipple shields, breast pads, baby advice books and a pump. She spoke softly of her disappointment that breastfeeding was proving difficult and regretted spending hundreds of dollars on a lactation consultant who helped her very little. She paid it though because she really wants breastfeeding to work.

My heart broke for her. I had been her a few months ago and knew that absolute desperation she was privately going through. It's a feeling no partner can ever fully understand because, well, they don't have the right equipment. Wanting to breastfeed and being unable to isn't like, say, wanting to buy a car and the finance not coming through. It is a deep want, a want that makes your bones and flesh and everything about you ache.

My friend asked me whether it was worth continuing and, like at her baby shower, I didn't really know what to say. The only advice I could offer her was to keep weighing up whether the benefit to the baby outweighed the cost to her. If the cost to her becomes too high, then perhaps it is time to consider the alternatives. But when to make that call is a highly personal one. I wouldn't dare to guess where her tipping point should be and when to heed it. I am the last person who should dole out advice on that one given the obsessional lengths I went to.

While I was driving away from her house, it occurred to me not only how far Little Old Man had come but also how far I had developed as a mother. Those early days were a world of pressure and self-imposed expectations over breastfeeding that I was very happy to have left behind. Rather ironically, it was only when I let go of that very motherly role that I gained so much more confidence in being a mum, simply through having more time to focus on other parts of me.

I drove to the supermarket to pick up a few things. As I walked down an aisle, I spotted a woman with a pram. I knew since it was a bassinet that the baby wasn't much older than a newborn. I approached where she was standing and slowed, noticing something strange. I pretended to reach for some tins while trying to work it out with some sneaky side looks.

It was then I got it. The stitching on her black tights was protruding and a tag was flipped out from the back. She had her pants on inside-out.

I wanted to giggle and then hug her out of some kind of universal motherly understanding. I decided against it out of fear she may think I'm a nutter or, worse, she was barely holding it together and would completely fall apart in my arms. I was making a concerted effort to leave behind awkward public displays of emotion since graduating from the newborn phase.

So I kept on walking and tried to see the scene in a positive light. Good for her, I thought. Maybe she's hanging on by a bare thread or maybe she was just absent-minded when she got dressed this morning. Either way, at least she still managed to make an appearance in civilisation.

Some days I struggle to get my mummy shit together. I would be a liar if I said otherwise. Yet it has been a long time since I've been so stressed out that the mere act of getting dressed or achieving a minimum semblance of normalcy needed to be congratulated.

I am under no illusions that this could all very well happen again with more teething or an illness. In that sense, I am far from smug. My current status as a semi put-together person very much rests on the fates given to me by the baby gods.

Yet, that said, I know it would be doing me a disservice not to acknowledge my present state rests partially on something else – the resilience I have built up through experience. Hard moments have happened often enough that I now tend to be able to roll with them or tell myself to hold on for a while longer rather than instantly fall into a crying heap. Yes, even with the lack of sleep, the poo-namis, the vomit, and ongoing refusal to eat solids. A hard moment is just that – a moment.

These experiences have reshaped me and how I approach life. Indeed, they have happened enough to forge who I am today – a mum, mostly comfortable in her own skin.

On the Move

Little Old Man has spent most of his waking time lately getting up on all fours and moving back and forth on the spot for hours. I call this action revving the engines, as it looks like he is getting prepared to take off. A friend with a baby the same age calls it dry-humping because it looks like what her dog does to her couch cushions. I prefer my interpretation.

Call it what you will, tonight Little Old Man officially graduated from revving to crawling! From one day to the next he somehow managed to coordinate all four limbs. It is like those last missing synapses in his brain connected and the impossible became attainable.

He zoomed across the living room, occasionally falling on his oversized nappy bum before correcting himself and continuing. He headed straight for everything he has obsessed over but was kept away from; cables, drawers, chair wheels, hard surfaces. Yes, he even managed to make it to the bookshelf. It was like he was mentally ticking off a list he had prepared of everything he would get his hands on once he was mobile. How very like his father. How efficient, how thoroughly German. Ok, I'm scared now.

I walked hovered above him like a Helicopter Mother, waiting to zoom in at the first sign of danger. I wasn't sure how much free reign to give him. It is easy to underestimate how clueless babies are about cause and effect. After the first night of crawling, I think it is safe to assume they know nothing and work from there.

The Hubby half-jokingly suggested that we buy him a safety helmet after we watched him struggle with navigating the world on all fours. He hasn't quite worked out, for example, that it is easier to go round a cushion and that there are some objects, like windows, where no amount of sustained head-butting will let him to pass.

Although said jokingly, I did check on the internet to see if a baby safety helmet exists. Turns out, they do, of course, but I decided to keep that information to myself until he has a big accident. I don't want him hurt but, at the same time, I don't want to stop him from learning basic physics.

So on he will crawl under his mother's watchful eye keeping a lookout in the background to ensure no permanent brain damage occurs. Sometimes in life the only way to learn things is the hard way, even for my precious Little Old Man.

Containment Lines

In my pre-baby mind, I used to see a playpen and images would flash into my mind of orphanages in former Soviet Russia. The kind where hollow-eyed children stared blankly into news cameras from behind the bars of their cots and straight into the viewer's heart. Their days made up of nothing but the occasional bottle being thrown their way by an overworked nurse and a longing to be held.

Perhaps the association was, in hindsight, a little harsh. Playpens aren't ideal but they are not *that* bad. Well, this is at least what I tell myself when Little Old Man shoots me that same hollow-eyed look from behind the bars of his. He plays on my heartstrings almost as though he consciously knows what he is doing.

When he does this stare, I feel like arguing back to him that he gets plenty of hugs, nappy changes, food and playtime with mummy. I am not some harsh, overworked Soviet nurse and he knows that, surely. It's just that sometimes I need to do other things than staring at him all day long in case he cracks his head open on a drawer. Things like making some lunch or going to the toilet.

Yes, yes, I can freely justify away why my child sits in a hexagonal jail cell on my living room floor. I wanted him to be a free spirit but I have caged him out of sheer practicality. As a full-time carer, I have to balance his need to explore and learn about the world at every opportunity with my need for the occasional moment of sanity. If he is in the hexagon, I know the damage he can do is limited.

While my child isn't as free-range as I envisioned, I like to think that at least he is a barnyard rather than caged baby. He does have more than an A4 size piece of paper to roam around on and a comfortable quilt from his nanna to cushion his many falls. And he gets out for several hours during the day to roam around freely. The playpen is very much the minority, not the majority, of his day.

Like many things in parenthood, the playpen a necessary reality of life with a baby. I want to give him his freedom but he has to learn how to use it safely first. When he has managed that, then maybe I might trust him enough to go to the toilet with him wandering the house. Based on present performance, I doubt this will happen for a while.

Perma-Jetlag

Except for The Golden Age, Little Old Man never quite got the concept of sleeping. At the moment his routine is to sleep a good block to around midnight, then wake every two hours until around 5 AM before intermittently grizzling to wake time.

When I am on shift, he seems to have developed an incredibly defined sensor for when I decide to sneak back to bed. He waits until I lay down, bring the doona around my neck and snuggle down into my sleeping position. Then, and only then, will he begin to grizzle again.

I ignore it for the first minute in the hope he will self-settle. It is a gamble because the longer I leave it, the more likely he is to wake The Hubby.

I don't know why they call it grizzling. He sounds more like a lame sheep, ready to be shot out of its misery in the paddock.

"Meeeeh, meeeeeeh, meeeeeeeh."

I uncurl from my sleeping position and start to get up. Then I freeze – there is silence. I wait, awkwardly, in my half-up position. I listen intently and just as I begin to hope I can lay back down…

"Meeeeh, meeeeh, meeeeh."

Damn it!

I throw off the doona and march back into his room. I stand over his cot unsure of what to do next. I have fed him, changed his nappy, rocked him and even sang lullabies through gritted teeth. I feel like screaming at him "WHAT DO YOU WANT?!?" but I know he doesn't have the answer. Nobody seems to.

I rub the side of his leg in an attempt to calm him from grizzle to sleep.

"Shhh, shhh, Mummy's here. It's ok, you can go to sleep now."

"Meeeeh, meeeeh, meeeeeh."

"Is everything alright?"

The Hubby stands yawning at the doorframe.

"I don't know what to do anymore, this is getting beyond a joke."

I begin to cry and scratch at my scalp in frustration. We've been going on and off like this for three hours now. In a run of bad nights, this is by far the worst. I'm at a complete loss.

"Go to bed."

"But it's my turn."

"Go to bed, put your earplugs in and try to get some sleep."

"That's really not fair."

"You are too frustrated to be of any use to him, you need a break."

It was true. Fair or not, I felt like I was near snapping point. I knew this was because I had broken my golden rule of only focussing on getting Little Old Man to sleep. I find when I just focus on him in that moment, I am far less impatient with the many attempts to get him to sleep. When I focus, however, on wanting to do other things, like sleep myself or get back to whatever it was doing before he started, then the annoyance levels rise in me quickly.

Perhaps it was the change in shifts or that The Hubby wasn't as worked up as me but he had Little

Old Man happily back to snoozing in twenty minutes flat. I was relieved but deflated. Worse still, I couldn't fall back asleep and dawn was only a couple of hours away. I had totalled around two hours sleep that night. The problem with being on-call is that it is hard to switch that part of the brain off when it is no longer needed.

I roll over and will myself to sleep. I toss and turn then toss again. I think back on the solution offered by the midwives in hospital – "sleep when your baby sleeps!" If only it was that simple. I have yet to discover how to make myself prone to spontaneous bouts of narcolepsy, except for those couple of times when I've fallen asleep in exhaustion on the toilet. Not the nicest place for a powernap, as it turns out.

My tummy rumbles back into awake mode and I go downstairs to have a glass of milk. Then I make the long, fruitless journey back to bed. I lay there and close my eyes, trying to block out every useless thought that crosses my mind.

I breathe in and out deeply ten times and count back from a hundred. At some point, in the middle of all my attempts to sleep, my body lets go and I fall into a light sleep. It's not much but it will be enough to get me through the next day.

In Theory

It had to happen. Little Old Man's sleeping patterns were beyond erratic. Neither The Hubby nor I had had a good night of sleep in months. I knew my insomnia was mostly caused by a lack of trust in my baby's ability to sleep for more than two hours at a time. By the time I struggled to sleep, I was up again to the sound of his cry.

We have a regroup in the morning after the night before.

"We can't go on like this…"

"I know."

"It's like we're back at the start."

"I know."

"So what do we do?"

The Hubby looks at me like he is expecting one of those maternal epiphanies I've never been able to produce for him. How should I know what to do about a baby that won't sleep properly? If I did, wouldn't I have deployed by now whatever secret motherly tricks I had up my sleeve?

I turn to the old *Baby Bible* and open up the chapter on settling. I start laughing at the text.

"Says here that babies over six months shouldn't be having bottles at night."

"Ha, he drinks about four!"

"And that they should go to bed at six or seven at the latest because they wake at dawn. If you get them to bed later, then you won't make them wake later."

I stop laughing and begin wondering. How does this book suppose that we choose the time our baby goes to sleep? I imagine it is easier with a child I could communicate with but a baby? They just do what they want.

The advice reminds me of when I have been asked what time I put my baby down to sleep. I was baffled by the question each time and my answer was uncharacteristically hippy – we just follow his lead. I felt like adding we do it because that's the vibe, man.

But it's true. We have been following his lead. It's what we have been doing since birth. If he's hungry, we feed him. If he's tired, we put him to bed. If he wakes during the night, we feed him. We do these things because that is what we have always done.

But what if the book is right? What if it should be us setting the structure now? He isn't a newborn anymore. Perhaps now is the time that we take the lead?

I see the error of my ways and what people must have been getting at when they asked what time he went to bed. I feel like a neglectful parent for not seeing what was so obviously right before me.

I read the rest of what my *Baby Bible* has to offer on settling. As usual, it mentions having a cup of tea when stressed. If I had a cup of tea every fucking time this woman suggests it, then I would spend my days racing to the toilet to relieve my post-pregnancy bladder of a five year old. I ignore the repeated tea tips and keep on reading.

"Says here that we should take away all comforters at night, which includes bottles."

"But what if he is hungry?"

"Well, he did manage to sleep through those three weeks without waking for a bottle. We know it's possible."

"Hmm true. What else?"

"We should also try controlled crying."

The Hubby rolls his eyes. He has voiced his scepticism in the past of this technique.

"We do our nightly regime and put him down when we think it is time for bed. If he starts crying, then we go in after five minutes and give him a little pat to calm him."

"And what happens when he continues to cry?"

"Then we wait another five minutes and go in again. Then we wait ten minutes, then fifteen minutes and we keep going until he is asleep."

"How long will it take?"

"It says here it can take between thirty minutes and upwards of two hours depending on the baby and the level of sleep disturbance."

"Knowing our luck we get the two-hour treatment."

"Well, it's worth a try. Whatever works, right?"

"Right. OK, let's give it a go tonight."

With that, we agree and await the night almost with excitement rather than the usual dread. For once we have a game plan other than just scraping our way through.

In Practice

"I. Need. To. Hold. Him. NOW!"

"You know you can't, it's not part of the plan."

"I know but…"

I pace back and forth outside Little Old Man's nursery. The door is closed but I can hear every breath he takes before launching into more cries of distress. Every inch of me wants to race in there and pick him up. But, as The Hubby so annoyingly pointed out, it's not part of the plan.

I remember my earlier promise to always try to be the bigger person in the room, even though I technically wasn't allowed into the room at present. I had to show Little Old Man the way.

Controlled crying sounded much easier on paper. Leave the baby to their own devices, they will calm down eventually. I recalled my earlier failed attempts when he was a newborn but figured I'd be much stronger now since the breastfeeding hormones are gone and I am used to the sound of a crying baby.

My plan was to maybe have a glass of wine instead of that cup of tea and kick back in the living room until the egg timer went off. I would then go upstairs to give him a small pat and some words of reassurance. I'm strong now, I thought, I can do this in a snap.

That worked fine the first couple of trips up the stairs earlier in the night. But by the time he had a few hours of sleep out of the way, he was reenergised and able to scream his protests out louder. By midnight, I was in bed and staring at the ceiling while counting down the minutes. When I finally went into his room, I was almost as distraught as he was.

"We must be doing this wrong. It should have worked by now."

"Well, your book did say it can take up to two hours. It's only been forty-five minutes."

"You mean this could go on for another hour?"

"I guess so."

The Hubby wasn't really offering much in the way of support. He had pulled a double shift the night before because I had a cold so I excused his lack of enthusiasm at 2 AM.

The crying continued and I kept my nerve, just. Two hours in and Little Old Man finally quietened into sleep. He next woke just past six in a very grumpy mood. I gave him a bottle and put him back to bed. He seemed to hover between awake and asleep. I left him to his own devices for another twenty minutes and then, once The Hubby left for work, I caved and picked him up.

I calmed him down and placed him in bed next to me since we had both been through a traumatic night. I figured if I was breaking rules, then I may as well break the biggest one. He calmed down for a minute but then started to make noise. A ball of frustration rose in me. I couldn't understand what he wanted. But then, maybe he was confused by what I was offering.

I placed him back in his cot, much to his wild protests, and closed the door once more. I then closed my door, put some earplugs in, shoved my head under the pillow and cried. Lack of sleep is more liveable once I'm into the day but it's always hardest to deal with at the beginning. It's like an old sporting injury that's a bit stiff in the morning but warms up eventually. Unfortunately, like an old sporting injury that gets knocked, it hurts all over again whenever I pull a bad night.

After a few minutes, I take my earplugs out and listen in guilt for his crying. I hear nothing. I walk to my bedroom door and open it – nothing. I then gently open his bedroom door and peek in. His bum is up in the air and his face is turned to the side. He is fast asleep.

I tip-toe back to my bed and quickly fall asleep, where I stay until he wakes two hours later. It seems we've exhausted each other out.

Later I reread my *Baby Bible*, which assures me that the first night is the hardest. I hope for everybody's sake that the crazy tea lady is right.

In Practice: Part Two

The big bonus so far with controlled crying is that we have fixed up a problem that we didn't even know we had. Namely, the time we were putting Little Old Man to bed. We had been leaving it up to him but, turns out, he is a bad judge and we were putting him to bed overtired.

On the second night of our controlled crying experiment it took far less grizzling for him to fall asleep. It was almost like another child. At 7 PM I found myself standing in the living room at a loss at what to do with this newfound silence.

I dug out the TV remote from among his toys. I should note that I don't approve of him playing with the remote because it is not designed for children but there is a healthy degree of resignation to its new dual purpose. Remotes are like the universal catnip for babies, they can't help themselves when they see one.

I wipe off the baby slobber and turn on the news. It is the first time I've caught the full bulletin in months. Afterwards, I enjoy a hot chocolate that hasn't gone lukewarm and have a leisurely conversation with The Hubby. There are no interruptions or distractions.

Bringing his bedtime back by almost three hours has given me triple the free time I was usually getting during the day. I used to have to wait until Sundays, when The Hubby and Little Old Man had some male bonding time, to have such a long block of time. Now I've had that block of time two evenings in a row and feel renewed.

The Hubby and I go to bed relaxed and ready for the night to come. Unfortunately, the great experiment starts to come unstuck at 1 AM. Little Old Man begins to cry, then settles into grizzling for forty minutes before completely losing it in a full-blown crying attack. I hold my nerve and continue to go in every ten minutes to do the same settling routine.

And then The Hubby enters the hallway where I am sitting.

"Maybe he is hungry. It has been a while since his last feed."

"No, the milk bar is closed between the hours of 10 PM and 5 AM. That's the rule."

"But he's been screaming forever. If I screamed like that, my throat would be too hoarse to go back to sleep."

I take a deep breath in. It's hard being Mean Mummy, even harder when your meanness is being pointed out to you. Little Old Man was trying every trick to plea for mercy.

"Can you please just go back to bed? I'm handling this."

"Ok, can I put my earplugs in then?"

"No, because you're doing the next shift and I'm not waking to wake you."

"Oh…"

I watch The Hubby retreat back into the bedroom and the warmth of his side of the bed. I feel a pang of jealousy and try not to imagine how good it must feel for him to snuggle under the doona. I am glad he walked away. He judged correctly that it was too late at night and I was too close to the edge for any further discussion.

After an hour and a half of screaming and settling, I can't take it anymore. I go downstairs for a glass of milk and to scream into a pillow in frustration at my self-imposed inability to pick him up and comfort him. I can't imagine what our neighbours think. I didn't much care at that point.

It is then that I hear footsteps across the floor upstairs. The Hubby is up and on the move. I get up off the couch and go upstairs to see what he is doing. He is leaning over Little Old Man's cot and trying to settle him by telling him it is for his own good. That's it. I officially feel like the worst mother to have ever breathed oxygen.

The sight of The Hubby trying to give sneaky comfort to Little Old Man makes me cave.

"Ok, let's try to feed him."

"It's up to you."

"Maybe you're right, I don't know."

I pick him up and feel an enormous pang of guilt. His body is taut with stress and his voice raw from screaming. I pop a bottle into his mouth and he starts to suck furiously. He gets about halfway through and then decides he has had enough.

"Hmm, maybe he wasn't hungry after all."

"Yeah, maybe he just needed a hug."

Ngargh! That's the entire point of controlled crying, it's all about the baby learning to settle themselves without being picked up all the time! By then though I am too exhausted to argue.

"Let me take over. You go back to bed, you've been up for over two hours now."

And so we reverse our roles. The Hubby takes my spot in the hallway and I get under the doona. Reality though doesn't feel as good as I imagined. I may be warm but my baby is still upset and we are both struggling with the same thing – an inability to fall asleep.

Thirty minutes later the crying subsides into a very tired moan. The Hubby returns to bed, either trusting this is the sound of impending sleep or being too exhausted to wait for confirmation. I pretend to be asleep so he feels like he has done at least one good deed for the night.

At some point I fall asleep, only to be awoken to the sound of Little Old Man randomly crying out. Daylight is peeking through the window so a couple of hours must have passed. I get up and have a quick shower to wake up.

The night wasn't as bad as the first but it sure wasn't close to the ideal. The experiment will continue. There is no other alternative.

In Practice: Part Three

Like the two nights before it, the third night starts out positively. Little Old Man is in bed and snoozing by 7 PM. The Hubby and I enjoy what is quickly becoming our together time before going to bed ourselves. Unlike the other nights though, the sense of optimism at our great sleep experiment has been replaced by a familiar feeling of dread at the night to come.

The Hubby nominates to do the first round. We confirm the ground rules – milk bar is closed between 10 PM and 5 AM (with a half hour leeway), no picking up except to quickly reposition, and only some pats and soothing words every five to ten minutes. That's it.

Little Old Man wakes just after 11 PM. The Hubby follows the plan, only soothing him when the grizzle sounds like it might escalate into something more. He is soon back in bed and feeling like he has dodged a bullet.

I fall asleep knowing that I won't be the lucky one. I have drawn the short straw of the 1 AM hellhole and it will be me, again, who has to feel like Mean Mummy.

Yet 1 AM comes and goes. The next time I awake it is to the sound of a grizzle. I look at the clock. It's 4:45 AM. I am so excited I literally spring out of bed. We've slept through the night, all three of us!

I go into Little Old Man's room. His grizzle has escalated into a cry and I prepare a bottle for him. It's a bit before the reopening of the milk bar but he hasn't eaten since 7 PM the night before so I figure it is fair enough.

He hungrily gulps down a bottle and half of another one. I change his nappy and rock him before placing him back in his cot. I can't believe my luck. He is going back to sleep!

I linger in the hallway for five minutes until he settles into silence. I then poke my head in to see him fast asleep.

I tip-toe back to bed and miraculously fall back asleep until I am awoken by Little Old Man babbling at 7:30 AM. It is the longest block of sleep any of us have had in months.

I go through the day trying not to get overly excited but finding myself almost punching the air in elation. I've read this technique is more of a circuit breaker than a magic fix and babies can easily regress if taken out of their routine. Yet if this is anywhere remotely near a new normal, I could get very used to it.

Fort Knox

The advent of crawling in our household has opened up a world of new obstacles and pitfalls. High on my anxiety-inducing list are the stairs. I have nightmares of Little Old Man spontaneously deciding to crawl head-long down a set of stairs when he is allowed to free-range. He can happily attempt to crawl up them with my hand poised near his backside. Yet crawl down unaided? Maybe when he's eighteen.

The Hubby has installed security gates at the top and bottom of each set of stairs and now our house now reminds me of the time I visited a medium security prison for work. The prison was segmented into zones and separated by guarded gates. As I walked through each gate, it had to be shut behind me as part of the security protocol.

Having my home feel like a prison though is a small price to pay for peace of mind. I can't believe I just wrote that but it is true. All I care about is knowing there is no way Little Old Man can tumble up or down the stairs so long as our gates are secured.

The other thing that we now need to be mindful of is anything within head-hitting height. When he is out of the hexagon, I am on constant patrol. The most innocent of things can be a hazard and I am amazed at how many sharp edges our home has at his head height. Crawling past cupboards, chairs and pulling books off shelves could all lead to head injuries.

While the dangers seem endless, I try not to be one of those mothers who must think out every last potential scenario. It's hard not to though when I am watching him move unsteadily across the floor. My eyes can't help but scan a few steps ahead for potential dangers.

Little Old Man's fervour for crawling and generally being in constant motion has led me to imagine what safer alternatives I could set up. My favourite idea is a horse training ring in the hexagon, with a stake in the middle and a rope around his torso. He could then go round and round in circles, burning up all that excess energy, while I safely sit back. The trick would be finding a way to encourage him to crawl in neat circles.

For his part, The Hubby suggested a baby-sized hamster wheel. Given the speed at which Little Old Man crawls, he also suggested we hook it up to some power generator and use the energy created to heat the house. This would create maximum output with minimum danger but harnessing the power could possibly be against some child labour laws.

In all seriousness, I really don't want to turn my home into some form of kiddy Fort Knox. The trick, as I have learnt, is to look one metre ahead of him when he is one the move. If I spot a danger, I won't move to protect him from every last one. Rather, I will target the really big ones and try to stand back so he can learn the rest. This won't be easy but I think it's equally as important for me to learn to incrementally let go as it is for him to crawl.

Refurbishment

Below knee-height, things in our house start to look a bit strange and out of place. Books have been stacked horizontally instead of in vertically descending order, knick-knacks have disappeared to higher levels and pot plants are oddly trimmed.

It is like a high-tide water mark that runs through our living room, into the kitchen and beyond to the dining room. The effect is subtle yet dramatic in the eyes of The Hubby and I. Together we carefully furnished the house and made it our home. The placement of every last piece was given due consideration in context of the overall feel we wanted to create.

Crawling has changed our priorities quickly and we rearranged our house with both his safety and our sanity in mind. He has since made it his business to point out every potential hazard and expensive breakable object which we as parents failed to spot. And, try as we might, we haven't been able to hide all the electrical cords and cables from him. It seems that it is not only remote controls which are like catnip for babies. No age appropriate toy quite stacks up against the excitement of gumming a live cable.

In an effort to combat this crawling menace, I have tried to get inside the head of Little Old Man. How would a baby think? What would be attractive to them? I have even got down on my own hands and knees to gain a better perspective on any low-hanging forbidden fruit.

Despite these efforts, I know the high-tide mark is only going to rise as Little Old Man learns to pull himself up and then finally begin to walk. My only hope is that enough time elapses in between to allow me to teach him what can and cannot be touched.

A Wobbly Renaissance

I wish I could say that all the desperate and sleepless nights of controlled crying are behind us and we all now peacefully sleep between the hours of 7 PM and 7 AM as promised in the books. Oh God how I wish I could say that.

The earlier positive signs dissipated and we were left again with a mixed bag of sleep. We have no idea going in what the night will hold nor do we feel any greater sense of control over how Little Old Man settles. It still feels up to fate whether any of us get some sleep, which is a rather unsettling context in which to find my own sleep. There is no upward trend – just the infinite flat nothingness of chronic sleep deprivation.

There are occasional flashes of hope – a couple of nights with three-hour blocks here or a sleep-in there. I desperately extrapolate these out into a potential pattern, only to then be thwarted by the randomness of his sleep yet again.

At the moment he is averaging four to five wakes a night. Some of those are pure settling but others are feeds. We caved on the feeds, particularly at the beginning and end of the night because he is still refusing solids. When we followed the controlled crying method to the letter, all we ended up with was two hours of screaming, three frazzled individuals and one empty bottle.

To deal with the continual wake-ups, we either take turns doing the graveyard shift or one of us does it all so the other can sleep the whole night only to return the favour the next night.

The slight problem with our system is that I lack the crucial Mamma Bear instinct. I remember reading once about a mother who slept through a truck crashing into her living room and only awoke when her baby whimpered. That is not me. As hard as it may be to fall into a deep sleep, once I'm there it takes a lot to wake me. Unless he is in the same room as me, Little Old Man needs to be screaming at full throttle to wake me from a deep sleep. This is rather unfortunate for The Hubby because his threshold for waking is a lot lower.

The result is that The Hubby is disturbed from his sleep if I've managed to fall asleep on duty. Lucky for him he seems to fall back asleep quickly enough but it is a disturbance nevertheless. We have both resigned ourselves though to the notion that this is the way sleep is from now on. It is slightly less depressing to accept the current reality than to continually build up false hope.

Yet I have done more than resign myself to the present situation. I fear his sleep will never correct itself and he will grow up to be one of those kids who always struggles to get to sleep. As the saying goes, the apple doesn't fall far from the tree. I've never been a great sleeper, worse now that I'm interrupted every two to three hours. Perhaps it is genetic, which is a subtle way of a mother blaming herself. Or perhaps, perhaps, he will grow out of it…eventually. I have to keep believing that.

Deflated

I love Little Old Man more than life itself but he has pushed me to the very borders of what I can handle and increasingly beyond. I have tried to be so patient and loving and everything that is expected of a mother. But I just can't do that all the time anymore with little sleep and a full-on cranky baby.

Some mornings he wakes with a smile and his excited penguin flapping. Regardless of how hard the night before was, this is usually enough to power me into the day.

At the moment though, most mornings start at around 5 AM with grizzling and by 6 AM he is up. Depending on how the night has gone, I either enter his nursery as the oasis of motherly calm that I imagine I am supposed to be and soothe him into a half-decent mood. Or, I go in there and say that I need a shower to wake up and will be back in ten minutes. When I choose this option, I shut the door and turn on the bathroom fan and heater so I don't hear anything outside the room. It helps a little to be able to reclaim the ability to choose when I start the day, even if I'm fighting off the guilt trips in my mind.

After one particularly bad night though, I was so cross at his continual grizzling that I went in and told him "Mummy has a failure to care right now", then had an extended shower. When my frustration had slumped into guilt, I felt so horrible even though I knew he doesn't understand what I had said. It was an acute moment of failure, where my vision of what I should be as a mother and the reality were at the furthest possible points apart.

When we have these starts to the day it is very hard to bounce back. Sometimes he blesses me with a two-hour morning nap and I take the opportunity to either sleep or force myself to do nothing but lay on the couch. This allows us to restart the day and work our way through.

On other days, he is without mercy.

There are many adjectives I can think of to describe parenting – some positive, some perhaps not fit for print. Yet if there was one word that most closely encapsulates the experience for me so far it would be: unrelenting. From the night after giving birth, when I was all post-op and dazed yet expected to breastfeed, I have been parenting without pause. I have not had a full day off in nine months. Hell, I haven't even had half a day off.

Rain, hail or shine, mummy has been on call and expected to deliver service with a smile.

I know this is what I signed up for in having a baby and to a large extent I just have to suck it up. It's just that a rather inconvenient truth remains that I am human and can't be on call all the time without there being some consequences to my well-being. What the alternative is, I don't know. We have no family here so any breaks I get are at the expense of an equally exhausted Hubby.

When I have a bad day, I always remind myself that tomorrow could be better. I try to draw a line with the sun so I can bounce into a new day. Yet the more months of our sleep drought that go by, the less able I am to find that bounce.

At the moment I see myself as a deflated ball, face-planting into the floor with full force over and over again with each bad night. There is no rebound in sight and the realisation is beginning to make me desperate.

Flatlands

I guess it came as no surprise that I eventually stopped trying to bounce back. My face remained stuck to the floor and I couldn't lift it high enough to gain a perspective. As far as I could see, sleep was never going to happen for me ever again. Little Old Man would never sleep properly and I would never get rid of my own struggles with insomnia. We were caught in a downward spiral.

At first I panicked about my lack of desire to bounce back. I had always kind of waited for it to happen naturally and didn't really make much of a conscious effort. A few hours sleep was usually enough to correct me. With a particularly bad period of sleep though, I lost that natural ebb and flow in my emotions.

But then a funny thing happened. I wondered what would happen if I just accepted my current low mood and let it be. I was sleep deprived and as a consequence my head was in a funny place. Trying to rebound in that state was only delivering ever-diminishing returns. To continue fighting against the same set of circumstances was not going to produce any other result. Some fundamental things had to change first, starting with his sleep.

I went to see a community nurse and signed up for a sleep course. I was told they would tailor a sleep program specifically for him and we can test it out for a week. If this doesn't improve things, our names would then be placed on a waiting list for a live-in sleep clinic.

I also booked an appointment to see a nutritionist. Little Old Man is nine months old yet still refuses any solids except for maybe sucking on a biscuit. Every day we perform a pro-forma act of stubbornness on both sides. I try to feed him carefully prepared purees and he does his best to avoid eating any of it. My suspicion is that the lack of solids is one of the reasons stopping him from sleeping through. His belly has outgrown formula as a single source of nutrition but he, for whatever reason, refuses to do the same.

As difficult as it has been to accept, I have also recognised that I can't be on call all the time. I have to let go, even if that means The Hubby needs to step in. We have begun to divide the night duties, not based on who got up last, but rather on who is less exhausted. I have also begun to train myself to see me-time as more necessity than luxury. If I can't gain energy through sleep, then I need to get it through something else.

Nothing is anywhere near sustainable or reinflated but at least there's some oxygen flowing in. I'm set to wait it out and hope my bounce comes back in time rather than try to artificially force it. All I have left right now is telling myself that we will find a way through this – we have to.

The Ugly Truth

It's just a phase, only a phase. He's teething. He's going through a growth spurt. He's just been in a portacot for a few days. He's struggling with solids. He's got a cold. He's got wind. Did I mention the teething?

I have used all the excuses in the book for Little Old Man's sleep issues. Over the months I have explained the broken sleep away as this phase or that. It was only when I was asked when his problems began that I realised they were there from day one. All those supposed phases added up to a continuous stream of sleepless nights, except of course for The Golden Age. The relentlessness revealed one ugly truth: Little Old Man is and always has been a crap sleeper.

He fights sleep at every turn. Oh how he fights it. And even when he finally gets there, he rarely stays settled. At the end of each sleep cycle he is up and grizzling like clockwork.

At the sleep course, the community nurse goes round the room to write down what the main issues are that people are facing. I consider my options of what to say when it is my turn. Except for a couple of mummy friends with their own sleep issues, I have stopped speaking truthfully about Little Old Man's sleep. If asked, I gloss over an answer and try to get out of the conversation quickly. I can't handle the sympathy or pep talks anymore, they make me feel like an acute and desperate failure.

I scan the room to see if there is someone else who looks like they are that stage or beyond. Whenever I have been scratching at the far side of desperation, I find myself searching out a baby situation that is worse than mine. Somehow it makes me feel a little bit cheerier to hear I haven't hit absolute bottom and it could always be even worse. Parents of twins usually do the trick.

As the nurse goes round the room though, it becomes apparent that nothing quite matches the length and relentlessness of Little Old Man's sleeping habits. I feel very sorry for the couple struggling with a sleepless three month old but my personal hell has been going on for nine months. Nine. Freaking. Months. It feels as though I've been on a very long haul flight and they've just tacked on to the final domestic leg with me.

Only one other woman manages to give me the illusion that I have it lucky. Her daughter is covered in eczema and cannot be left to self-settle because she scratches her sores and bleeds all over the cot. Her story is truly awful and a knot of guilt forms in my stomach for wanting someone to be worse off than me.

Then the nurse turns her attention my way. I am on the brink of tears but remember my promise to leave behind public outbursts of emotion.

"So what have you tried to get baby to sleep?"

"Everything. Controlled crying, rocking, singing, comforters, no comforters, dream feeds, sleeping in the room, music, white noise. You name it, we've given it a shot. He has been waking about five times a night for the past five weeks and two or three times for months before that."

"Hmm. And how is he at the moment?"

"He has a cold so he's really all over the place."

"Have you tried squirting breast milk up his nose? It really helps with blockages."

I frown at the nurse and quickly begin to lose faith. This was sold to me as a chance to draw up a personalised sleep plan based upon individual issues. So far though it has consisted of listening to other people's problems and watching the same DVD shown in the newborn sleep course. I look out the window and question whether it would have been more useful to have instead slept in the car for a couple of hours.

What am I doing here anyway? Didn't I just resign myself to the fact that Little Old Man will never sleep? Why am I fighting again? I fight his sleep almost as much as he does.

I don't know the answers. All I know is that I don't have any energy left to spend on futile fights anymore. I could watch the DVD again, have a cup of tea and go home to start over but with what? I've got nothing. I'm a spent force quite content feeling sorry for myself.

The nurse wraps up the group by going round once more and asking everyone what strategy they will implement when they get home. I say my plan is to harass the contact given for a referral to the residential sleep clinic. A couple of people laugh but I'm serious.

On the drive home a thought passes through my mind: if I smash my car into that tree, then I would be admitted to hospital for at least two days and could therefore sleep. Luckily, despite the insanity of sleep deprivation, there is a small part of my brain that still knows such thoughts should exit as soon as they enter. I also know that such thoughts are a big red flag. I drive on safely home and ask The Hubby if I can be excused for an extended siesta.

The morning did not deliver the fundamental change that we so desperately seek. It's not in my nature to be pushy but I know I need to ram my way into that sleep clinic as soon as possible. I can't resign to never sleeping again nor can I continue to tread water in the hope things will right themselves with enough time. We need a reboot and we need it now.

Zen Baby

When I find myself at a physical and emotional low ebb, it is easy to lose sight of why I am going through all this. Luckily, Little Old Man is always around to remind me with his beautiful face and inquisitive personality. He may be a terror at night and sometimes during the day but he can also have moments that make my mummy heart soar.

Babies are wonderful little creatures. Intense and impractical at times, yes, but wonderful too. They represent the best of humanity because, for a fleeting moment, they are free of the prejudice and assumptions that weigh down the adults around them. As such, they are far closer than any adult to seeing people and things as they really are. This gives them the capacity to unwittingly share the world around them from a completely different viewpoint.

Every so often Little Old Man will stop crawling or trying to climb stairs long enough to examine something I hadn't even noticed. A leaf on the ground, the way the sunlight casts a shadow, the reflection of our silhouettes in the water, how the wind bends the trees outside our living room window, and the discovery of every little tag attached to his toys and clothing.

The smallest of details are the most fascinating to him and, at the same time, the most likely to have been overlooked by me in my rush to somewhere else. Before he came along, I thought I would show him the world but it turns out he shows me plenty of it too from his perspective and amazement at the newness of it all.

The things he shows me are simple but they all serve to remind me of how overly complicated my thinking can get. One of my brain's favourite hobbies is to worry about the future or situations I have limited control over. Yet there is only so much point to stressing out about such things. When I do, then I invariably end up in a kind of tunnel vision with zero perspective, much like I have been in over his sleep or earlier on over breastfeeding.

If there's one thing my Buddha Baby has taught me, it is that sometimes the best way to stop stressing is to slow down and be aware of what's around me right now. It's pretty obvious that there's not much fun to be had in only seeing my problems to the exclusion of all the good going on. If I don't consciously stop myself from worrying, then I will overlook this stuff.

My attempts to slow down and avoid tunnel vision have had varied successes. Sometimes I'm able to and other times I'm a hopeless stress head. I remain nevertheless committed to trying.

My ultimate goal is to make an unsteady leap of faith and believe that everything I am worrying about will sort itself out, somehow, with much less stress and micromanagement on my part. That feels like a long way away but it's a goal all the same. In the meantime, I'm quite content with every so often literally managing to slow down to smell the roses that my son has so kindly highlighted to me by shoving them in his mouth.

Oversupply

When I was pregnant I was told not to worry about buying baby clothes – particularly the smaller sizes. Apparently there is nothing women love more than buying other women baby clothes. The smaller the better, as there is a correlation between size and the cuteness factor.

This advice turned out to be accurate. I was inundated with hand-me-downs and gifts of itty-bitty newborn clothes from all corners of my life. It was touching and overwhelming all at once. What I suffered in undersupply with breast milk, I more than made up with an oversupply in clothing. The pile was so large that I quickly lost any overview of what clothes I had in what size.

Instead of being logical and sorting out the sizes though, I decided instead to follow my hormones. And my hormones said one thing: shop! Well nest, actually. But in my head I translated this to mean beat up my credit card while I still had a full-time wage and the spare time to do so.

As the pregnancy progressed and my mobility became limited, I turned my shopping efforts onto the internet. Our post box was filled with onesies and cute pram sets freighted from all over the world. Come to think of it, perhaps I should also add a couple of tree plantings to the list for these carbon-heavy purchases.

When I finally got round to sorting, I realised most clothes fell in the zero to six month range. After that there were some clothes for six to twelve months and then nothing by eighteen months. The majority of larger clothes were thanks to hand-me-downs.

Since his birth, I have tried to ensure Little Old Man wears each outfit at least once to assuage any oversupply guilt. This not an easy task to achieve. It requires me to keep an eye on what clothes are currently rotating through his drawers as well as regularly checking through the next pile.

And checking the next pile doesn't mean just checking the size – no, I have to physically hold up each item and guesstimate whether he is big enough for it now. For while baby clothes come in standard sizes, the designs and cuts are as varied as adult clothing. A size 00 in one brand may be a size 000 in another. Adding to the confusion are the clothes from other countries, which range wildly in interpreting how big a baby should be at a certain age.

I have been caught by this a few times, particularly with outfits from Le Smug Shark. Some of the six month old clothes she posted to me looked fit for a newborn. It would seem tat French babies are as petite as their Mamas.

The other problem is admitting that it is time to retire a favourite onesie or pair of pants. Despite having so many clothes to churn through, there are a few items that stick with me and are hard to let go of. Usually they are those rare pieces that are cute, easy to put on and comfortable for him. I get attached to seeing him in these outfits and it is only begrudgingly that I move them into the potential next child and/or charity box.

Little Old Man grows so fast that this mourning process for his clothes happens on a near weekly basis. Sometimes my reluctance to let go gets to the ridiculous stage. At this point, buttons pop and I make him wear long grandpa socks to cover the gap from once long pants turned capris. One onesie I was particularly attached to got so small that, when he sat, the buttons popped and his nappy burst out of the gaping hole.

Even for my own part, I have had trouble retiring a much-loved maternity skirt. It is full of holes on the band at the top and continually needs to be hitched up in the absence of a big pregnancy belly. Yet somehow I manage to wear it multiple times a week – it is comfy and goes with everything. I am ashamed to say that I have previously put the skirt in the bin, only to fish it out later and transfer to the wash basket. My next attempt will involve cutting the skirt so I'm not tempted to repeat this process. I guess I really have to learn to let go better.

As the months pass, the piles become more manageable in size. In a few more months I will be at the stage where I may have to actively buy clothes once more. Well, unless I get online first and bump up my piles. I somehow doubt I will ever get down to the last onesie.

Camping Out

We have lived through the insanity and clawed back a little bit from the edge. Little Old Man's sleep patterns have settled back from a manic five times a night to three.

The slight easing in night duties has given us an opportunity to regroup and think of a new strategy for dealing with the situation. And that strategy is – drumroll please – a camping mattress in the hallway outside Little Old Man's nursery! Genius! Why did we not think of this before? We don't need our bed for collective sleep in any case, so why do we both get in it each night and frustrate ourselves?

Instead, we have divided the night into two camping shifts. When one of us is not on shift, they get to sleep in the bed with the door closed and earplugs in. We have trialled our new system for a few days now and the early signs are positive.

In essence, what we have done is given up on waiting on Little Old Man gifting us with sleep and fashioned a way for us to give it to ourselves. Sacrificing half the night on a camping mattress for a block of guaranteed sleep in a bed may seem an odd exchange but it far better than what we previously lived with. And, while it's still not the reboot we need, the new strategy is something more liveable in the interim.

Wrestle Mania!!

"If you just lay still for ten seconds this will all be over. Ok, let's make it five seconds!"

I am back again at that sadly desperate point of pleading with a baby. But it is no use. Babies know neither mercy nor logic.

Little Old Man has been squirming, turning, writhing, wriggling and convulsing on the change table for a good five minutes. The accompanying protests are most likely audible throughout the neighbourhood but I fail to care anymore. We are too locked in battle.

We circle each other in our intractable stubbornness. All I want to do is change his nappy. All he wants is to move and be anywhere but here. Like I told him in my exasperated yet strangely calm tone though, if he was still for a matter of seconds it would be done. But no, we'd rather bat at shadows on the wall or reach for the tissue box while driving Mummy insane.

Little Old Man has ramped up his carousel antics on the change table into something that can only be described as wrestling. I can't even lay him flat as the starting position anymore. He is already twirling in my arms as he descends towards the mat – his eyes and hands searching out a point, any point, of distraction.

If he wants to go somewhere or touch something, then it will happen unless I pick him up as the ultimate red card. But I can't dress him while holding him – I'm good as a mother but not that good, not yet at least. I have also not yet developed the same X-ray vision my mother used to have. Just give me time.

I have seriously considered watching a few wrestling matches to reinterpret the moves into more baby-appropriate ones. I need to find a way to gently counteract or contain the strength of his movements so he remains still for long enough to change his nappy or outfit. I garner parenting advice from various sources but never did I think Hulk Hogan would be one of them.

At a touch under ten kilos, he certainly punches above his weight. I am amazed at how much of my strength as a fully grown adult is needed just to keep a handle on him.

Today I was holding up his ankles to wipe his bum. Usually this is a position he can't leverage great movement from but he has learnt some new tricks. He flexed his trunk upwards and twisted it along with his head to the side. He then grabbed on to the table and started to pull himself up.

His movement created a split second where I had to decide between trying to maintain control through holding his ankles or letting go altogether so I could gain more control round his ribs. I moved swiftly, knowing he was merely millimetres away from falling off the change table.

I held him to my chest and breathed a sigh of relief. Little Old Man seemed oblivious to the chaos his actions caused and continued to arch backwards in search of whatever distraction he was aiming for.

Other than wrestling, the only trick I have left is distraction. He is presently in love with a magnet from the fridge, which I let him suck on freely but only at change time. Alas this magnetic attraction is beginning to wane and he has yet to indicate a new distraction of choice.

I guess this is all a nice way of saying that, like many things in parenting, I have no clue what I should technically be doing. I try to be firm but friendly with him but all the while I am in half panic under the façade of confident parenting.

How do I beat him at his own game? Or tell him, for that matter, that this actually isn't a game? How do I get him to focus? How do I stop him from doing crazy kamikaze moves on the change mat? I can't, really. He's still a baby.

Half Bounce

After a couple of weeks of the camping mattress solution, both The Hubby and I feel slightly more human. Perhaps me more so than him given that The Hubby usually nominates for the harder morning shift to fit in with his work.

I don't want to jinx it but I feel at least my own sleeping problems are less acute. My insomnia doesn't seem to bite as hard now that I am free to sleep half the night in peace. When I'm on duty I can manage to sleep lightly but I know that I could be woken at any minute. I accept this defined period of the night for what it is rather than struggle with the old vague lines between on and off duty that we had when The Hubby and I shared a bed.

Sleep deprivation is a strange thing. When I'm in the midst of it, my mind is a foggy mess and the world seems like it will never, ever be right again.

There is a sense of permanency that fuels my desperation. Nothing will be good again. Sleep will never happen. I will never feel human again. This perma-jetlag will plague me forever.

I think all these things despite having learnt countless times over in the past ten months that sleep deprivation is a transient state of mind. It is incredible how quickly I can recover to functional levels with just a couple of hours of sleep. Four hours is the sweet spot. If I can get a block of four hours then I feel like a woman renewed.

Luckily, I have managed to accrue a number of such blocks since we started the camping mattress strategy. Yes, there is a part of me that really, really still needs a long lie down and possibly a holiday involving copious amounts of cocktails by the pool and a great babysitting service. Yet I feel like a solid buffer has been placed between me and that head space where I felt like driving into a tree was the most logical way to get some rest.

Ideally, the camping mattress will go one day and The Hubby and I can return to sleeping in our own bed. Even more ideally, this will occur because Little Old Man has discovered the joys of sleeping through the night. For now though, this is the best we've got. It may not give me a full bounce but at least it has shown that, with some sleep, there's a little bounce left in me yet.

A Certain Diplomatic Incident

I swear Little Old Man will grow up to be a comedian. As he has shown on many previous occasions, he has an amazing sense of timing. Today was no exception.

A friend of mine will soon be leaving Canberra after her husband's diplomatic posting ends. By way of farewell, the ambassador's wife at the embassy of their home country extended an invitation to her closest friends for lunch.

I have been invited to similar functions before and know through experience that, despite the call for informality, you always wear your Sunday best and behave accordingly. These are not the kind of functions where you can put your elbows on the table. And you certainly don't slouch. Ladies who lunch, as I have learnt, don't slouch. Ever.

The greatest challenge has been mastering the fine art of idle chitchat with typically intelligent, urbane and articulate strangers. I struggle with conjuring up topics of conversation that are engaging yet altogether harmless. I either end up appearing dull or awkwardly oversharing in some subconscious rebellion at the stuffiness of the situation I perceive myself to be in.

This time though I enter the embassy with no such concerns. A baby will offer the perfect conversational foil. Most people love babies and asking the same questions about them. Is he crawling yet? Is he on solids? How are you finding motherhood? I have my answers ready to go, complete with a few well-practised jokes that I know are comic gold.

Little Old Man and I work the room like old pros. He thankfully went down for his morning nap as scheduled and is now happy to smile and coo for an appreciative audience. Sometimes I feel bad for wanting him to perform, like he might think I see him as some kind of performing seal. But then I remember he doesn't even know what a performing seal is and I feel a bit better. Besides, he seems really in the mood for attention.

I set him down on the parquetry wooden floor and he crawls across to a woman who is sitting on a chair. She bends down to say hello and he pulls himself up to kneeling position, arms outstretched for her to pick him up. He is practically begging for her attention as though he never gets any at home. She obliges and he laughs – much to the amusement of everyone at the table.

My son, the star performer. I don't even have to bother with the idle chit-chat. Everybody is content to just watch him drool and grab at the neatly laid out cutlery.

And then lunch is served. A waitress comes over and asks if I would like her to show Little Old Man the kitchen so I can eat my lunch in peace. Why yes, certainly! Don't mind if I do enjoy a lunch without chowing down fast and helicopter parenting at the same time.

I am so chuffed by the unexpected babysitting that I even allow myself a glass of wine. The situation is far removed from my usual routine of sitting on the couch in tracksuit pants eating leftovers and playing my sad little phone apps for intellectual stimulation. I savour the moment in adult world because, well, haven't I earned it?

I certainly did that very morning. Little Old Man did something in his nappy that was off the chart. It was…well, let's just say it was. We both ended up needing a shower and wardrobe change.

The smelly grossness of the morning was worth it though. I enjoy my wonderfully expensive wine like a mummy Cinderella and banish thoughts of having earlier been covered head to toe in shit. I also savour it because I know there is no way humanly possible that Little Old Man has any poo left in him to evacuate. I am safe.

The waitress comes back as the plates are taken away and hands over a jovial Little Old Man. He has apparently been having a grand old time in the kitchen flirting with the chef.

"I even squished up some raspberries and fed them to him off my finger. He loved it!"

"Ohhhhaha, really? How did you manage that?"

"Don't know. He just ate it."

I want to press this woman for more information about her technique. I am still deploying aggressive marketing techniques to convince Little Old Man to let even the blandest bit of slop into his mouth. And she got something as wildly exotic and colourful as raspberries into him? How? Tell me, woman! But she has already disappeared discreetly back into the kitchen.

Little Old Man begins to rub his eyes and look a little less perky than at the beginning. I take this as my cue to bundle him up before he gets cranky. I stand up from the table and walk over to my friend and the ambassador's wife to thank them for a lovely lunch.

And then it happens.

I hear a splash, then a dry-retch. Well, actually a wet-retch. Then I hear an audible gasp across the room and I look up to see the eyes of twenty women in their Sunday bests looking at me and Little Old Man. All conversation stops. I quite possibly even hear cutlery drop in shock.

I look down and Little Old Man's face is as red as the raspberries he gorged himself on in my absence. I panic and rub his back, which brings forth even more vomit. He then breathes in deeply and sneezes, spraying vomit in a greater radius than his projectile efforts. His colour returns to normal almost instantly and he lets out a cry. I know he is alright.

I glance at the damage around me. The parquetry floor he had been crawling on is covered in white formula vomit and half-digested red fruity bits. I move my arm to get a better look. The crook of my elbow has been cradling Little Old Man and, unknown to me, is loaded with another lake of vomit. As I move, it slaps audibly onto the floor and all over my shoes, adding to the disaster zone.

Everyone in the room unfreezes and begins to talk again. The exorcist baby showstopper number has come to an end. Like his bowels, there is nothing left in him to give. The raspberry waitress comes out with towels and kindly offers to take him so I can 'freshen up'. It is really a kind offer since we are both covered.

I am relieved that he is ok. He has only had a couple of upchucks like that in his lifetime – once with avocado and another time with peach. It's like a piece gets stuck somewhere in his oesophagus and will only dislodge with some concerted vomiting.

Each time this has happened we have both been left wary of food afterwards. The nutritionist we went to see seemed to fancy herself as a bit of a child psychologist on the side and hypothesised that these traumatic choking incidents were behind his reluctance to eat solids. I hope she was wrong because this would set him back months.

Apart from the relief, I am also feeling absolutely mortified. Of all the places he could have done this he has done it in one of the most socially proper settings imaginable. At least I was standing on something waterproof and not the antique Persian rug off to my left. His timing may be good but it's not that good.

I freshen up as best I can and go to hug my friend farewell before remembering I am a mess. She looks at me in sympathy and says it really wasn't that bad even though we both know it was. I turn and apologise sincerely to the ambassador's wife but, rather diplomatically, she waves it off.

"Oh my dear, I have raised three children. This is par for the course."

"Thank you for your understanding, really."

I feel like adding she can send me any floor polishing bills but figure it's probably poor form to mention such trivialities.

Maybe I was a bit wrong in approaching these events as unforgivingly stiff affairs. I have, after all, just being involved in the biggest social faux pas I could imagine. Yet she saw what happened in a more forgiving light than my self-conscious self ever would allow – a simple case of a baby being sick. In doing so, I saw her for what she was beyond her formal title: a mother.

I could also see that she was right. There will be moments where Little Old Man happily plays along as the centre of attention and things go smoothly. But for every smile he can also be cranky, frown or empty his orifices in all the wrong places. That's just the lottery of life with a baby. I can only enjoy the good if I also accept the flipside, even if that does involve the occasional diplomatic incident.

Sock it to Me

Life with Little Old Man can sometimes feel a bit like ground hog day. Every day we face the same set of unspoken arguments. No, you can't eat dirt out of the pot plant. Yes, we are going to try to eat this rice cereal. No, please no not another poo. Yes, you can destroy your father's collection of German grammar books.

One of the biggest and most frequent arguments we have relates to the smallest of his accessories: socks. I shouldn't actually call it an argument. It is more of a fundamental difference of opinion.

Despite it being winter and miserably cold, Little Old Man would prefer nothing more than to go through life barefoot and free. He protests at the imposition of socks on his chubby little toes and fails to see the practicality of warm feet. I, on the other hand, see all the point in the world.

I inform him each time I put them back on that socks keep are an awesome invention for keeping feet warm. Without them, the rest of our bodies would be unable to maintain a perfect body temperature. Humans have suffered for millennia the plight of sockless feet and it is only modern mankind that has been able to rise above their chilly ancestors. Or something. Just keep your bloody socks on this time, will you??

I hear myself giving this thinly veiled lecture in a happy voice and feel like such a mother. I swear I am only one small step away from tucking in his shirt at the back to prevent his kidneys from getting cold. I never did discover why my mother was so obsessed with me not getting cold kidneys as a child. What would have happened if I did?

Albert Einstein said that the definition of insanity is to repeat the same thing over and over while expecting different results. I have recognised the slight insanity in running after Little Old Man to put his socks back on for the umpteenth time. As such, I have devised other ways to keep Little Old Man's feet warm other than engaging in direct sock-to-foot combat.

My first attempts involved putting baby shoes on. This slowed his sock pulling efforts down a bit until he figured out how to rip off a shoe with his mouth. It was really quite coordinated of him.

Then I double-socked him, pulling both socks way up high over his pants in a grandpa manoeuvre. Depending on the pants involved, this can hold for up to two hours before he finally manages to free his feet from bondage.

I swear whoever manages to invent a sock that does not fall off through crawling will be an instant millionaire and the demigod to mothers everywhere. Double that fortune if said sock cannot be pulled off and drooled all over in the backseat.

While I may not have invented anything, I think my third solution comes close to solving the sock problem. Given how cold it is, I now dress Little Old Man in a full cotton onesie with built-in feet as an undergarment. This may not be as thick or warming as socks but it sure beats him going barefoot for most of the day.

Now to find a solution to Little Old Man tipping over the bin...

This is Not a Drill!

"What is your problem?!?"

Little Old Man has been screaming his finest for over an hour. He has refused to go down for his morning nap despite rubbing his eyes and giving me every other textbook indication that he is tired. He has had a bottle, a nappy change, I've sung his current favourite go-to-sleep song (*Auld Lang Syne*) over a dozen times, I've rocked him...nothing, nothing penetrates his upset cries. It feels like I've landed at the worst New Year's Eve Party ever.

He has worked himself beyond Strangled Cat and into a new zone of distress that he has only reached a couple of times before. I call it The Distressed Elephant. He crawls around his cot on all fours before stopping to rock back and forth while crying. For whatever reason the action reminds me of maladjusted zoo animals, elephants in particular, that make the same movement to relieve their boredom and anxiety.

I adapt my own form of Distressed Elephant and pace the room. What is wrong? Why won't he go down? Why must he always fight me? Why does he do this to me?

The last question is a dangerous one, as it flips the situation into him against me when really he is just a baby and acting out of instinct rather than malice. I see the question as a red flag to leave the room for a moment to regroup.

Away from the nursery I find the nearest pillow and punch down hard then scream into it. Our household would be in serious trouble if someone ever set up a Royal Society for the Prevention of Cruelty to Pillows and Cushions. It may be wrong but sometimes a quick whack to a pillow is the quickest way to release pent-up frustration. Actually, it probably isn't wrong as this action doubles as a form of housework. Our couch has never looked so fluffed up and inviting!

I feel so inadequate for not being able to remain calm and to in turn calm him down from whatever state he has worked himself into. I wish I had the insight and patience of a saint but I don't. I'm just an ignorant mum with no idea of what else to try. His crying is out of all proportion to his usual day nap protests.

I decide to try nothing for ten minutes and close his door. I head for the bathroom and turn on all available fans and heaters so I can't hear him. Then I get in the shower and let the hot water sting away my tears. I am back in the zone where I feel the most like a failure as a mother. Retreating to the bathroom feels like defeat every time even though I know logically there is nothing else I can do while we're both so tense.

For my part, I have to calm down by letting all the frustration and upset go through me. I figure he pretty much needs to learn do the same.

I hop out of the shower and hear his urgent cries have subsided to half-arsed wails. The tightly wound coil in his chest is slowly releasing itself. I go in to his room and sit there, humming *Auld Lang Syne* until he begins to snore peacefully.

An hour later he is awake again and still grumpy. I look at the clock and decide to call a friend to meet me for lunch. I have to get out of the house. Like with sleep deprivation, a grumpy baby is easier for me to handle when out and about.

I meet up with my friend and tell her about the morning I've had. I am still at a loss about what his problem is. He doesn't have a temperature and all the usual care boxes are ticked. It is like he has had a personality transplant.

My friend bends over Little Old Man and tries to get him to crack a smile. He deadpans her then looks the other way. Undeterred, she decides to look a little closer and sticks a finger in his mouth.

"Well, there's your problem right there."

"Huh?"

"See those two white lines on his gums? They are his teeth."

"Oh..."

"He's teething!"

I feel like such a fool. Why had teething not even entered my realm of thinking as a possibility? He is ten months old for goodness sake! All those earlier false starts put the idea completely out of my head. Either that or I must've really believed it when I thought he had no teeth in his head. But Gummy McGummy has teeth alright. And they are sprouting forth.

I take Little Old Man out of the pram and give him a hug, whispering an apology into his ear for not working it out for myself. A ball of guilt settles into me and I feel like a candidate yet again for World's Worst Mother. If I had known the cause then perhaps I would not have become so frustrated with his random screaming marathon. I would have given him teething gel, pain relief, more hugs and way more sympathy.

The situation is an example of the many moments where I wish he could communicate and

I'm guessing he wishes the same. It must be so frustrating and I really need to remind myself to see the world from his perspective, even when his behaviour is pushing all my buttons at once.

I ring The Hubby and let him know teething is back on and that, yes, it really is happening this time. This is not a drill. He is excited yet unsure of what we can expect next in terms of sleep and mood. I tell him we're just going have to learn to be extra patient and give him leeway until some teeth appear. Ready or not, Little Old Man is about to get his chompers.

Roadrunner

My earlier guilt trips over the playpen have gone away. It's not that I got used to caging Little Old Man into a defined space but rather the playpen ceased to be. Well, at least in its original form.

Little Old Man worked out pretty quickly what we were doing when we placed him in the playpen and cried for his freedom accordingly. I tried to resist letting my guilt cast me in the role of prison warden, even when he grabbed at the bars and pouted his protest. No no, this is all for your own safety my dear child. I am protecting you, not inhibiting your inquisitive spirit.

The battle of wills has ultimately proved futile. As much as I hate to admit it, I caved. Little Old Man's curiosity and determination to explore the world would not be quashed by my desire for the easy safety of a playpen. So The Hubby and I have been negotiating where the boundaries of safety should lie and coming up with ingenious solutions to enforce them. We have strived to find a balance between sensibly cautious and overprotective.

The playpen was disassembled into pieces of fencing and tethered in front of areas deemed dangerous or expensive if broken. Other contraptions have also sprung up around the house, such as cardboard rings around the base of pot plants and baby locks for drawers.

Now we have a free-range baby except for a few exceptions. Everyone seems happy with the solution. The only slight problem is that Little Old Man does not follow the 'out of reach out of mind' line of thinking. Rather, he sees the barriers set up by The Hubby as a fun challenge and sets about disassembling them.

With age he is becoming more crafty and quicker at outsmarting his father. Undeterred, The Hubby seems to also see the situation as some kind of fun challenge and concocts even more intricate designs when his last ones fail.

The setting up and demolition of barriers is a daily occurrence in our household. It is as though father and son have pitted themselves against each other as Wile E. Coyote and the Roadrunner. Sadly, The Hubby is the unlucky coyote in the relationship and never quite manages to slow down his little roadrunner for very long.

If it was solely up to me, I may have tried the playpen solution again but I haven't and probably won't. In a strange caveman way they seem to be bonding over this common challenge and I don't want to interfere in the process.

All that is left for me to do is occasionally hum the *Roadrunner* theme when another contraption fails. That and try to maintain The Hubby's sense of humour about it all.

Meep meep!

Redesign

Apart from safety concerns, there are upsides to having a curious child. It is forcing us to be creative not only with safety but also with how to keep him entertained.

An upturned laundry basket, as it turns out, is perfect for him to push around and practise his walking on. Empty egg cartons keep him occupied for hours. And almost nothing beats the fun of bashing around a soup spoon on tiles. Well, except perhaps for getting one's hands on the Holy Grail – Mummy's smartphone. Yes, the very same one I occasionally send texts from while Little Old Man circles my legs for undivided attention. Bad mummy on her smartphone!

Little Old Man has toys, lots of them, but none of them seem quite as attractive as a real object. He learnt fairly early on to distinguish between toy and object. He flatly rejected his toy phone and keys and is insistent on drooling all over my real ones. Perhaps the bright colours and plastic feel gave them away as inferior copies – although I'd never admit this to The Hubby given his viewpoints on all things non-wooden.

In his clamouring for whatever he could wrap his chubby little fingers around, I realised that his desire for real objects was not something to be fought against. It just needed to be rethought. Why can't he play with a wooden spoon or a saucepan? Just because household items aren't designed as toys doesn't mean he can't have fun with them so long as they are safe to play with.

If he is so keen to explore the world around him, then I am more than happy to hand him some choke-free pieces of it.

Teeth!

After months of speculation, it has finally happened. Little Old Man has teeth! Not just one but two bottom teeth have emerged over the past few days.

Teeth, real teeth!

Up, Up and Away

I am sitting on a plane with Little Old Man strapped onto my seatbelt. It is like being tethered to a whirlwind and there is little chance of out-manoeuvring him. He bounces excitedly off the seat in front and onto my chest, before using me as a launch pad onto the neighbouring passenger. He is excited by this confined new game and starts the circuit again.

I make mental calculations of how long it will take him to alienate every passenger within a five row radius. Or, worse still, how long until I become *that* mother – the one with the screamy baby that everyone rolls their eyes at.

I'm hoping this doesn't happen but I don't know how Little Old Man will react to flying and air pressure. Today is our first trial. To add to the insanity, I am also flying solo to meet up with my mother for a couple of days in the sun. There is no hubby to help out with the baby and act as a buffer between me and her.

The plane bumbles along to the runway and I will it to hurry up. Maybe the roar of the engines as we take off will be enough to quieten him.

The plane stops for that moment at the end of the runway before take-off. I take this as my opportunity to pop a bottle in his mouth in an attempt to counter any ear popping. No dice. He is far too excited to sit still for a bottle.

We tilt upwards into the sky and I wait for the screaming to start. But there is nothing. Little Old Man restarts his bouncing game, blissfully unaware of the feat of engineering he has just experienced for the first time.

The seatbelt lights go off and a crew member walks by to see how he is going. She helped me get seated and is genuinely interested in making sure he is ok. It is people like her that have made me a massive fan of humanity since becoming a mother. Some people will go out of their way to help me or steal a smile from Little Old Man. For her efforts, the stewardess is rewarded with a chewed emergency landing booklet that Little Old Man excitedly hands over.

"He's fine. If there's anything to worry about, it's usually the descent."

"Oh…"

"But it's usually only if the baby has a blocked nose or something that air pressure becomes a big issue for them."

"Oh good, he's got no problems in that department."

I feel assured and the rest of the flight passes by with me trying to entertain Little Old Man within the confinement of my personal space. The biggest winner turned out to be a sick bag I fished out from the seat pocket. The crunchy sound of the plastic-coated paper is endlessly amusing, it would seem.

I look down at the nappy bag wedged between my feet and smile on all the age-appropriate toys I crammed in there. I also see the corner of a nappy and shudder at the memory of our one in-flight hiccup – a trip to the bathroom to test out my wrestling skills on a tiny change table perched perilously above the toilet.

The plane starts to descend and Little Old Man rubs his eyes. The excitement has worn off and his body clock remembers naptime is overdue. I hold him tight in my arms and rock him as I sing *Auld Lang Syne* softly into his ear. I don't want to know what the person in the seat in front of me thinks. I'm pretty sure they've worked out by now though that I am travelling with a baby.

I focus on calming him down and continue to rock and sing rhythmically. It is calming for me too after the anticipation of our first flight together. His movements start to slow. I close my eyes and continue my hypnotising hold on him. In moments like these, I like to fancy myself as a snake charmer bringing an overworked cobra under my spell. But perhaps that's just me again.

I open my eyes and look down at my sleeping boy. The horizon edges further up the window and twenty minutes later the plane safely hits the ground with a thud. Little Old Man continues to snooze sprawled out across my lap. He has managed to again be oblivious to the engineering feat that returned him safely back down to earth.

With a bit of help from the friendly stewardess, I slip him half dozing into the carrier and disembark. A trail of contentment drool extends out from his lips and onto my sleeve. So much for my fears of being the one with a screamy baby.

The Puzzler

"I bought gripe water. I thought this could be why he can't sleep."

"Uh, thanks Mum."

I place the bottle among the formula I packed for him, not quite sure what to do with it. Gripe water sounds vaguely familiar but only in a historical kind of way, like the plague or pox. I imagine its use to be about as forward thinking as the medicinal use of leeches and mercury. I make a mental note to later ask Dr Google to confirm or deny my suspicions.

The gripe water is the third sleep solution my mother has handed me since arriving at the hotel. I can't quite work out if her enthusiasm for getting Little Old Man to sleep better is for my overall well-being or for her sleep over the next couple of nights. Maybe a bit of both.

"I also bought some food pouches for him. Maybe he isn't eating many solids because you keep cooking him up vegetables."

"Uhhh…"

"You need to start on something they will like."

She holds up an array of baby food pouches filled with chocolate puddings and custards. I have nothing against baby custard but I am mindful that it is hard to foster a love of vegetables while feeding them a mono-diet of custard.

But I accept the pouches without a word of protest. There is no point in arguing with her. After all, this is the woman who fed Little Old Man the cream out of a chocolate éclair aged six months and then proclaimed he had no problems with eating solids. And she is also the woman who, at 74, still refuses to eat vegetables and picks at her plate with all the disdain of a toddler if any dare to make it on there.

I try to smile through her well-intentioned meddling. I've had plenty of practise at this pose. I love my mother dearly and know she means well but her ideas on how to feed and raise a baby are very divergent to mine. She is stuck somewhere between the Victorian and space ages. In return, I suspect she thinks I'm a parenting hippy weirdo.

The more things she pulls out of her bag of tricks though, the more I begin to see myself reflected in her. I see in us the same obsession to find the solutions to my baby's woes. It is like we have made him into a puzzle and all we need is to find the right pieces to solve the sleep mystery.

I can mock her all I like but the reality is that at times I have approached his issues in exactly the same way. The only difference is that my solutions are slightly more conventional.

"Mum, maybe there's nothing wrong with him. Maybe he is just being a baby?"

"Nonsense. He should be sleeping through and eating solids by now. I also got this teething rattle which my chemist swore by. She has three kids now, you know…"

I recede back into the smile and nod routine and keep my epiphany to myself. I can see why it is so tempting to buy everything in search of an easy solution. Nobody likes to have an unhappy baby, particularly when you feel powerless to change the situation. Baby stores cater to this by offering so many solutions that, depending on how deep your pockets are, you could quite easily spin out endlessly from one solution to the next.

At the risk of sounding defeatist, maybe there's only a limited point in trying products to solve their woes. I have found Little Old Man has a remarkable knack of righting himself when given the space to do so without running interference. Maybe if I had more patience and learnt when to step in and help him, the bigger challenges would correct themselves too.

My mother digs further into her bag in search of some homeopathic teething gel. I know Little Old Man will become her own personal guinea pig over the next couple of days. The Mamma Bear in me feels like protecting him but her snake charms and gripe water are harmless to a baby. They only stand to harm a mother who believes and puts all her desperate hope into them. And I'm not one of them. Not anymore, at least. I'm done with turning my son into a puzzle.

The Great Divide

"He's fine, just leave him."

"But…"

"He's fine!"

I am at snapping point, trying desperately to hold onto civility and not yell at either my baby or mother. They are both testing me though – hard.

We are on the last night of our getaway and I am counting down the hours till I can board the plane in the morning. I am feeling The Hubby's absence acutely. I have lost count of the number of times I wished he would magically appear at the hotel door and offer to take over so I can have a break on my supposed break. Not that I didn't realise beforehand, but his absence underlines just how much he does with Little Old Man and how well we work as a team. As a solo parent, well…

For her part, my mother has limited mobility so there's not much hands-on assistance she can provide. I know this frustrates her so I try not to let my own frustrations over Little Old Man's antics show. Yet that is proving difficult when she continues to speculate on the cause of Little Old Man's issues while also providing running commentary on my parenting skills.

As for Little Old Man, he is having a great time exploring his new surroundings. So much so that he has forgotten the need for day naps. He practically bounces round the hotel room walls in excitement and has found a new passion in swinging back and forth on cupboard doors. He alternates this with pulling threads in the carpet until bald patches appear.

When my mother sees him doing these things, she can't jump up in time to stop him. Instead, she tells him firmly to "Get down! down!" He listens to her commands about as much as her poorly trained dogs do. The only constructive thing her yelling does is tell me it is time to get back into the living room quick smart to save him or the furniture from harm.

My efforts to settle Little Old Man to sleep have become a favourite commentary topic. When I let him cry, she sighs heavily and looks agitated that she can't leap in. She doesn't understand why I would leave a baby to cry for so long. When she voices her concern, it is as though she has a direct tap into my motherly sense of failure and can trawl through the most sensitive parts with ease.

"The poor little mite. He's so upset."

"It's the method."

"You can't leave a little baby to cry like that. He doesn't understand."

"It's the method, Ma."

"When you were a baby…"

"When I was a baby was a long time ago. Things have changed since then."

"When you were a baby you slept straight through from the hospital. I'd pick you up asleep around 10 PM for a bottle and then you'd only wake in the morning."

"Well that's helpful to know."

I pick up Little Old Man after thirty minutes of screaming and walk him round the hotel room to calm us both down. It is not part of controlled crying but I feel the pressure of my mother's silence. The lights are low and I can barely see her silhouette. But she is there, looming as large as my guilty conscience and sense of pressure to succeed at settling my baby. I feel angry at her presence. If she had lived just one night in my shoes, she would not be so quick to pass judgement on how I am handling this. Yet, by that logic, I shouldn't be that quick either.

I don't usually feel the need to prove my parenting skills but with her it's different. I want to show her there is potential and reasoning in my methods. Teaching him to self-settle into sleep is hard but a gift that will remain with him for life.

Even though I haven't said these things to her, I can well imagine what her response would be. If the method works so well, then why isn't he asleep? Why can't you manage to settle him? Why can't he settle himself for that matter? What is wrong with the picture?

It is for these reasons I don't say a word. She has me pinned even in unspoken conversations.

Chicken

After one day back home, Little Old Man has turned back into the calmer and better behaved version of his travelling hyper-self. For lunch he even voluntarily ate a significant amount* of chicken potato mash. It was a moment of personal triumph after months of patient cajoling. He ate savoury and it wasn't a rice cracker!

A few hours later I met the downside of babies eating meat. There are no words to describe the stench that was awaiting me in his nappy. Only one word really suffices. Wow. Just wow.

Stench be damned. He ate chicken! He ate it!

* More than three teaspoons in one sitting without vomit, feigned disgust or choking.

Anniversary

The Hubby and I celebrated our wedding anniversary today. Pre-baby, this used to involve one of us shouting the other to a fancy dinner at a restaurant of their choosing. The favour was then returned in reverse the following year.

Doing anything civilised after sunset now though is out of the question. So we changed tact and decided to go out for lunch. Drawing on my restaurant experience, we also take up a friend's offer to look after him 'anytime'. It helps that our friend has a son the same age so Little Old Man can have a play date. Kind of a win-win for everybody, hopefully.

On the big day we drop Little Old Man off with my friend and I try to restrain myself from running through everything in his nappy bag. I cover the basics and take the cue to stop when she starts shooshing me out the door.

"Go! Have a good time! Don't worry about him, he'll be fine."

I stand tentatively at the threshold of her door. This is the first time that both The Hubby and I have left Little Old Man in the care of someone else. I take a few steps towards the car and hear no protest. It can't be that simple. Surely he would throw himself at the door begging for me to take him? I look back in behind my friend to see Little Old Man chasing their dog.

"I have my mobile on me if you need me."

"Go!"

"Ok, ok I'm going! Thanks."

The Hubby and I drive off to enjoy a long lunch together, just the two of us. It's an odd sensation to not have Little Old Man's pram sidled up to our table. The Hubby and I chat without rush and actually manage to cover non-baby topics. We talk about my eventual return to work and agree that I should start putting feelers out for a new position in my organisation. Life is too short to sit in a job you hate, even part-time.

I feel lighter for having made the decision, excited even. I am sure I will miss these days when I am back at work. The grass is always greener, as the saying goes. Yet for the first time, sitting there with The Hubby, I can see there are positives to be had from both worlds if I navigate them well.

The Hubby made me promise not to obsessively look at my mobile. I will admit though that I may have gone to the ladies under the guise of needing to go but really only wanted to check my mobile for missed calls. There were none.

Our anniversary lunch reminded me of his insistence during the early days of us eating meals together at the table. With a baby it is so easy to lose sight of each other in the midst of chores and child-minding. But it doesn't have to be an either/or equation. We can still go out as a couple, just not as spontaneously or in the same way as we used to. Not yet, at least.

Our lunch also reminded me that, before Little Old Man came along, there was The Hubby and I.

We still exist, even though our resources are presently stretched. And we will continue to exist, long after Little Old Man has grown up, moved out and hopefully established himself with his own family. He is our world but we are each other's too.

We finish off a lovely meal and slowly wander back to the car. I really enjoyed the time out together and relaxed more than I thought possible. Ok, maybe I should also admit that I did sneakily check my phone a second time while he was paying the bill. But that is still a pretty good effort for me.

Back at my friend's place I enter the living room, hoping that my lunch high won't be destroyed by the reality of a distraught baby. I see Little Old Man and smile in relief. I really should have more faith in him. He is standing up happily pushing over a stack of magazines while his playdate rips them up. Little Old Man has apparently spent most of his time watching their dog and shrieking in excitement at the moving fur target. At no point did he fret or cry out for us.

"He has had an absolute ball."

"Really? Phew."

"There's nothing to worry about with babysitting. He's a very happy little boy."

I walk over and pick him up. He happily wriggles about in my arms and we thank my friend for babysitting, offering to return the favour anytime.

Who knows, I think optimistically, perhaps we could even make this a regular thing.

Leap of Faith

My earlier persistence at getting into the residential sleep clinic finally paid off. The Hubby, Little Old Man and I have checked into one for four days. We were offered a spot and wavered on the need during a short bright spot before finally submitting to having to go through with it.

I hesitated over the sleep clinic so much because it meant placing myself back in the hands of midwives. The trust I lost in them postnatal never returned and I had thus far had avoided any contact with them. All medical-related issues, milestone checks and immunisations for Little Old Man still ran through my doctor. I quite happily cut out any midwife interaction after the hospital, preferring the science of medicine to the conflicting opinions and meddling of midwifery.

Yet desperation pushes people to desperate measures. Little Old Man's sleep and feed issues had moments of hope but, overall, he is still a crap sleeper and an even crappier eater. I knew there was no point just checking in and arching defensively at every piece of advice. If it was to be of any help, I had to listen openly and give their methods a serious attempt. This was only ever going to happen if I first made that very difficult leap of faith and trusted in midwives again.

Before entering the clinic, I reminded myself of how far I had come since last dealing with midwives. After the birth I was high on drugs and hormones, traumatised, and had zero idea of what to do about the screaming bundle of love beside my hospital bed. I was vulnerable beyond belief.

Skip forward eleven months and the picture is completely different. Yes, we are struggling with Little Old Man's sleep and feed patterns but the rest is rock-solid. I have grown into a confident mother of a charming, strong and clever baby boy. I can tell when he's tired, hungry, happy, pooing, curious, bored and happy. I know his cries, can read the thoughts that run across his sweet little face and have learnt the hard lesson of patience in the face of a screaming baby at 3 AM. If a method of my parenting is up for discussion, I am confident to enter an informed discussion and explain why we have been doing things a certain way and be open to any tweaks.

Secretly, I am hoping that our stay at the sleep clinic will do more than cure some of Little Old Man's issues. I hope it will also help me see that midwives aren't the big bad wolves my mind has made them out to be. Their conflicting opinions in the hospital and afterwards with breastfeeding were less than helpful but should be seen in the context of what I was living through. I still would have struggled even if their advice was perfectly designed for my situation.

Maybe mending my view of midwives in four days is too ambitious or maybe I will be pleasantly surprised, who knows? All I know is that I am unpacking our bags at a sleep clinic and, for the first time since the birth, I am willing to give midwives another go.

Lunch Date

I am sitting at a table with Little Old Man. He is eating a sandwich and I am doing the same. Well, he is eating a sandwich as best as a baby can. It is nevertheless a surreal scene of triumph.

A midwife, Carolyn, has set up this most unlikely of lunch dates. She suggested we try him on a sandwich and some vegetable sticks. I would eat the same to model for him how it's done. I couldn't help but laugh at the thought and hope her CPR accreditations were up to date. The notion of Little Old Man eating anything not pureed within an inch of its life seemed absurd.

I readied myself for his refusal followed by suspicious acceptance, gag, choke, and gag again with the potential for one of his mega vomits. Yet he took the sandwich from her outstretched hand and put it straight in his mouth. When it fell on his lap, he took a piece of parboiled carrot and had a go at that. I could see bits being chewed off and moved to fish them out of his mouth.

"No, give him a chance to chew."

"But he only has two teeth. He'll choke."

"He may gag but this is perfectly normal."

"Even if he vomits?"

"It's better for him to vomit than not. It shows that his body is getting used to handling food and can get rid of something blocking his throat. Gagging and learning to swallow are actually very important to speech development. As long as they don't go blue in the face, it's ok."

Her last add-on does not help calm me. I imagine Carolyn is going to pull out a reference card for overprotective parents with graded colours that a baby's face can turn before intervention is necessary. I would intervene at flush pink but she seems to be asking me to leave it until he is purple with bulging eyes.

I suspend my suspicion and try not to stare. I can't help it though. My son is eating a sandwich! A revolution is happening before my eyes. Carolyn hands him a prune, which he squashes in his hand before rubbing it through his hair.

"It's alright, he's just exploring."

"But…"

But no buts. He is a complete mess yet she has managed in five minutes more than I have in months. I begin to feel like an idiot for complaining that my child doesn't eat food. Maybe if I had been wild enough to have given him actual food, then he may have eaten some. Yet I was afraid to do so after his many vomit sessions, topped off by that certain diplomatic incident involving raspberries.

Little Old Man begins to gag and my hand moves towards him.

"Leave it. He'll work it out."

I put my hand back down on my plate and pick distractedly at my sandwich. I put it to my mouth and watch him from the corner of my eye. The previously stuck food is now rolling round in his mouth and he is busy staring at the baby in the next highchair. For the first time I feel a flicker of trust in his ability to navigate solids.

Carolyn explains that it's important I offer food but it always remains up to him whether he takes it from my hand. She encourages me to choose something from his snack box to try. I look for the squishiest item but they are all decidedly solid. I pick up a cheese stick and stretch out my hand.

We have had so many struggles over food and I have willed him to eat so often that the pressure between us has at times been too much. Now I feel almost sheepish as I offer up the cheese. If only he could understand how sorry I was for pushing him and that I only did so with his best interests at heart. I fully expect him to refuse anything I offer out of suspicion but, to my surprise, he takes it.

To the outsider it is really no big deal – a piece of cheese and nothing more – but to me it marks a new beginning. For the first time he has shown an active interest in the food I am offering. There were no tricks used to shovel puree into his mouth – it was as transparent as an offer can be. Here is a piece of food, take it or leave it.

I pick up my sandwich, smile at him and we continue eating our lunch.

Love Light

For some reason I haven't quite worked out, the ducted heating and in-floor heating at the sleep clinic are turned up to maximum. This means the inhabitants are being heated from above and below with no chance of escape. Parents wander round in singlets and thongs despite the barely double digit weather outside.

On the first day the clinic struck me as being like a tropical oasis. On the second, I came to view it more like an overheated hellhole populated by screaming babies and their zombie parents.

It is easy to see the babies playing and forget they are here for a reason. No matter how sweet and angelic they are during daytime hours, they all turn into sleep vampires come sunset. You can hear their protests cranking up each night along the clinic hallway. And while their challenges with sleep and eating may vary, they all have one thing in common; they have drained the life-force out of their parents through months of broken sleep and sometimes also food refusal.

I feel self-conscious at first being myself in this place but relax a little by the second day. It will be our home for four days so I may as well get used to it. I get down on the floor in the playroom and crawl after Little Old Man then lay on my back, much to his amusement. He places his hands on my forehead and stands up over my face. He then wobbles as he lowers himself to give me a big sloppy trout kiss on the nose before swiping drool across the rest of me. We laugh and I thank him for the display of affection. He has a while to go before he is coordinated enough to give a regular kiss but I know the sentiment is there.

When we checked in I was given a list of tired signs. This afternoon I put him down for a nap on only one sign and he fought the nap for an hour before I gave up. The midwife had willed me to continue but I deferred to my own judgement on his behaviour. There was no way he was going to go down, he wasn't tired enough to give in easily.

I pick him out of his cot and come back out to the playroom, deciding to wait for two tired signs before trying again. He eventually does show two signs – eye rubbing and clumsiness – and I ask another midwife, Liz, to assist me in settling him.

The concept here is to learn through doing, with the midwives guiding my moves from outside the nursery as necessary. I picked Liz to help because I found her advice so far to be well-timed and most reasonable. There is something about her. I can tell she gives advice not only as a textbook midwife but also as a mum.

I go about settling Little Old Man, singing and stroking his side as he yells out in protest. I pit myself as a calm and comforting force in the face of his crying hysteria. Unlike at home, I don't walk away for allotted times and let him work himself out. I stick it out and calm him down to the point where he turns his desperation down a few notches to a half-arsed cry.

Responsive settling takes time and patience but I feel reassured that it is ok to pick him up if he gets too upset. Before the clinic, I had in mind that I could only touch him as a very last resort and struggled badly with the sense of frustration and futility this rule created in me.

I keep on patting and watch on in amazement as Little Old Man begins his slide into sleep. I gently lift my hands from his relaxed body and go out to Liz, who has been whispering tips from the bedroom. I tentatively start to talk, unsure of how far I should extend my trust to her.

"God, I'm such a failure. If he got out of control then sometimes I left him to cry because I couldn't handle it. I didn't think I was allowed to touch him. I thought letting them cry it out was how you settled a baby."

"You're not a failure, you just needed to learn better settling techniques that's all."

"How could I have left him like that though? I am meant to be the bigger person in the room but sometimes I couldn't hack even being in the room. He deserves so much better."

"Hey, you're a great mum. I've seen you playing with him, how he seeks you out and reacts when you hold him. Sleep and eating are things you can learn but this, it's precious. You have given him the greatest start in life he could possibly hope for. Don't beat yourself up over this."

"Yeah I guess so."

"No seriously. I see babies in here who don't respond to warmth and those are the ones I worry about. They don't know what to do with affection because it is not regularly given to them. They are the saddest part of this job because I can't fix that. Sleep and feed issues, sure. But teach a parent how to love their child? No way."

I have seen one of the babies she is talking about. Her mother is in the clinic for a parenting assessment and does everything technically correct. She feeds her baby and puts her in clean clothes yet even a layman like me can see something is missing.

The girl is about Little Old Man's age and I smile and chat with her like I would do with any baby. Yet she never responds. There is no light in her eyes, only dull recognition at someone else's gaze. I don't know the back story but the result on display is heartbreaking. I smiled at her mother at the beginning too but she was the same. No response. There is no warmth in their interactions. It is as though love left the room a long time ago or perhaps, for whatever reason, was never there.

Liz catches my eye and reaches for my arm. I feel she is peering right through my defences with no effort and I shift uncomfortably. Perhaps she has seen the look on the faces of so many other mothers that she instinctively knows its meaning.

"You need to be kinder on yourself, Meagan."

"Yeah I know. That's not the first time I've heard that."

"Well, listen then."

I look away and nod. She is right, I know she is.

Coming Down

My son is an addict – a junkie for the bottle. I can see now I have been his enabler, feeding him at all hours of the day or night based upon his cravings. But no more. The time has come for him to go cold turkey and learn the hard lesson of self-settling sans bottle.

It is 4:30 AM on night three of the sleep clinic. Little Old Man has needed settling eleven times till this point and has now moved into full-blown tantrum mode. As was the game plan, he was given a bottle when he woke around midnight and he hasn't had one since. The idea is that we want to stretch his feed till breakfast time, where he will be offered solids first and then a bottle.

The night before I caved at 5 AM and gave him his breakfast, which he promptly threw on the floor. I then offered the bottle and he drank a few sips before crawling off to play. I felt tricked by his earlier screams, which I had interpreted as hunger. I could tell from his behaviour that he wasn't really hungry but rather he just didn't know how to settle back to sleep without a dream feed. In its absence, his body woke up fully in confusion about what to do next.

Tonight though, there will be no more caving. I knew going in it would be hard on us both but he has to learn how to settle without the bottle. All night he has been grizzling and in need of some kind of settling – from simple shh'ing at his door to rocking him to singing and patting him gently. I feel completely trashed yet determined not to lose a night of sleep for nothing. He will go until daybreak without a bottle.

The midwife on duty, Helen, is mildly annoying but I am relieved for the company. Perhaps with some foresight of what was to come, I sent The Hubby home the night before to get some proper sleep. At least one of us had to be functioning to keep the program going.

Helen suggests that maybe I should give him a bottle since we've both made a super effort until now. Her words are tempting but I decline, pointing out what happened the morning before. She suggests I pick him up since he has taken to rattling the metal bars of his cot in rage. I do so and try to hold him still enough to rock but it is useless. He is jerking his body about too much in angry screaming fits.

I remember back to when I first started formula feeding and all the not-so-nice names I had given it, among which were 'kiddy cocaine'. It is at that point I realise he is like a junkie coming down. I'm sure though breastfeeding mothers have similar issues with night feeds — it is not the bottle itself but the comfort of the feeding, however it is delivered. So technically he's a comfort junkie.

The analogy, as weird as it may be, is enough to keep me determined and not get frustrated. I am helping him get over a very hard habit. With my guidance, we will ride this storm out together.

I turn Little Old Man to my hip to see if a new position might calm him. All of a sudden he sees a door handle and begins playing with it. Ohhh how shiny, see how it clicks open then shut. He is so fascinated that he stops screaming and begins to play. I look to Helen in the half dark outside.

"See? He doesn't need a bottle, he's not hungry."

"Good, keep rocking him…now is your chance to settle him."

I rock and sing *Five Little Ducks* to him repetitively. I am so tired that I lose count of how many ducks went swimming one day and make up the numbers up as I go. In the back of my mind, I wonder how Mamma Duck could be so errant as to allow her baby ducks to go swimming despite them continually going missing day after day. Maybe they don't sleep well and she doesn't mind one less squawky baby duck to mind.

Little Old Man yawns and brings my thoughts back into the nursery. I slowly place him back in the cot and gently hold him in place, stroking his leg rhythmically. He begins his half-arse cry but I keep going, hopeful at this first sign of sleep after 90 minutes of screaming. The half-arse crying ends and he begins to snore. I continue patting and shh'ing for a while longer before trusting the peace enough to withdraw my hands. He is asleep.

I leave the nursery to find Helen still standing there. I half expect some words of encouragement since she's been my advisor and sleep confidant this marathon night. Instead, she is peering at my formula bottles and picks one up.

"How do you prepare a bottle?"

"Huh? Like the instructions say – boil water, let it cool, add formula, use."

"No, no, no. You must add the formula to boiling water and then ice it down to the temperature you need. These are the guidelines to stop bacteria growing in the milk."

"Says who?"

"The World Health Organisation."

I grit my teeth and try to hold back from screaming at her to get the fuck out of my room. The only thing stopping me is that I don't want to wake Little Old Man.

"You're...you're telling me this now? After this night?"

"I'll find a pamphlet and leave it in your file so you can read it through in the morning."

"Yeah great. Thanks."

I start walking towards the door as a sign for her to follow me. I am shaking with sleep deprivation and rage. The fucking World Health Organisation. I remember feeling beholden to their six-month exclusive breastfeeding guidelines until I worked out they have to make guidelines broad enough to apply to mothers living anywhere between Bangladesh, the Kalahari, France and Australia.

I get into bed angry and unable to sleep. I am beyond overtired. I close my eyes and try to at least calm down. The night may have been hard but functioning through the day with next to no sleep will be even harder.

After an hour or so Little Old Man stirs. I look over towards the window and see daylight peeking in through the curtains. No matter how shit I feel in the day ahead, the night has been a success. We have made it to daybreak without a bottle.

Fishbowl Parenting

A red flag must have been put in my file for my bottle preparation and lack of sleep. When Little Old Man and I emerge for breakfast, I am approached immediately by a midwife. I have zero desire to talk to her. After the formula advice, I have begun shutting down and feel the urge to flee. But I can't. We have one more night left and I am determined to see this through.

"I heard you had a rough night."

"Yes, but we're here."

"Well, if you need to see a counsellor then I can arrange one."

"Err, thanks but I just need some sleep."

"It's ok to ask for help."

"I know but I really just need some sleep."

"Ok, well here's the brochure Helen promised on how to prepare bottles. It is worth reading."

"Thanks but I'll follow the tin instructions."

The midwife looks more concerned at my open dissent of her advice and goes away to talk to another midwife. They both glimpse back at me before walking away, probably to decorate my file with even more red flags.

I know I look haggard and drawn. The sight in the bathroom mirror when I got dressed was not a pretty one. But I am really, truly just tired. If I felt anything underneath the tiredness it would be happiness and relief. We both pushed on through and broke the bottle for the first time. If I had given it to him at 5 AM, things would be more desperate and perhaps I would benefit from speaking to a counsellor. As it stands though, I know the lack of sleep has served a valid purpose and I am willing to pay the price.

As I soon discover though, saying you don't need to see a counsellor is like falling over and trying to reassure people that you're alright. The more you try to convince them of the contrary, the less believable your words sound. It leads them to be even more concerned than if you had just submitted to the offer in the first place.

But I wasn't going to give in on this one. I came here with no trust of midwives. I have gained a little trust back but not enough to let a stranger trample into my inner world at their suggestion. If I'm struggling, I know where to go. And this place is not it.

The price to pay for my stubbornness is a feeling that my every move is being watched as though I may crack at any moment. I want to go out for a long walk to get away from this fishbowl but it is raining. Instead, I take Little Old Man into our room and close the door. The Hubby is coming soon.

I play with Little Old Man on the floor in an effort to distract myself from my exhaustion. I will make it through, I tell myself. I always do.

Release

The Hubby arrived later in the day with lunch and some sleeping tablets. I don't normally resort to pills but I have found that sometimes I can get so overtired doing graveyard shifts that I pretty much need an elephant dart. When I am so tired it is as though I have broken the switch in my brain that enables me to drift off to sleep. The only way to reset it is to knock myself out altogether.

I slept most of the afternoon, waking again for dinner before trying to get to sleep again a few hours later. It was little use. My insomnia was biting hard in the sleep clinic. The proximity of Little Old Man's cot to our bed meant that I heard every whimper and deep sigh from him. This set my inner Mamma Bear into overdrive and I couldn't stand down, even with earplugs.

I tried to sleep on a couch in the common room but there was too much noise from parents and babies commuting to the nurses' station for assistance. The breaking point was when a mother came out holding her twins. She looked over at me and said she had seen me earlier and was concerned. I realised I had become the woman that made other women feel better about their lot, even the ones with insomniac twins.

I moved back into bed next to The Hubby and curled into a ball of desperation. Sleep, sleep, sleep! If only my body would give over to my will.

Eventually it did at around 2 AM. I slept for three hours before being woken by Little Old Man's morning attempt for a bottle. The Hubby settled him back with a lullaby, which worked on me too. This was a miracle in many respects, not least of all because The Hubby's off-key singing is not exactly what I would describe as soothing.

The next thing I remember is The Hubby waking me to take over at 8 AM. Little Old Man was outside being fed breakfast by one of the midwives and he had to go to work. I was tired but not as trashed as the day before. It would be easier to get through, especially since I knew we would be checking out. I got dressed and went to join my son at the breakfast table.

My time at the sleep clinic was intense but highly productive. I have faced and dealt with all the things I have let slide at home because it was easier to keep going with poor habits than to fix them. In hindsight, I see that The Golden Age was when he was on the right track of sleeping through the night but we reverted back to newborn night feed habits when he stumbled. Switching back onto the right track again wasn't easy and would take time to establish but at least we have started.

I have learnt better settling techniques and slight improvements to what I was already doing. This has taken the pressure down greatly because I no longer stand helplessly outside his door or stomp off to the shower when I can't handle his screaming anymore. My goal with his sleep has shifted to calming him to the point where he can babble peacefully off to sleep rather than cry himself there. Nobody likes to cry themselves to sleep, it's not a nice way to go.

After breakfast I pack up our things into the car and sign some paperwork to release us. A midwife walks me to the door and reminds me to take breaks and look after myself. She hands me another copy of the bottle preparation guidelines along with a wad of pamphlets for community support programs. I sense she is about to launch into one last lecture and I cut her short.

"Thanks for the stay. I think we've improved."

"You're welcome."

My feelings towards midwives remain cautious and mixed. I got on well with some but was grated into thinly veiled rage at others. I settle on viewing each as an individual rather than dismissing them all as a profession of nut bags. That would be an injustice to the good ones out there, like Liz and Carolyn or Lovely Linda from the birth.

I get in the car and drive off with the windows down. The cool breeze hits my face and my mind feels the sharpest it has since entering the heated parental purgatory. At a set of lights I turn to the back to check on Little Old Man. He is munching on a plastic ball and babbling away. He hears my voice and smiles instinctively in its direction.

The sparkle in his eyes makes my mind go to the little girl. I feel so sad for her and can only hope her future brightens. But I also know the reality is that she represents just one of many children who aren't given the best of starts in life. There's a reason why child protection agencies exist in every state and territory. For a whole range of reasons, perhaps some beyond their control, not everyone can cope well enough with the intense demands involved in raising a child.

Seeing this darker side of parenting upfront has made me reassess my own attempts at parenting. For the first time, looking back at Little Old Man in his car seat, I see his development since birth as not some fluke. It is the result of loving guidance and work from The Hubby and me – a point not to be dismissed lightly.

The lights go green and I turn back round. As I drive off I find myself thinking that I'm not a failure. To the contrary, I'm actually a good mum.

A stressed and at times overtired and clueless mum but a good one all the same.

Back at the Start

I find myself wishing yet again that this was the part where I could say that we all slept happily and smugly ever after. Unfortunately, sleep and babies do not always equal such a simple equation. With Little Old Man it seems that progress in the sleep department is all too often followed by regression.

The first few days after the sleep clinic were promising. Little Old Man woke around midnight for his one permissible feed and then quickly went back to sleep until daybreak. It was a miraculous turnaround and I felt like the pain of cutting the night feeds down had been worth it.

And then it all went downhill. He started to wake at 2 AM to scream his lungs out for a couple of hours. It was as though he had calmed into a new sleeping routine and then awoke one night, acutely aware that he had forgotten to protest the situation. None of the settling techniques we had learnt at the sleep clinic calmed him. He stood indignantly at the cot bars and screamed out into the cold, long nights before us.

This went on for four nights until he turned the screws even harder, screaming for an hour after the midnight feed then from 3:30 AM to 6 AM. He was then up by 6:45 AM. It was a gruelling time. I had entered the sleep clinic exhausted and left with zero energy in reserve. I was in a worse state than in the newborn phase. I had nothing left to give after almost a year of broken sleep.

The early mornings were the hardest. I would cry uncontrollably in despair at the long day ahead. After the sun came out it got a little better but I was still prone to burst out crying at the smallest of things. I was so exhausted I began to fall asleep in random places again. The toilet once more became my go-to narcolepsy haunt, along with standing up against a wall in his nursery. I became frightened of driving long distances in case the same happened there.

Things got even more desperate when I lost the one thread keeping me together – hope. I saw that the sleep clinic hadn't fixed Little Old Man's nightly antics. If anything, they were worse. And his mood during the day declined since he spent half the night screaming and not sleeping. He was now full-on work day and night.

I then reached for my mobile to text with some of my sleep deprivation buddies. These were other mothers also going through sleep dramas with their babies. We would all text each other day or night for support. Our bubbles of awake felt a little less isolated when they were connected to other bubbles out there in a sleeping city.

As I scrolled through my list, I realised that one by one they had all dropped away. All their babies had managed to get it together and sleep through the night. My friends were now part of the sleeping city. It was only Little Old Man, all alone, who was holding out and making me scrape by in my deflated bubble.

My only possible source for sleep deprivation buddies were a couple of friends with newborns. At that point, right there, I lost hope.

To Sleep, Perchance to Dream

"Why is he doing this to us? Why won't he just sleep? Why? I don't understand what we are doing so wrong. We've tried everything."

I lean on The Hubby and cry in frustration. It is 4 AM and Little Old Man has been giving us his all for an hour. The Hubby suggests letting him settle on him and they both fall asleep on the lounge. He admits that he has been settling him this way for the past couple of mornings just to give himself a break.

I feel a sting of anger at him undermining the technique and then pity that he felt the need to hide this from me. I must come away sounding like a sleep militant at times. I try to soften.

"Maybe, maybe…let's just see what happens if we put him in bed with us. I know, it's wrong and crazy but it will be easier lying down."

"Isn't that the biggest no-no in the book?"

I remember my previous failed attempt at co-sleeping and wonder if it is worth a shot. I also remember the midwife back at the hospital, who chastised me for letting Little Old Man fall asleep on me at the ripe age of two days. She warned I wouldn't get him out of my bed until he was four years old. A little extreme, I think, in hindsight.

"Yeah I know but something has to give. If we create another problem, then I'd rather deal with that one than the problem of having no sleep."

"Whatever works, I guess."

"Within reason. I don't want him in with us the whole night, just from this 4 AM scream time."

"Ok, let's give it a go."

So that is how we came back to breaking the cardinal rule of sleep school and, in the process, brought some sleep and sanity to our house. Little Old Man rolled over in the space between us and promptly fell asleep for four hours. Any reservations I had about not being able to sleep myself didn't eventuate. It wasn't a deep sleep but a sleep all the same.

Like with the camping mattress idea, letting Little Old Man sleep part of the night in our bed was not a long-term solution. But it was enough to give us back a buffer.

His sleep has improved in the weeks since. He still has good nights and bad. The trick is to remember that everyone has to fall asleep eventually. Humans simply cannot function without sleep and we all have to get there in the end, even ratbag babies and insomniac mothers.

The other trick is to remind myself not to build up or lose all hope based on one night and that, even if it really doesn't feel like it at times, he will eventually get to the bigger goal of sleeping the night through. After all, he can't be an 18 year old man waking every few hours crying for his mummy to feed him a bottle. At some point, this period in his life has to have a natural end.

Sleeping through is a logical conclusion but also a hopeful dream – one I can't let go of again. As I have learnt, it is too precious and soul-destroying to lose hold of. The sleep will come. It has to.

Cruisin'

Little Old Man has taken to leaning on walls during playtime and cruising along bits of furniture. With some encouragement, he has also held our hands and taken a few wobbly steps.

He keeps practising being vertical with the same repetitive zeal he displayed when learning to crawl. Like with the crawling, I suspect that last extra bit of something he needs to complete his training will randomly appear one day. Then he will begin to walk through our living room as though he has always done so. In the meantime, he will continue to cruise and practise soft landing on his nappy.

We are mindful of the new heights Little Old Man can now reach with his cruising. The high-tide water mark in our house that was set with his crawling has moved further up. Cutlery and placemats have been pushed into the middle of the dining table, books taken off the coffee table and reading glasses have found a new home above the microwave.

Our proactive moves have made us think of ourselves as quite clever. We felt completely unprepared when he started crawling but thought we had it all sorted for the latest developmental leap. As it turns out though, we are merely parents and not mastermind strategists. We cannot foresee all potential risks and, like our son, sometimes we have to learn the hard way. In one instance, it was the very hard way.

Since Little Old Man's birth, The Hubby and I had a habit of hanging particularly stinky nappy bags on the door handle rather than putting them in the nappy bin to fester. The next person who went out then placed the offending bag in the outside bin. Our disposal system worked brilliantly for almost twelve months until Little Old Man could reach that high.

At first I heard him banging on the front door and thought nothing of it. Then I heard the sound of plastic being hit. Before I had time to register what the noise was, there was a squeal of delight. I looked around the corner to see him standing there, hands covered in brown goo, with a big smile on his face. He had batted and pulled at the nappy bag until the contents spilt out. I ran over and stood before him momentarily, unsure what to clean first.

Many parents who I've told this story to have laughed knowingly and said it is only the beginning. I dread the thought of what we might next learn the hard way. At least we can rest assured that it probably won't involve nappy bags.

A short time after the incident, The Hubby had thought up a new baby-proof stinky nappy disposal. He seems confident but I am aware that our little Roadrunner can be surprisingly crafty. I hope he is right though. After all, nobody wins from a self-styled game of poo piñata – least of all the ones who have to clean up.

The Birthday Boy

"Blow out your candle! Ok…breathe on your candle. Never mind, Mummy will do it for you."

I lean in with Little Old Man on my lap to blow out his birthday candle. At the same time I am trying to smile casually and prevent him from driving his fist into the cake. I feel like one of those snowplough mums, pushing challenges effortlessly out of the way of their offspring. But I'm also parenting under pressure. There's an audience of friends and family waiting with cameras poised in anticipation. They want to capture the exact moment when Little Old Man officially turns one.

Although I find the situation terribly constructed, I'm just as keen to capture the moment. Turning one is a big milestone – big enough to require cake, even if the birthday boy doesn't really register with excitement the impending sugar high.

As I cut the cake, I think back on the blur of the twelve months behind us. It is hard to believe that a year ago today Little Old Man made his rather dramatic entrance into the world. In some ways it feels like an eternity ago, particularly in the sleep department, but then in other ways it seems like only yesterday.

Little Old Man has grown so much since the hospital. Only when I was hanging up photos for the party did I really see how far he has come. He has transformed from helpless newborn with a bad case of bobble head to confident toddler on the verge of walking. Intellectually too, his view of the world around him has grown enormously. He can now point to what he wants, say with a whimper or a scream how he feels, and get excited at new discoveries.

Yet Little Old Man isn't the only person to have grown in this past year. While he has been busy stretching his own boundaries and horizons beyond measure, he has also done the same to mine. I remember the moment of panic and uncertainty at the hospital over whether I was cut out for this motherhood gig. With his existence to push me, I have learnt nurturing skills and endurance that I never dreamed I was capable of in my pre-baby life.

The ride has been incredible but rough. His birth threw me down to the lowest points I have ever been physically and mentally. Supported by The Hubby, close friends and the Mother's Group, I did eventually bounce back despite all the sleep dramas. I resumed my daily walks, lost a lot of the pregnancy weight and put any memories of the delivery well in the past.

You could even say that I peed my pants and lived to tell the tale.

With the candle blown out and photos taken, I stop to savour the moment. Parenting is hard work. Hard. Fucking. Work. But it is also beautiful work – the most beautiful and fulfilling work I have ever had the honour to undertake.

I look over to Little Old Man to see him entertaining an appreciative audience. As I watch, I feel proud – of him, of us, and of the different challenges we have faced as a family and overcome. The Hubby and I have done a good job. We have loved, fostered and guided his development as best we knew how. The result is a beautiful child inside and out.

That is not to say there isn't room for improvement in the second year. I wouldn't want to call myself out as a smug shark at this late stage! No, I know I have lots to work on. My patience levels for a start. And there's still the sticky question of how I am going to find the time to plant the forest of carbon neutralising trees I promised to allay my conscience.

Despite a few tweaks though, we have a pretty solid base to work from. Our commitment as parents will see him move healthily along the trajectory from baby to boy and one day into a young man. He will grow and make The Hubby and I grow as humans along with him.

Yet, no matter how much he grows, there is a special place in my heart where he will always remain my Little Old Man.

Happy birthday, gorgeous boy. I love you more than all my words and deeds could ever hope to express. You are my son and greatest pleasure in life – even if at times your sleep patterns make the idea of shipping you to Somalia in a box seem like a logical temptation.

Love you always, stinky bum.

Xx Mum

www.ingramcontent.com/pod-product-compliance
Lightning Source LLC
Chambersburg PA
CBHW051933290426
44110CB00015B/1963